STANDING FLOWER

STANDING FLOWER

The Life of *Irving Pabanale*
An Arizona Tewa Indian

EDITED AND ANNOTATED BY

Robert A. Black

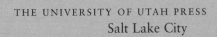

THE UNIVERSITY OF UTAH PRESS
Salt Lake City

LIBRARY OF CONGRESS CATALOGING-IN-PUBLICATION DATA

Pabanale, Irving, d. 1972.
  Standing Flower : the life of Irving Pabanale, an Arizona Tewa
Indian / edited and annotated by Robert A. Black.
      p.   cm.
Includes bibliographical references and index.
    ISBN 0-87480-689-5 (alk. paper)
    1. Pabanale, Irving, d. 1972. 2. Tewa Indians—Biography. 3. Indian
reservation police—Arizona—Hopi Indian Reservation—Biography.
4. Indian judges—Arizona—Hopi Indian Reservation—Biography.
I. Black, Robert A., 1927–   II. Title.
    E99.T53 P33 2001
    979.1'35—dc21

                                                    2001001942

06 05 04 03 02 01
 5   4   3   2   1

THIS BOOK IS DEDICATED
TO THE MEMORIES OF
Edith and Sylvan Nash

CONTENTS

Contents

ACKNOWLEDGMENTS

I am grateful to the many individuals and institutions who helped make the completion of this book possible.

It gives me great pleasure to acknowledge the support of my Hopi and Tewa friends, who shared their knowledge and personal reflections so graciously. Paul Kroskrity, Robert Euler, and Hank Liese read the manuscript and made invaluable editorial suggestions; I received much good advice from these friends. I owe a great debt to the late Alfonso Ortiz, whose warm support and counsel underscored the importance of bringing Pabanale's life history to print. Al is deeply missed. Jack Dynis and Gregory Herek provided artistic ability and computer expertise; they are extremely patient friends.

I am especially indebted to the Museum of Northern Arizona in Flagstaff, its director of many years, Edward P. Danson, and subsequent directors for enabling me to work and live at the Research Center for many seasons. The museum grounds, nestled beneath the majestic San Francisco Peaks, inspired me. To Katharine Bartlett and Dotti House, directors of the Museum Library, I owe special thanks for their boundless knowledge and generous help. Thanks also go to Sue Bekke for her help in preparing the manuscript.

The D'Arcy McNickle Center for the History of the American Indians at the Newberry Library in Chicago provided a fellowship for work on this life history. Fred Hoxie, the former director of the center, and the library staff helped make my stay there most productive.

I am especially grateful to Jeffrey L. Grathwohl, director of the University of Utah Press, for his encouragement and support of this book. I also wish to thank Kimberley C. Vivier for her careful and sensitive editing of the manuscript.

A number of foundations provided financial support for summer work on the project. My thanks go to the Wenner-Gren Foundation for Anthropological Research, the American Philosophical Society, the Skaggs Foundation, and the Jacobs Family Fund.

Finally, I am indebted to my wife, Kathleen Cave, for her encouragement and superb editing skills. 'Is kwakwhá i pas lomáwuuti.

INTRODUCTION

The old man sat on a creaking kitchen chair in the home of his daughter, Edith Nash. It was a typical Pueblo dwelling of adobe and stone, located in the village of Sitsomovi atop First Mesa, a narrow, fingerlike projection rising some six hundred feet from the desert floor on the Hopi reservation. Wearing a battered western hat, he leaned forward, his dark leathery frame resting on an oversized cane as he listened intently to his daughter's words. He sat quietly in the room as Edith told him about this *pahana* (white person) friend who would listen to him and record the story of his life.

I first met Edith Nash and her husband, Sylvan, in 1957 when I was a graduate student in anthropology. Sylvan became my mentor when I began learning about Hopi rooftop announcement making, the topic of my Ph.D. dissertation at Indiana University. We worked closely together for many summers, and his family and I became good friends. After receiving my degree, I returned regularly to the Hopi country to engage in research and renew old ties, and our friendship was strengthened.

During one of my visits, in the summer of 1966, Edith asked me if I would "take down" her father's story. She proceeded to tell me some of her father's accomplishments: "He did many important things for the Hopis in his life; he was a policeman and a judge." In 1935 he helped write the Hopi constitution, and he was among the first delegates to the newly established tribal council. From 1940 to 1949 he was chief judge of the Hopi Tribal Court.

Edith was concerned that no one in the villages was interested in his story. She hoped I would record it so it could be preserved for her children and for future generations. I accepted her invitation out of respect for her feelings. I was also excited by the prospect of getting to know her father and learning about his life during the early twentieth century, a crucial period in reservation history.

My introduction to Irving Pabanale was formal that day. Edith said, "This is our friend, Bob Black; he is going to work with you." He raised his head in response, saying, "My name is Irving Pabanale. It means 'Standing Flower' in the Tewa language." He was pleased that I would be recording his story and made it known that he wanted it published so that his "Hopi people" would know what he had done for them. He also indicated that he wanted to tell his story in English to demonstrate his command of the language. Thus began an unusual relationship, that summer day in 1966, one that was to last until Pabanale's death in 1972 at the age of ninety-one.

We started the next day, driving down to Flagstaff, where I was a research associate at the Museum of Northern Arizona. I was able to arrange accommodations for Pabanale there, providing an ideal setting for our work away from the confines of First Mesa and the attendant lack of privacy. As we began, I was aware of his preparation for this event. His style and manner of delivery indicated he knew exactly what he wanted to say. Earlier Edith told me he had organized his narrative orally and had rehearsed it repeatedly. His manner of presentation reflected this prior preparation. He spoke slowly and deliberately. There was an understated reserve in his diction: every thought was expressed carefully and unhurriedly. There were no digressions, only occasional pauses in his delivery to correct a word or phrase or collect his thoughts before continuing. His voice was level and unanimated; he used few hand or body gestures. He addressed me as Mr. Black and requested that I play back recorded portions of the tape for his approval. After several days he grew tired and asked to be taken back to his village. I was able to work with him at the museum several more times that summer.

At the end of my stay he asked if I planned to return next year. I assured him that I did, and he said he would look forward to working with me again. When I returned the following summer, he told me he had remembered some additional details that he wished to include in his story. He was thus able to fill in some gaps and expand on previously mentioned events. At other times during our sessions, when I asked him to provide more information on a topic, he was usually reluctant to elaborate. He invariably replied that this was all he could remember or that he had nothing more to say on the subject.

His narrative did not provide a sense of internal unity. Each episode was relatively brief and self-contained, intended to offer only a glimpse into his varied life experiences. These vignettes did not culminate in an introspective appreciation of his life journey.

At the end of the summer of 1969 Pabanale felt that he had rendered a fairly complete account of his life and that he had nothing further to add. He indicated that he wanted his book to include photographs and a number of folktales he remembered from childhood and had told his children. His active life spanned half a century, and he was gratified that the record of his experiences and accomplishments had been preserved.

Irving Pabanale's narrative was recorded on a Uher monaural battery-operated tape recorder on five-inch tape reels. It was transcribed verbatim from the tapes, copies of which were deposited in the archives of the Museum of Northern Arizona Library in Flagstaff and at the Library of Congress. Pabanale's story is presented here as he related it. No syntactic, stylistic, or grammatical changes were made, nor was any portion enhanced or deleted. It is thus available for others to examine and analyze from different perspectives.

A few comments are appropriate at this point regarding the repetition of phrases and words throughout the text. Although, as H. David Brumble points out, "the use of repetition grates upon the modern ear" (1988:11), it is very much a part of the traditional style of storytelling in many Native American communities and is highly valued by the Arizona Tewas and the Hopis. These patterns of repetition have been preserved throughout the narrative, as they provide insights into the ways the English language is reshaped to reflect Arizona Tewa narrative style. The more traditional Arizona Tewa rhetorical styles emphasize repetitive structures in which stories are very straightforward, with little description or elaboration.

Pabanale's Story

Pabanale begins his life story with the statement, "I would like to tell something of my life from my childhood up until today. I will tell it as near as I can remember." He then locates his Tewa ancestors in time and place, describing their migration to First Mesa and the consequences of this historic trek. He arranges the subsequent episodes chronologically, emphasizing his experiences and contributions to the Hopi people.

Pabanale can best be described as a culture broker, a cultural middleman who learned to act as an intermediary between the native culture and the sources of American power and influence. There have been several successful culture brokers among the Arizona Tewas and the Hopis, beginning in the late nineteenth century. Tom Polacca was the first Arizona Tewa to play this role, in the late 1890s. Polacca adopted Christianity, founded the settlement of Polacca (named for him) below First Mesa, and was responsible for establishing the first day school and trading post on the reservation, also at Polacca. In more recent times Albert Yava was certainly the most outstanding and successful culture

xiii

broker. His life history, *Big Falling Snow* (Yava 1978), is testimony to his and the Arizona Tewas' accomplishments and contributions to Hopi life.

Pabanale achieved modest success as a manipulator of the sources of Indian and American influence. There is a sense of pride and personal satisfaction in his narrative regarding his participation in the seemingly strange world of white America. Like Albert Yava, Pabanale had a sense of the historical validation of the role of the Tewas in Hopi life. Despite the cultural differences that strained relations between the two groups, the Arizona Tewas emerged as leaders in Hopi affairs.

Pabanale's early life was a departure from traditional village experiences. He began attending the reservation boarding school at Polacca in 1895 and moved on to the Phoenix Indian School in 1900. After running away because of homesickness, he returned to the school of his own volition. Pabanale appears to have accepted his new experiences with satisfaction. He fondly remembered how in 1904 he learned to play the B-flat cornet and traveled with the school band, giving concerts on different reservations. After a concert at First Mesa his adopted Paiute uncle, Talasayo, kept him from returning to the school, hiding him among the rocks near First Mesa.[1] He stayed with his uncle and was also cared for by his older brother, Nelson.

As he grew older, Pabanale became restless and wearied of reservation life. He wanted to travel, to explore and learn more about the white man's world. He revered his brother Nelson, who had gone his independent way some years earlier and whose achievements Irving sought to emulate. Pabanale traveled and traded, taking pride in his self-sufficiency. He probably was drawn to government service because of his brother's position as a policeman. Following in Nelson's footsteps, he gained the reputation of an aggressive law officer. His duties included checking Navajo camps for alcohol and, in 1918, forcing the conservative Hopis of Hotvela to be dipped in vats of sheep disinfectant, which was believed to help prevent the spread of influenza.

Nelson Pabanale left the police service in the 1920s and took training as a medicine man and healer. He persuaded Irving to do the same, and Pabanale soon began to practice medicine on First Mesa. Some people in his village, however, doubted his assertions that he was trained in the traditional medicine societies at Santa Clara Pueblo on the Rio Grande.

In 1936 Pabanale was invited by First Mesa leaders to assist in drafting the first Hopi tribal constitution, authorized by the Indian Reorganization Act of 1934. This work brought him into contact with representatives of the Bureau of Indian Affairs, men such as John Collier and Oliver La Farge. He was later elected a delegate from Tewa Village to the first Hopi Tribal Council. His most noteworthy position of power and prestige came in 1940 when he was selected to be chief judge of the Hopi Tribal Court. The new court, established under the Indian Reorganization Act, operated free from interference from the Bureau of Indian Affairs, and tribal members were entitled to confirm or recall judges.

In this instance Pabanale's efforts at culture brokering were not totally successful. His tenure as judge, from 1940 to 1949, was controversial. Concerned with upholding government regulations as they applied to the reservation, he earned the scorn and enmity of many conservative Hopis, who believed he imposed stiff sentences for minor infractions and was inflexible about relaxing the restrictive government grazing regulations.

Pabanale did not abandon his traditional roots during his years of government service. He was initiated into the Hopi Wuwtsim Society as a young man and continued to participate in Hopi and Tewa ceremonies.[2] In effect, he straddled American and Indian cultures. When he helped write the new constitution, he was concerned that it include provisions to preserve Hopi traditional life. But at the same time, he was a strong advocate for an elected tribal council, a concept foreign to Hopi culture and considered suspect by most people of the tribe.

Pabanale was neither a marginal progressive nor a staunch conservative. He was a pragmatic innovator. He reached his mature years when accelerated culture change was affecting most of the Hopi villages, especially on First Mesa. With the imposition of an artificial political unity, village life on the reservation became less insular. As the influence of outside agencies became more pervasive, the Hopis' lives changed radically.

Pabanale's active public life came to an end in 1949 when he resigned his office as judge. At the time, he was widely recognized as an influential public person by his peers as well as by people both on and off the reservation. His ensuing blindness and subsequent inactivity gave him time to reflect on the events and accomplishments of his years of service. Pabanale's implied purpose in telling his life story was to play the role of the respected elder. From the start, he assumed a "take charge" stance with regard to our relationship, controlling the narrative process. This approach was a form of traditional Tewa teaching, in which I was the apprentice sitting at the knee of the teacher. He was there to teach me about his life; it was my role to listen and learn. The narrative was

xv

strictly his agenda, and it defied collaboration; I was a facilitator. Since it was self-initiated and self-selected, it was "complete," and there was no need to add significantly to his initial telling.

By controlling his narrative, Pabanale was celebrating his claim to fame—his status as a successful culture broker. This agenda may account for the absence of substantive data concerning his early life and his reticence about his childhood experiences and participation in clan and village ceremonial activities. In Tewa culture, telling the story of one's life is a way to appreciate a person's external accomplishments. In Western culture, in contrast, a life history is not a record of outside achievements as much as it is a way to get inside a person. In socio-centric societies like that of the Tewas, people are reluctant to talk about themselves or attract undue attention. They are much more comfortable talking about their social groups.

The life history of Pabanale's nephew, Albert Yava, *Big Falling Snow* (Yava 1978), illustrates this concept. Yava was very much a part of the social fabric of Tewa-Hopi life. True to the structure of formal Tewa discourse, he talked about his clan and his society but not about himself. Yava made the distinction explicit: "What I have told you may not seem to be anything more than a lot of recollections, traditions, opinions and observations. Maybe that's all a person is, a collection of these things. I tried not to put myself forward too much, though I am sure some people will think I did not talk about myself enough. In our Indian way of looking at the world the individual isn't important, only the group. We forget the names of our heroes and villains, while remembering what the group did, for good or evil, and how it met challenges and dangers, and how it lived in balance with nature" (1978:139).

Yava valued extending ties with missionaries and government agents, and his narrative is characterized by a fearless assessment of the fundamental cultural differences between the Hopis and the Tewas. Nevertheless, Yava believed in close interactions with the Hopis in matters pertaining to ceremonial life and the protection of Hopi and Tewa lands. He was concerned that the traditional teachings of Tewa life would be lost if government schools were accepted, but he felt that some things about the white man's ways had to be learned if the next generation was to survive (Yava 1978:10–11). He was careful not to reveal his personal feelings about events in the life of the Tewa community, but he commented at length, from the perspective of an observer, about kinship ties and village history, contacts with other tribes, land conflicts with the Navajos, and differences between Tewa and Hopi values.

xvi

Pabanale also valued his ties with the outside world, but, unlike Albert Yava, he tells his story as a reporting of his own accomplishments. Pabanale paints on a broad canvas, carefully blending memories of an active and noteworthy life marked by public recognition and personal satisfaction. He saw the federal government as an omnipotent structure with influence over most avenues of native life. In his narrative there is a persistent thread of respect for and dedication to the precepts and representatives of federal power on the reservation and the privilege of being part of this authority. The transition from warrior-protectors of the Hopis to interpreters and go-betweens enabled the Arizona Tewas to exert considerable influence on their Hopi neighbors. As Yava points out (1978), the Tewas developed a kind of skewed reciprocity with the Hopis and the Americans. They willingly served as intermediaries between the Hopis and the numerous representatives of the outside world—Indian agents, missionaries, and school officials. They were astute power brokers, stepping into a void where their particular qualities were needed. In keeping with the Tewa role, Pabanale saw government service as a means of furthering some of his personal aspirations, such as earning recognition and respect from white officials and having a voice in the creation of new policies.

Toward the end of his life history, in the chapter "The Problem with Alcohol," Pabanale addresses a deeply felt concern about drinking on the reservation. He is speaking to all members of the tribal community—on all mesas—with the statement, "I would like to say that it is a great and considerable problem that permits me to speak in behalf of my Hopi people concerning liquor." His strongly voiced admonitions were related to his deeply felt religious beliefs and the effects that alcohol had on his kinsmen. In this address Pabanale speaks from the position of a respected elder whose status entitles him to state his views on various issues. He was what the Tewas call a *séño*, a respectful term for a mature older man.

The Distinctive Nature of Pabanale's Life History

What makes a life history unique? Each narrative is the work of a creative process of sifting, selecting, and ordering memories of events and experiences into a unique pattern. In all life histories the narrator has a special agenda to fulfill, guiding his or her life story in predetermined directions and imposing distinctiveness on it. In Native American accounts these considerations of one's life can integrate the mythic with

xvii

the substantive: reminiscences about tribal origins, migrations, the place and circumstances of coming of age; the dreams, experiences, and disappointments of becoming an adult; and the struggle to achieve wisdom and contentment as one grows older.

Pabanale's narrative makes an important contribution to a native assessment of life for two reasons. First, it does not suffer from the editorial distortions common among "as told to" accounts. It is an accurate and unchanged representation of his original story. Second, his narrative, unlike many Native American life histories, chronicles the life of a cultural innovator in an increasingly bicultural world.

Pabanale introduces himself first as a Tewa, then as a Hopi, and informs the reader that he is a descendant of those intrepid migrants who came to the Hopis nearly three hundred years ago. He then relates the account of this migration in all its fascinating detail. This is the framework that Pabanale constructs around his personal role as a Tewa cultural innovator. He does not dwell on the traditions of tribal life or clan and ceremonial duties; he says, in effect, that he saw his life as different. He did not conform to the cultural status quo but embarked on a life journey that was peripheral to the traditional Hopi world, sidestepping a strict and insular tribal life to pursue his own imaginative agenda. Pabanale is the antithesis of the stereotypic "Indian." His account illuminates another perspective on native life, that of a person who worked at the interface of two cultures. He sought and achieved personal advantage and some distinction in the American world of opportunity and change.

The Setting

The Hopis are a Pueblo Indian tribe of more than eleven thousand people. Their thirteen villages sit atop three fingerlike projections, or mesas, that extend southward from the extensive Black Mesa highlands in northeastern Arizona. Black Mesa itself is part of the massive arid Colorado Plateau to the north.

The mesas are close to the Four Corners area, a sacred region for the origin of ancestral Pueblo peoples. Today it is the place where the four states of Arizona, New Mexico, Utah, and Colorado come together. Many prehistoric sites of ancient Pueblo cultures, both large and small, are to be found here (Cordell 1984; Cordell and Gumerman 1989; Ford, Schroeder, and Peckham 1972; Ferguson 1996). Long before the arrival of the first Spaniards in the Southwest, the Hopis were ancient occupants of the region, where they have lived some two thousand years (Adams 1978:1).

Entering the Hopi country from the east, one encounters the first of the three Hopi mesas, numbered consecutively First, Second, and Third. On First Mesa are the villages of Walpi, Sitsomovi, and Tewa Village (formerly called Hano), where Irving Pabanale grew up. Below the mesa and adjacent to state highway 264 is the modern community of Polacca, founded in the 1890s by Tom Polacca, the first member of Tewa Village to adopt Christianity and build his house below the mesa.

Some fifteen miles to the west, on Second Mesa, are the villages of Musangnuvi, Supawlavi, and Songoopavi. Like Walpi, Second Mesa villages were relocated on top of the mesa during the late seventeenth century for protection from the Spaniards (Ellis 1974:57).

Eight miles west of Second Mesa lies Third Mesa, on which are located the villages of Orayvi, Hotvela, Paaqavi, and Kiqötsmovi. Orayvi claims to be the oldest continuously occupied settlement in North America. The analysis of ancient pottery from the area indicates that Orayvi has been occupied since A.D. 1150 and possibly earlier (Levy 1992). In ancient times Orayvi had a population of one thousand or more; today it has fewer than one hundred residents (Ellis 1974:33). Toward the end of the nineteenth century, internal factionalism grew between progressives—those friendly to the whites and willing to have their children sent to government schools—and the staunch conservatives, who resisted all government intrusion (Levy 1992:79, 93–94, 160–61; Whiteley 1988). In 1906 the two opposing factions split permanently, resulting in the partial abandonment of Orayvi and the establishment of new villages by the antagonists.

The progressive faction moved below the mesa and established the town of Kiqötsmovi (known previously as New Orayvi). It is currently the seat of tribal government and the headquarters for the Hopi Tribal Council. It is a secular village, quite removed from traditional Hopi culture. In 1907 the conservative faction from Orayvi established the village of Hotvela a few miles west of Orayvi. It remains a traditional Hopi town, although some of the age-old ceremonies are no longer performed there.

In 1909 a less conservative faction from Hotvela moved away to found the town of Paaqavi, a mile from Hotvela. The remaining Hopi settlement, Munkapi, was established as a farming colony by the people of Orayvi in the 1870s. It is located some forty miles to the northwest of Orayvi, near the Navajo town of Tuba City. It is a choice location for farming since it has a year-round water supply, which is used for irrigation on a communal basis. Munkapi itself is divided into two distinct factions: lower Munkapi considers itself anti-government and conservative whereas the upper village is recognized as a progressive settlement. The two communities are physically as well as ideologically separate.

This is high desert country. The elevations of the Hopi mesas range from 4,500 to 6,500 feet. The climate reflects the altitude and dryness of the region, with cold snowy winters and hot dry summers. Below the mesas, numerous washes drain the sandstone-capped Colorado Plateau and provide varying quantities of water year round. The Hopis have traditionally been farmers, relying on hardy cultigens planted in protected areas close to springs or washes. Floodwater farming is the most important farming technique (Hack 1942:34). Seeds are planted in areas where flood runoffs from streams spread out to cover large fields with water. Another successful method of crop production is sand-dune farming, a form of dry farming. Sand dunes contain a relatively high degree of moisture and are used for crops especially during times of erosion when floodwater farming is not possible. Because of high winds, brush windbreaks are constructed and held in place by large stones to protect the plants (Hack 1942:38). In addition to maize, beans, and squash, the Hopis grow chilies, tomatoes, melons, peaches, apples, and apricots— fruit crops introduced by the Spanish. Many are dried and stored for use throughout the year. Today much of the Hopi diet consists of Anglo-American foods.

The English language, as well as Hopi, is universally spoken throughout the Hopi country, including Tewa Village. The Hopi language belongs to the Numic branch of the wide-ranging Uto-Aztecan language family. Members of this dispersed family extend from the valley of Mexico through California, the Great Basin, and the Hopi mesas. The Rio Grande Tewa language and its close relative, Arizona Tewa, belong to the Kiowa Tanoan family, which includes the Pueblos of the Rio Grande as well as the Kiowa of Texas. Rio Grande Tewa is considered a single language with village dialects.

The Arizona Tewas have a special status among Pueblo peoples. They are the only group known to have survived the Pueblo diaspora of the eighteenth century intact, retaining their language and many elements of their culture. In the almost three hundred years that Southern Tewa has been spoken at First Mesa, it has undergone changes in grammar and vocabulary, and today it is considered a separate language, Arizona Tewa. It is spoken by about half the members of the community

(Kroskrity 1993) and can still be understood by their Rio Grande relatives.

The Arizona Tewas are a unique minority and an integral part of the Hopi community of First Mesa, where they persist as a cultural island within the broader Hopi sphere. Their culture includes elements from the Rio Grande Tewas as well as from the Hopis. Over the years, they have accommodated themselves to Hopi social and religious life, but their participation has been by choice, not coercion. As part of this accommodation, the Arizona Tewas adopted the Hopi matrilineal clan system, allowing them to interact more effectively with the Hopis, especially with regard to intertribal marriages and ceremonial participation. Tewas and Hopis have similar kinship systems, with extended families grouped into matrilineal clans, in which affiliation and descent are reckoned through the female line. Clan membership cuts across villages and mesas, and clans maintain strict rules of exogamy. In addition to regulating marriage, clans serve as guardians of rituals, ceremonial knowledge, and associated paraphernalia and regalia (costumes and katsina masks). The society is crisscrossed as well by a large number of non-kinship fraternities or societies that have important responsibilities in conjunction with the clans in the complex ceremonial cycle.

A Brief History of the Arizona Tewas

For almost three hundred years, the Arizona Tewas have lived among the Hopis of First Mesa as a separate community, having migrated from their northern Rio Grande villages around 1700. This relocation is unparalleled in the history of the Pueblo Southwest. In the past, migrating groups in this region have tended to merge with larger communities, resulting in the absorption of the newcomers and the loss of their cultural and linguistic distinctiveness. The Arizona Tewas, however, have successfully preserved their language and much of their Rio Grande culture to the present day.

A primary factor in this cultural continuity was the perpetuation of the Arizona Tewas' migration history through oral narrative. This tale was conveyed from generation to generation in the Tewa language to all youths undergoing initiation rituals. The account of that memorable journey describes the Tewas' travel to First Mesa at the invitation of the Hopis and the events that led to the establishment of Tewa Village atop First Mesa.

Irving Pabanale appropriately begins his life story with a version of

xxi

the migration legend that he learned from his father. It is a fitting prologue to the reminiscences of his life experiences and accomplishments as an Arizona Tewa. His account attributes the migration of the Tewas to the urgent pleas of the Hopis for help in fighting the Utes and Navajos, who were raiding the First Mesa village of Walpi.

Ancestors of the Arizona and Rio Grande Tewas—Tanoan-speaking peoples—are believed to have entered the Rio Grande valley sometime after A.D. 700, having moved away from their homes in the San Juan River area near Mesa Verde (Ford 1972:31). They proceeded to diversify culturally and linguistically as they moved south, separating into three language groups—the Tewa, Towa, and Tiwa—in the Kiowa-Tanoan language family. Kiowa-Tanoan is estimated to have had a population of some ten thousand speakers in 1634 (Hammond and Rey 1953).

After A.D. 1300 one group of Tewa speakers settled in the Galisteo Basin, south of Santa Fe, while the other Tewas remained in the north, in the San Juan area. As early as 1583, these Southern Tewas were designated *Tanos* by the Spanish, who recognized them as a separate administrative group, apart from other Tewas. The Tanos themselves acknowledged their distinctive cultural status, calling themselves *T'anutowa*, "live-down-country people." This designation of the Southern Tewa branch refers only to habitat, not to language (Harrington 1916:576). There seems to have been little linguistic difference between the northern and southern groups. Don Diego de Vargas, who reconquered the Pueblos in 1693, reported that the Tewas and the Tanos spoke the same language (Espinosa 1940:76).

The full impact of the Spanish conquest was felt following the ruthless colonization of New Mexico by Don Juan de Oñate in 1598. The Spaniards imposed harsh restrictions on Pueblo social, economic, and religious life. The Tanos were especially hard hit by the Spanish colonial program because of their proximity to Santa Fe, the headquarters of the regime in New Mexico. They were required to provide considerable tribute and services and were prohibited from participating in their native ceremonies and dances. The padres zealously pursued the forced conversion of the Pueblo people to Christianity, especially among the Tanos. By 1630 some ninety missions had been established in dozens of Pueblo towns (Hodge, Hammond, and Rey 1945; Scholes 1942).

The situation grew worse with the implementation of the *encomienda* system, which contracted out native labor (Hackett 1937: 260). The Spanish resorted to repressive measures, including imprisonment, lashing, and hanging, to counter Pueblo resistance to conversion (Schroeder 1972: 51). The disruption of social and economic life contributed to the spread of intervillage strife and factionalism, adding to the frustration and resentment of the Pueblo people. In addition to the spread of smallpox epidemics throughout the region (Leonard 1932:35), an unidentified pestilence killed more than three thousand Indians, or more than 10 percent of the Pueblo population, in 1640 (Scholes 1936:324).

By 1643 only forty-three Rio Grande Pueblos survived of the more than ninety that had existed around 1600 (Forbes 1960:139). The population declined from thirty to forty thousand to about sixteen thousand (Hackett and Shelby 1942:xxxi). In this period of upheaval Apache bands, aided by the recent acquisition of the horse (Schroeder 1972:52), stepped up the pace and intensity of their raids.

Unrelenting suffering and fierce antagonism to Spanish rule brought matters to a head in 1680 with the outbreak of the Pueblo Revolt. All the Pueblos, including the northern Tewas and the southern Tanos, were actively involved in the fighting. The Tanos were the first to attack Santa Fe, which they occupied until 1692. With the expulsion of the Spanish from New Mexico, the Pueblos gained a twelve-year respite from colonial domination. Inter-Pueblo dissension began to escalate, and hostile groups formed alliances. The Pueblos of Pecos, Taos, and Jemez and the Keres villages of San Felipe, Santo Domingo, and Cochiti were allied against the Tanos, Tewas, and Picuris (Twitchell 1914:2:276; Espinosa 1940:110).

The retreat of the Spaniards also led to increased Apache raids on the outlying Pueblos, and the attacks could not be effectively repulsed by the fractionalized, feuding villages. Consequently, the southern Tanos were forced to abandon the Galisteo Basin and relocate to the northern Tewa country. Here they found no respite from Spanish oppression, Apache raids, and epidemics, however. In the period 1664–74 de Vargas brought a group of colonists to establish the second permanent Spanish civil settlement in New Mexico (Reed 1952:16). To make room for the new arrivals, he evicted the Indians from San Lazaro and located the colonists in the new Spanish-Mexican village of Santa Cruz. The evicted Tanos were forced to move in with the natives of nearby San Cristobal. In retaliation, they burned the church of San Cristobal and killed some missionary priests. This incident sparked the unsuccessful revolt of 1696, in which the Tanos of San Lazaro and San Cristobal were joined by the Jemez, the northern Tiwas, and some Keresans (Simmons 1979:186).[3]

The Tano population dispersed after the failure of this latest uprising. Tanos from San Cristobal joined with other northern Tewas in migrating to the Hopi country, where they founded the Tewa community of Hano on First Mesa around 1700 (Reed 1943a:73).

The Tanos/Tewas were reported to be at First Mesa in 1701 and most likely were involved in the attack on Awatovi (see Brew 1949 and Montgomery, Smith, and Brew 1949). Awatovi was one of the largest Hopi towns in the Spanish province of Tusayan and sat atop Antelope Mesa, to the east of Walpi and First Mesa. Awatovi overlooked the broad Jeddito Valley, the main trade route to the Zuni villages and easily reached by the Spaniards from their headquarters in Santa Fe. From 1540 to 1628, missionaries frequently visited Awatovi and the other villages. In 1629 the mission of San Bernardino was established at Awatovi under Father Francisco de Porras, who was killed in 1633. Little is known of the early mission period; the records of the mission were most likely destroyed after the Pueblo Revolt (Bartlett 1934:56, 1–12; Hodge 1907:119).

When the Spanish reconquered New Mexico in 1692, they received a friendly reception at Awatovi, and several friars were later sent there to perform baptisms. The Spanish revitalized the former mission and proceeded to spread Christianity among the receptive townspeople. Hopi leaders from other villages, however, were greatly concerned by the threat of another Spanish intrusion into Hopi life and the violation of native customs and beliefs. In November 1700, it is believed, Hopi warriors from Orayvi, Songoopavi, and other villages joined together to attack and destroy Awatovi. They burned the village to the ground, killed the men, and took the women and children to distribute among the other villages (Hodge 1907).

In the early eighteenth century the Tewas began to make their influence felt as both antagonists and protectors of the Hopis and later as activists in the process of cultural and political change. For further details on the culture and history of the Tewas, see Dozier 1966, 1956, and 1954; Ellis 1967; Ford et al. 1972; Kroskrity 1993; Ortiz 1979; Reed 1952 and 1943a; Schroeder 1972; and Yava 1978.

Structure of the Book

Irving Pabanale's narrative, Part 1, offers vignettes of his life as traveler, trader, adventurer, political activist, law enforcer, and upholder of the white man's authority. His purpose in telling his story—to be remembered for his accomplishments—is evident in the frequent asides with which he concludes segments of the narrative, saying, "This is what I did at the time" or "This is what I did for my people." The text is at times disjointed and sketchy, and it is impersonal and devoid of emotional detail. Yet from it we learn a great deal about the important changes that took place in the lives of the Hopi and Tewa people. The chapter titles were added later, but the divisions reflect how Pabanale told his story.

Part 2 contains the texts of seven folktales Pabanale told his children and wanted included in his story.

Part 3 supplements and clarifies the events, places, and situations mentioned in Pabanale's text. The chapters here are presented in the same order as those of Part 1. For example, Pabanale's account of the legend of the Tewa migration is augmented by ethnohistorical annotations based on archaeological and ethnological research.

Three distinguished tribal members—Dewey Healing, Emory Sekaquaptewa, and Abbott Sekaquaptewa—contributed their personal assessment of events and individuals mentioned in the text, providing interesting insights from a native perspective. Dewey Healing, a Tewa, was a highly respected village official who worked to preserve traditional values of Tewa culture. He labored ceaselessly to secure the reestablishment of the Hopi Tribal Council after it was disbanded. Healing served as a councilman and as chairman of the Hopi tribe. Emory Sekaquaptewa, a Hopi, was very supportive of the project to publish Pabanale's narrative and provided invaluable assistance. Abbott Sekaquaptewa, Emory's brother, served as chairman of the Hopi Tribal Council (1964–76) and of the Hopi tribe. As a board member and chairman of the national organization Futures, he worked with prominent Americans to raise money for the education of Indian children. He also founded and edited the Hopi newspaper *Qua Toqti*.

The appendixes provide a content analysis of the known variants of the Tewa migration legend and comments by Emory Sekaquaptewa on drilling for oil on the Hopi reservation.

Aerial view of First Mesa. Tewa Village is in the foreground. Photograph by Milton Snow. Courtesy of the Museum of Northern Arizona Photo Archives, Flagstaff.

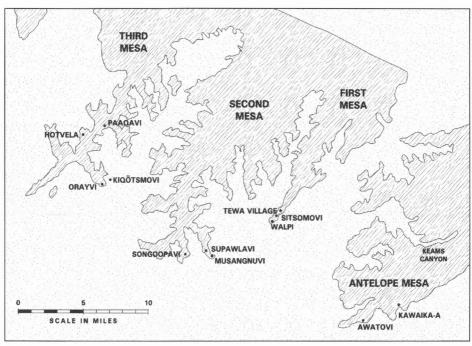

The Hopi mesas and villages. Frederick J. Dockstader, *The Kachina and the White Man*, rev. ed., 1985, p. 12. Courtesy of the University of New Mexico Press. Updated by Jack Dynis

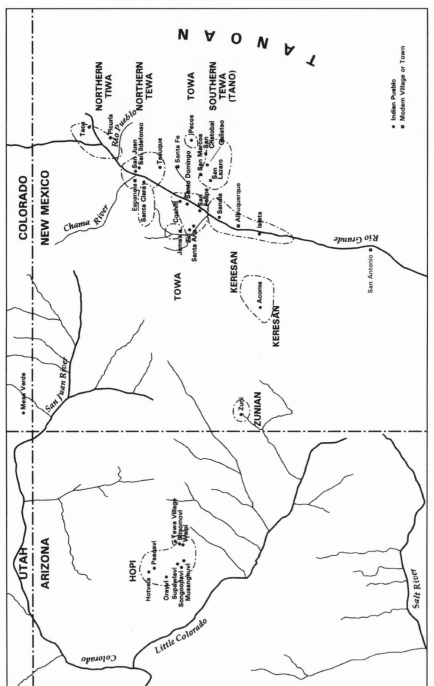

Hopi villages and Rio Grande Pueblos, with language family designations. Elsie Clews Parsons, *Pueblo Indian Religion*, 2 vols., frontispiece, vol. I, 1939. Courtesy of the University of Chicago Press. Amended and updated by Jack Dynis.

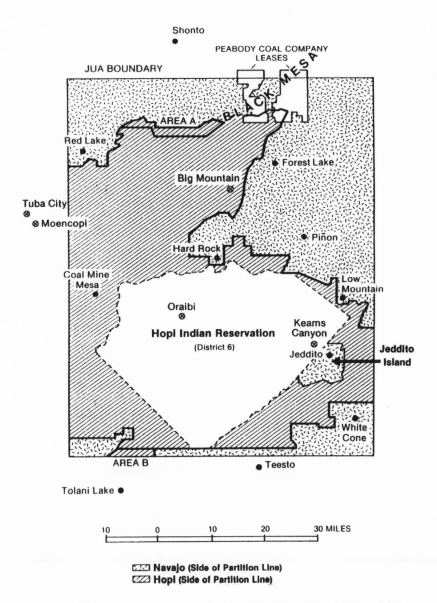

Partition of the Joint Use Area. Ward Churchill, "Genocide in Arizona? The 'Navajo-Hopi Land Dispute' in Perspective," *Critical Issues in Native North America* 2 (Dec. 1968): 119, graphics by Steve Brown. Courtesy of IWGIA, Copenhagen.

ABOVE: Tewa Village, First Mesa, around 1880, looking north. Photograph by John K. Hillers. National Anthropological Archives, Smithsonian Institution, Washington, D.C.

TOP RIGHT: Tewa Village, First Mesa, around 1880, looking south. The village of Walpi is in the background; the middle area will eventually be occupied by the village of Sitsomovi. Peaches can be seen drying on a Tewa roof. Photograph by John K. Hillers. National Anthropological Archives, Smithsonian Institution, Washington, D.C.

BOTTOM RIGHT: The Keams Canyon Day School and students around 1890. To the left is the Thomas Keam Trading Post. Photo by Ben Wittick. Courtesy of the Museum of New Mexico, Santa Fe.

Irving Pabanale (*hands together*) with three reservation policemen.
Photographer unknown. Courtesy of the Museum of Northern Arizona Photo
Archives, Flagstaff.

Nelson Oyaping, chief of Hopi police and older brother of Irving Pabanale, around 1915. Photographer unknown. Leo Crane, *Indians of the Enchanted Desert*, 1925, p. 315. Courtesy of Little, Brown and Co., Boston.

I hereby certify, That _Irving Pabanela_ and
Josie Coompepe, known by me[a] to be the persons described in the
above license, were married by me[a] in our presence[a] on the 22 day of _June_, A. D. 1909,
at _Polacca, Ariz._, in the State[a] Territory[a] of
in compliance with the laws of said State or Territory.[a]
by declaring in our presence their intention to live together permanently as husband and wife.[a]

WITNESSES:

George Cochier

Jane Kawonhonema

Name, _J. B. Epp._

Official designation, _Ordained Missiona_

Address, _Oraibi, Ariz._

(a) The unused words should be crossed out.
† If marriage is by a clergyman or by a magistrate the officiating person must sign this certificate, giving the title authorizing him so to do, and his address.
If marriage is by declaration, two adult witnesses must sign this certificate.
The above license, with the return of marriage, must be immediately returned to the Agent who issued it by the person who solemnized the marriage or by one of the witnesses.

5—178.

(TO BE GIVEN TO APPLICANTS FOR LICENSE TO MARRY.)

No. 1.

MARRIAGE LICENSE.

Moqui Agency.

Arizona. State Territory.

License is hereby issued for the marriage of the following persons:

	MAN.	WOMAN.
INDIAN NAME	Pabanela.	Coompepe.
ENGLISH NAME	Irving.	Josie.
NAME ON ALLOTMENT ROLL		
AGE	25	20
RELATIONSHIP TO EACH OTHER	None.	None.
BLOOD OR NATIONALITY	Indian.	Indian.
TRIBE OR CITIZENSHIP	Hopi.	Hopi.
NAME OF FATHER	Secatyauma.	Isia.
NAME OF MOTHER	Charlaco.	Wela.
PREVIOUS MARRIAGE	None.	None.

THEY WISH TO BE MARRIED

1. By a clergyman[a] civil magistrate[a] in accordance with the laws of this State[a]; Territory[a]; or

2. By declaring (in the presence of adult witnesses, who shall sign the certificate) their intention to live together permanently as husband and wife.[b]

WITNESS MY HAND, this 4th day of June, 1909.

Name, _Horton H. Miller_

Official designation, Superintendent.

(a) The unused words should be crossed out.
(b) This second form of marriage to be used only when it is impracticable or very difficult to obtain the services of a clergyman or civil magistrate.

Marriage Certificate No. 1 issued by Superintendent Horton H. Miller, Hopi
Indian Agency, Keams Canyon, Arizona, for the marriage of Irving Pabanale
and Josie Coompepe.

Pabanale with his wife, Josie, and daughter Edith in the 1920s. Photographer unknown. Courtesy of Edith Nash.

Pabanale (*left*) with Timothy Tumosi, a fellow policeman, in the 1920s.
Photographer unknown. Courtesy of Edith Nash.

Pabanale at the San Diego Fair around 1920. The Plains headdress was adopted by Pueblo people, including the Tewas, for social dances. Pabanale is wearing the policeman's badge. White official and photographer are unknown. Courtesy of Edith Nash.

Pabanale (*left*) with guests and Walpi Bear clan chief, Kootka, in the 1930s in Sitsomovi. Photographer unknown. Courtesy of the Museum of Northern Arizona Photo Archives, Flagstaff.

Pabanale's grocery and "curio" store in Sitsomovi around the 1940s. Courtesy of the Museum of Northern Arizona Photo Archives, Flagstaff.

The Hopi Tribal Court in session. Chief Judge Pabanale is seated at the extreme right. Photograph by Milton Snow. Courtesy of the Museum of Northern Arizona Photo Archives, Flagstaff.

Pabanale as chief judge of the tribal court, early 1940s. Photograph by Milton Snow. Courtesy of the Museum of Northern Arizona Photo Archives, Flagstaff.

ABOVE: Edith Nash, daughter of Irving Pabanale, holding one of her prize-winning pottery trays. Photograph by Christy Turner II. Courtesy of the Museum of Northern Arizona Photo Archives, Flagstaff.

TOP RIGHT: Pabanale with Robert Black at the Research Center of the Museum of Northern Arizona, 1969. Photograph courtesy of the Museum of Northern Arizona Photo Archives, Flagstaff.

BOTTOM RIGHT: Letter from Irving Pabanale, witnessed by his daughter, Clara Belle Lewis, giving permission to the editor to publish his narrative.

Pabanale at the Museum of Northern Arizona, 1969. Photograph by
Robert Black.

STANDING FLOWER

The Coming of the Tewas

My name is Irving Pabanale. My last name means "standing flower" in English [*po'bi-neli*—"flower standing"]. I would like to tell something of my life from my childhood up until today. I will tell it as near as I can remember.

I will first tell about how our Tewa people came to Hopi land years ago. Of course, I can't say the exact year; however, I will tell what our old people used to tell us, and right at the present time our older people are still telling about how they came to the Hopi land. It must be somewhere around four hundred years ago at the time when the Spaniards came and went through this country, led by a man by the name of Coronado. That was when we Tewa people were called to come to the Hopi land. As I have said, I will tell just what I learned from my older people, as they were the ones—my clan [*phe'towa*—Stick clan] were the ones—that brought the people from near San Juan. The place is now a ruin. The name of that place where our people had come from in those days is called C`e'wadeh; that's a Tewa name. It is a white strip in the middle of a high rock, which is why they named it C`e'wadeh. That was the place where our people were living.

In those days there were a lot of enemies coming to the Hopi land and to the mesas where they were living. Finally, they got together, the Hopi chiefs, and they wondered where they would go for aid, for someone to help them. They were talking among themselves and then they said that there were some people that were good in fighting. They said that they would go to them for aid, to help them to fight, as there were not many Hopis left, and so they got busy. One time, then, two men were asked to go over to New Mexico to these Tewa people for help. One was a Snake clan man and the other a Hopi Bear clan man. They were sent; they were chiefs also. And so they were sent to New Mexico to these Tewa people.

Of course, I can't say how they went, but I'm telling it according to what I have heard from our people, which was handed down from generation to generation. So they were sent there and they came to that place about a little after sundown. They were standing at the plaza wondering where the chief was living. As they were standing there, a Tewa man came to them. They had blankets around them, these two Hopi men. He asked them who they were. Then they said that they were Hopis. "And what intention have you got to be around here this time of night?" They said they came to see the Tewa chief. "All right," he said; the Tewa man said to them, "I will take you to the chief." And so he took those two men to where the Tewa chief was living. It was a house three stories high where he was living. When they came in there, the chief was sitting there at his home. When they came in, the chief was looking at them. Then he told them to sit down and so they sat down. Then the Tewa man told the chief that they were Hopis. "Well," the chief asked, "what kind of a tribe are the Hopis?" Then the Tewa chief asked them what was their intention in being there. They said, "We came for your help; we have a lot of enemies coming to us and we are not very many left, and so we got together and talked among ourselves and we thought we would come for aid. We heard that the Tewa people were good fighters and so that's why we came over here for you to send your men out to the Hopi land where we came from." The Tewa chief said, "Is that what you came here for? But I don't agree with you. I don't want my people to be killed by enemies, so I don't agree with you two, and so you can go back." This is what he said to them the first time when they came there.

So they came back home and the Hopis on the mesa got together and asked them what they had found out. They told them that the Tewa chief didn't want them [his men] to come there. Then the Hopi chiefs said, "Once is not enough. When you want anything, you can't get it right away and so you will go again." In a couple of days they went again—the same men, the Snake clan man and the Bear clan man. And that was the second time they went over. When they came over there, they knew where the chief's home was; they went directly there. When they came in, the chief looked at them and recognized that they were the same men; then he asked them to sit down. So they sat down and again the Tewa chief asked them what they had in mind in coming over to them again. They said, "A couple of days ago we were here and asked for your help. We want your men to come out to the Hopi land to help against the enemies that are coming there. This is what we said when we were here the first time," they said.

Again he said, "I told you I don't want my people to be going out where there are enemies. I don't want to expose my people. And so you can go back." And they came back again. They told the other chiefs what the Tewa chief had said. Then they said that they would again go over and so in a few days they went back again. In a few days they went again and the Tewa chief noticed that they were the same men that came there before. He asked them what they were there for. They said the same thing, that they came for help, for the Tewa to be sent out to the Hopi land. This was the third time. Then he said to them, "What kind of life are you having up there in the way of food? Is the food plentiful?" And the Hopi said it was. This was the question he asked them at the third time. Then he said to them, "What do you think our reward will be? You don't say anything about that and I can't send my men for nothing to attack the enemy." And so they said, "Well, we have to go back and find out." And so they went back again and they told the other chiefs what the Tewa chief had said. Then the Hopi chiefs said, "We were ignorant for not saying any reward." The chief said to the others to come to his house the next day, after when they had their breakfast, and to wash their hair and to come over there to his house where they would work on some feathers, as the Hopi usually do. The next day the others washed their hair and then went over to the chief's house—the head chief of the Hopi. They came there and they were working on feathers, making their *pahos* [prayer sticks] and other things.[1] The chief made one *paho* about six inches long and made two others that were short—from the middle of your hand up to the middle of your finger. He made a long one and two short ones. They call that *sakwavaho* [blue prayer sticks]. One, he carved at the tip and he painted it yellow or orange and made two dots on it and another dot down below. That's how the *paho* was made. After he got through with them, he tied those two short ones together and then fixed a turkey feather behind the two *pahos*. The other long one had four feathers attached to it, and that one was painted blue.

After they finished that, the chief who made the *pahos*, the prayer sticks, said to them, "Now when you go again, you take this along." Of course, the Hopis know what those *paho* represent. That long one represents land and those other two short ones represent population. One of them is carved as a female and the other one is a male. They got ready to go again and the Hopi chief told them to take along those li'l *atö'ö'ö*, they call them [woven capes]. They're embroidered red, blue, and white. They took that along with them and also those prayer feathers when they came to the Tewa. When they came a little after sundown, the chief

5

was still awake, for that was the custom of the chief; he didn't go to sleep until late, after all the people are in bed, then they go in bed. That was the custom of the Indian people.

They came there and he was looking at them and he knew it was the same men. They had something under their arms. They sat down and untied what they had and they said, "This is what we brought." That's what they said to the Tewa chief. Then he was looking at them, and he said, "I don't know what they are; what kind of stuff is that; what do they represent?" Then they said, "This long one represents land and these two that are tied together represent population; one is a female and the other one is male, and these short feathers represent raindrops. And so this is what we brought to you if you agree to your men coming out." The Tewa chief said to them, "This is what I want, but when you first came here, you offered nothing. You did not say what reward you would give if I sent my men. Now, I agree with you, but I have to have my men call out and notify the people for so many days." This is what the Tewa chief said to them. "And so you will go now. We will have to call out to the people tomorrow morning and tell them that they will get ready in eight days; then we will start from here." That's what the chief said to those two Hopi men. So they came [home]—they turned back. When they came home they told them that they [the Tewas] agreed to come, and so they were glad of what they got—of what they want.

The next morning, one of the Tewa men called out when the sun rose, as that was the custom. Whenever they're going to announce anything, they call out to the people when the sun rises.[2] He called out and told them to get ready, that they were going out to the Hopi country, to help them, for the enemies were coming to them. "Get ready in eight days," he told the people. They were making their bows and arrows and what equipment they use in fighting—their spears and their headdresses, and all that.

In eight days when they were going to start, the chief went over to the other side of the river where they would go, and he made an announcement. He said that those who would go would come from a certain row of houses, not all of them at that time, but just half of them. And so they were coming across the river to the place where they were gathering together. When they were about to start, there was a lady coming from the other side of the row of houses. She was not included to come, but she came there and said that she was going to follow them because she wanted to come and she had a baby on her back, and so they said all right. "If you wish to go, it's up to you," they said to her. After they got

6

together, a man that was the head of those people there—he was a Stick clan man—said he was going to lead the group. And so he sprinkled cornmeal and put the feather down on the cornmeal, in the way of saying that that was the road that they were going to start on.[3] They started from there in the afternoon.

The first day they went as far as Santa Clara. There is a big point that I know of; that is where they stayed overnight. So the next morning when they got up, they asked, "Which people were going; what clans were going?" They found out there were eight clans, the Stick clan, Tobacco clan, Sun clan, Katsina clan, Cloud clan, Sand clan, Cottonwood clan, and the Butterfly clan. They were the ones that were coming out. So after they found out how many clans were coming, then they started again. They were coming among the Pueblos that were living out that way. Whenever the drought is gone, they come to a village or a place where the people are living and they get their food that way, they were coming out. Finally, they got to Ganado [a Navajo town in Arizona forty-six miles northwest of Gallup, New Mexico], and that's the place, it was told to us, that they buried some *paho*. The Tewa people did that.

Before they started again, the Tewa chief said, "No telling; they might treat us mean and if they do treat us mean, they might drive us back home sometime. Then we will come and stop here and here is the place we will stop instead of going way back to our own place." This is what the Tewa chief said to the crowds before they started from Ganado. So, from there they start again. Finally, they got to where we call Keams Canyon [eight miles east of First Mesa]. They got there and went down the valley and they heard some noise like water running. It was making a big noise and so they asked two of them to see what it was. So the two went over there to where the sound was. They came there and there was water about one foot high. It was boiling water. It looked like it was boiling, but it was not boiling. It was still water but it was standing about a foot high. That's where they stayed that night. Then the chief told two men to go down as far as they could, to find out if they were near the Hopi mesa. So the spies [scouts] went down as far as the last point before Polacca; there is a point there, the last point you come to when coming to the mesa. They got that far and saw a light. Then they went back and they told their people that they would be there the next day. The next day they got up and had their breakfast and they came down to that valley and went as far as where they call Blue Bird Hill. That's where they stopped until all of them were gathered there. The

Hopis were watching for them to come and they saw the crowd on that Blue Bird Hill. "It must be them," they said. The two Hopi chiefs got ready and came down to meet them and the Tewa people started down from that Blue Bird Hill, on straight toward the mesa.

They met one another at the wash, about a mile from the foot of First Mesa. That's where they met them. Then from there the Hopi chiefs took the lead bringing them, and got them over to where there is a high rock. They stopped there and the chief said that they were going to stay there as there was a spring a little ways from there which they will have for water. So that's where they stopped; they didn't take them up on the mesa. And so they were living there; they made their little homes there, and they lived there for some time. Pretty soon their food was all gone. They had no farms and they were hard up in the way of food. Then they came up on the mesa, to the Hopi women who were making some food. They said they were hungry. It was said that when the Hopi ladies were stirring their cornmeal, and when it was hot, they would take one of their stirrers and hand it to the Tewa, to get the cornmeal on it. But it was too hot and they couldn't get the food; then they told them that they weren't hungry.

This is the way they were treating them until the enemies of the Hopi were coming. They were always on the lookout for them. They saw a light over at where they call a midpoint, that evening, and they noticed that the enemy was coming. So the next morning, early in the morning, the two Hopi chiefs got up and went down to where the Tewa people were staying. They came down there and said to them, "Now we came down here to you people as you are here to help us against our enemies. They are coming again and we came down to ask you to come and meet them." The Tewa chief said, "No! How can we attack the enemy when we are hungry? When we come up on top of the mesa for food, you don't give us food and so we are not going to fight." The two chiefs were standing there and they said, "Well, this is what you came here for and so we came down for your people to help us." Again the Tewa chief didn't agree. Then the third time when they asked them to come, they said, "All right; as we have come here to help you, we will try to drive away the enemy for you."

And so the Tewa chief called out for the men to dress up in their war costumes. They painted themselves with red paint and had war bonnets and spears, bows and arrows and quivers. They also had shields that they protected themselves with when they are fighting. In those days, there were no guns or anything like that, just bows and arrows that they

8

fight with. And so they gave a big yell and were all dressed up and followed the two chiefs up as far as the Gap; the Gap is still there.[4] That's
where they sat down. They looked on the other side of the Gap and it
was about a mile and a half where the enemy was coming; they could
see them. Some were on horseback and some on foot. The Tewa came
to the two Hopi chiefs and the two chiefs said, "They are coming close
now." "All right," the Tewa chief said, "we will try to drive them away,"
and they came down to meet them. As they were coming close to where
those enemies were, the Tewa chief said to his men, "We will try and
just drive them, until I announce where we will throw them down,
because what we are going to fight for, for them [the Hopi], is the land,
and I don't want the land to be bloody. When I announce for you to kill
them or throw them down, then you start to kill them." And so, they
just drove them—they were shooting at them and making all kinds of
hoot noise. Finally, they drove them back; they were driving them up
that valley, up to Wepo.[5] To the west of Wepo was the place where the
enemy camped that night and some of them went up that hill—a sloped
sandhill—and the Tewa went after them and drove them back down.

When they were going a little way above Wepo, the Tewa chief
announced for them to throw them down if they can. Then he said,
"The first one that you throw down, you must put a rock there where
he fell." That's what the chief said to his men. So they went on fighting
up the valley and pretty soon a call was heard that one of the Tewa men
was thrown down. The chief asked, "Who is he?" They said, "A Sun
clan man." The chief said, "Let his body be there; a man's body lays
anywhere, as he is a man. Let the coyotes eat his body and let his skull
be there." That's what the chief said.

Then, on the fighting went. Another one was thrown down. "Who is
he?" the chief asked. It was a Cottonwood clan, a Katsina clan man.[6] He
said the same thing, "Let him lay there. He's a man and his body can lay
there." So they went on again. Pretty soon another Tewa was killed. He
was a Stick clan man. Those were three men who were very well known,
who were thrown down. They were fighting up the valley towards the
north until they went about nine or ten miles, when the enemy chief
stood up and said, "We will retreat," motioning with his hand to quit
fighting. But the Tewa chief said, "We will not retreat," and they went
on fighting until a man called out, "That will be enough," so then they
stopped. The enemy got together in a group. There was just a few men
that were left with their chief. Some Tewa were killed, of course, but not
very many. When they stopped fighting, the enemy said, "Who are you

9

people? No one ever has done this to us. Who are you people; what tribe are you? You have pretty near killed us off, but one of us has to go back and tell what has happened and so that will be all; don't fight anymore." And so they were talking with one another from a little distance.

Then a Tewa man said, "We are Tewas," and he asked, "Who are you?" And the chief of the enemy said that they were Ute Indians. "We are brothers but we have done away with our young men." That's what the Ute chief said. "No wonder, you are good fighters. Now we must come to one another, making four steps, putting down our bows and arrows, and another four steps, putting down our spears and knives, and another four steps, when we will put down our shields. Then we will meet one another." That's what the Ute chief said to the Tewas.

The Tewa people said, "We must guard our chief. They might jump on him when he comes to that chief." So the two guarded the Tewa chief when they were making those steps. The Ute chief first made four steps and put down his bows and arrows, and so the Tewa chief did the same. The last steps that they made, they put down their shields. Now the Ute chief said, "Now I got nothing in my hands." So they came to one another and the Ute chief put his hand out and shook hands with the Tewa chief, and then again said, "I'm sorry we have done away with our men. Why didn't you say that you were Tewas, as we are recognized as brothers, and now we have done away with our men."

Now after they had put down all those weapons, the Ute chief got his bow and gave it to the Tewa chief. That bow, it was said, was made of elk horn. The Ute chief told the Tewa chief that the bow he gave him will never come to rot. "Then you give me your bow," he said to the Tewa chief, and so the Tewa chief gave him his bow, which was made of oak. Then the Ute chief said, "We will never fight again. Now we know one another, we are brothers, but we have fought, not knowing who you were, and so now we are going back," the Ute chief said. So they turned back and went north with the few men that were left of them. Then the Tewa chief said, "Let's go back, but we must go back on our tracks where we fought; then when we come to where we first threw down that man, that's where we're going to stop until we all get together, and then we will go on again." So they started to come back, and those Ute Indians went away towards the north. We don't know where they came from, but now days we know they must have come from Cortez [in the southwestern corner of Colorado], where the Ute country is.

So the Tewa people came on down on the tracks where they fought. When they came to the Ute man whom they threw down first, they opened him up at the breast and took out his heart, and the others that were lying there, they scalped them.[7] They scalped them, and they were bringing the scalps. When they came to the place where they met the Utes that morning, the chief stopped and waited until all of them got there, and then he said to them, "Now we're going up to the Gap where those Hopi chiefs are, but wherever I stop, you must stop there, too. Then we will go on after what I may do there, at the place where I stop." And so they were coming about a mile below that gap, and he stopped there. There was a little ridge there, a sandhill. There he stopped and then he dug a hole clear up to the elbow on his right hand. He dug a hole that deep and then he put the heart of the Ute Indian whom they first threw down, in there. They put some scalps in with the heart and then packed it down tight. The chief said, "The ones who will be living may know what will grow up on this hill; maybe a tree of some kind."

The Tewa chief then asked his men how many of the enemy each had killed, and they stated how many they had thrown down. It's said that after they fought, they went up to where they first threw down the Ute man and they stacked up some rocks there—about six feet high. Then they went up to where they retreated that time when they were fighting. There was a stack of rocks about six feet high, too. That is the truth of what they had done at that time, fighting with the Ute Indians. It's just a little way beyond Wepo.

They went to the foot of the mesa—before you get to the top there's a high rock leaning against the wall. That's where they went, and they drew a round shield, a Ute shield, on that rock. They carved lines near that shield for each one that was killed. That is our record; that is proof of what the Tewa had done when they got here.

Well, from there the Tewa came up to the top of the mesa and the Hopi chiefs were still waiting for them. When they to came to them, they greeted them and the Hopi chiefs said, "Now we believe that you are good fighters. We are glad that you drove away the enemy, and so you can make your home up on this mesa. You can come up from down there and make your home here." Then the Tewa chief said, "Why should we make our homes on that other mesa? If we make our homes up there, you may have an enemy come to you again and you will be gone before we know." Then the Hopi chief said, "That's right. Well, let's go up," they said. So they came up with the group of Tewa men; they came on top of that mesa. When they came to the top, the Hopi chiefs started to go back towards the Gap and then they stood up there, on top, where they thought they might give the Tewa a place to make

The Life of Irving Pabanale

their homes. "Here, this is the place for your people to make your homes." Then the Tewa chief said, "Are you crazy? How can we live in a little place like this? This is just a point; when we increase in population my people might be falling off the mesa, and so I don't agree with you." "Well, that's right," the Hopi said, and they took some more steps. They must have walked about fifty yards. That's where they stood again. "This much of it is plenty," they said. "I said that is not enough," that's what the Tewa chief said. They had come from the fight and were talking in a loud voice. So the Hopi chiefs went on and started again. And stepped the same distance, and they said, "All right, right here. This will be the divider," and that was the fourth time. "I think that will be all right," the Tewa chief said.

The Hopi chiefs said, "This will be the divide for building your homes; the divide between the Tewa people and the Hopi people. The Hopi won't make their houses beyond this divide. But if a Hopi lady marries a Tewa man and wants to be a Tewa, she will fix her hair like the Tewa women. And if a Tewa woman marries a Hopi man and wants to live where the Hopis are living, on the other side of this divide, she will have to fix her hair like the Hopi women." This is what they said right there where they were standing.

And so that was the divide made at that time, from both sides. The Hopi and the Tewa villages will be put according to where the divide is. So this was said there at that place where they were all standing.

A Hopi chief reached inside a blanket he had around him and took out a short piece of corn. He got some of it off and chewed it. He chewed the corn and then he told the Tewa chief to open his mouth. So he did. Then the Hopi chief gave him the corn that he had chewed. After the Tewa chief had swallowed what the Hopi chief had given him, that Hopi man gave another piece of corn to the Tewa chief and asked him to chew some and have the Hopi chief swallow it. The Tewa chief said, "No, because I'm ugly and you are a nice-looking man, you might vomit if I give you my chew. I had a hard time to swallow yours and so I don't want to give you any."

This was said at the time when they arrived from the fight. The Tewa people went down to where they were staying. When they came down there, it was late, about sundown. Then the chief called out to the people to come to the plaza. When they came there, he dug a hole again, clear up to the elbow. Then he asked every one of them to spit in that hole. And so they did; they spit in that hole. After they did that, then he packed it down tight with rocks and bushes and other stuff. Then he

12

said to the people, "I will tell you why I have done this. If the Hopis learn our language, they might mistreat us. They won't have any respect for us." That's what the Tewa chief said to them. "And so this is going to be hidden away; they won't learn our language." And that's where the language is buried, you might say—the Tewa language.

This is what had happened. Two days afterwards, they got ready and came up on top and they made their homes there. And it must be true, the way the Tewa language has been hidden away underground. The Hopis, they don't talk the Tewa language, but all the Tewas, from children to grown-up people, talk Hopi because the Tewa man had swallowed what the Hopi man had given him when he chewed the corn. And so, this is how come we Tewa people are still living with the Hopi, because those people who came from New Mexico, from C`e'wadeh, were the ones that fought for the Hopis.

The Hopi Snake clan knows it; the Hopi Bear clan knows it. So I hope what I have said will be taken into consideration. I hope it will be true as the way our people tell us who brought out the group. It's the Stick clan that brought out those eight [Tewa] clans.[8]

This has been written in different books which I have read, but none of it tells how many clans came out to Hopi country. But I have stated now what clans came from New Mexico, to help the Hopi people. Of course, from then on they had fights with the Apaches, too. But this is where they gave them the land. That's why I'm telling what I learned from my old people, my uncles and old grandfather.

The Early Years

I must have been very young when my mother and father passed away.
I don't know when I was born, but I was very young when they passed
away. My father was Sikyatngowma; he was a Tewa. I was told he was
an ambitious man; he was a farmer. He got sick and died, and my
mother, Shalako, she passed away soon after that. Then my brother,
Nelson, and my uncle took care of me. My uncle's name was Talasoyo.
He was a Paiute Indian but he had a Tewa name.

In those days, you know, when the Paiute Indians had a famine, they
took their children and gave them away for something to eat. That's
how come we had that man, Talasoyo, at our place.[1] Our old uncle
bought him from his mother and father, and Talasoyo was living in our
house in Tewa Village. After, when those houses were built down below,
in Polacca, by the government, he went down there to live. I was living
up there [in Tewa Village] with my brother and also my sister. She was
Albert Yava's mother, Iyetsawa. In those days, all people who were
blood relatives lived in one house, so I was living with them—Albert's
mother, my brother, and my uncle, that Paiute man.[2]

We were going to build another house in Tewa Village. First, we said
that we would go and get some logs. Of course, I was not yet able to do
any hard work but I heard them saying that they would get some logs.
They went up to Piñon—beyond Piñon—to get the logs. In those days,
they dragged the logs by burros and horses. They brought them that way
out here to First Mesa, and brought up rocks from down below, on their
backs. They built a home there and I was still living with Albert's
mother. She was kind to me and so I enjoyed my life when I was young.

When I was about five years old, I reckon, a white man came out here
to the Hopi reservation and was asking who to see to build a schoolhouse for the young children. He came to the Hopi chief first, but as he
couldn't find him, he found a man by the name of [Tom] Polacca. He
was a Tewa man. He had two houses built on the hill at the foot of First

Mesa, on Corn clan land. Polacca agreed that they could use one of those houses for the children to come to attend school. This was a day school. So that is where I went to my first school with my cousin Albert Yava.

In those days the little children were told to go to the cornfields and the watermelon fields where their fathers and brothers go. The people urged their little children to go to the farms regularly every morning, especially when the corn is ripe and the melons are ripe. We had a black burro with a short tail which we were using all the time when we go to our watermelon patch and our cornfields—those of our fathers and brothers. One time, we went to go to our field and as we were there, walking around, soon it was noontime, dinnertime. So I told my nephew Albert to go and get the burro. He brought the burro—she was a tame burro—and I was milking the burro. After I milked the burro, we added some water to the burro's milk. Then we put our piki bread,[3] which we might call "corn flakes," into the water and milk and that's how we had our dinner. We usually did that every time we went to the fields.

I was in day school about a year at Polacca [1895], and the next year I was sent to Keams Canyon where they had been building a schoolhouse. Keams Canyon is about thirteen miles from here. I was sent there by my brother, Nelson. When I came there, there were some other children there, too—some Navajo children and some Hopi children. As I was very small at that time, and as there were three others that were about my size, we all were dressed in dresses, since they did not have clothes to fit us. We had some older girls who took care of us. Every morning they washed our faces before we went to breakfast.

In 1895 a school building and a dormitory were built, with the teaching down below. It was two stories high, which we people had never seen before, and we were proud of that building. Pretty soon there were some other buildings and houses put up.

The reason why I was sent to Keams Canyon, to boarding school, was because I was an orphan at that time. My father and mother died nearly one year after the other. I was in school at Keams Canyon at what they used to call Old Plant. It's way above where the buildings are now. That's where I was attending school in 1898. That time there was smallpox, see, and the four of us ran away from school and I was on the mesa. Then they quarantined the place at Keams Canyon, so we didn't go back.

And so we had the smallpox.[4] There are two different kinds of disease in smallpox. Some that are little ones and some that are big ones. The

15

ones [people] that have the little ones, they lose their skin entirely, but the ones that have those big smallpox, they didn't lose their skin. That was found in that disease we had. What they used on me and my cousin was horse's fat; that's what they were rubbing on us. That's good for that; that's what cured us, see. So whenever they kill a fat horse, they give it to the people, and in those days they were doing the best they can for the people. They had confidence in the people.

I continued there until 1900, and some children were going to be sent to nonreservation schools from here. There were two other Hopis from Songoopavi and two Navajos that were going to nonreservation schools. The school team was ready to take us and we went on the wagon going to Holbrook. The first night we stayed at a place called Bitahochee—a Navajo name. The next day we went on until we came to Holbrook, late, where we had our supper. A man by the name of Shoemaker was the one who took us to Holbrook. After we had our supper, a train came from the east. We got in the train and left Holbrook. The man who took us to Holbrook said to us, "You folks are going to the Phoenix Indian school." We got to Phoenix early in the morning, about three o'clock.

They were waiting for us at the depot and they took us to that school. There were different kinds of Indians that were attending the school, but there were just a few Hopi girls and boys there at the time. We had a few Navajos there from Fort Defiance, also some Maricopas, Pimas, Mojaves, and there were some Osage from Oklahoma there, too. We also had some Indians from Central America; they called them Yucca [Yaqui] Indians. They were half-Mexican and half-Indian. After a couple of weeks at the school I got lonesome; I got homesick. One Saturday night, as I was in bed, I was thinking what to do because I was lonesome. The next morning was Sunday and we went to breakfast. When I was at the table I made two sandwiches instead of eating. I had only a little to eat, but I had two sandwiches in my coat pocket.

We came out of the dining room and we were dismissed by the officers. Then I went around where they had the Holstein cows for milking. I was standing around there and I made up my mind to go home to Polacca. I had a chum, a Mexican boy, and I went to him and asked him if he had any matches. He gave me a box of those small matches. There was a rose that was pictured on the box. I also had a can that I got around the kitchen where they throw slop. So then I sneaked off.

I went towards north until I came to a canal. I took off my clothes, went into the canal, and got some water. I got to the other side and dried myself and put my clothes on. It was Sunday morning and, of course, I

16

had my uniform on. On I went, thinking I was going north. As I was going, ahead of me was a big mountain which they call Camel's Back. I came to Camel's Back about 3:30 and was looking around for a place to stay. I went around and I found a big rock leaning against a high rock wall that was standing. I found that place and then got some rocks and closed it off on one side and left the other side open. That's where I stopped and took off my coat. I put my water in there and then went out from that place to pick up some bushes around there so that I could have a fire that night. That's all I did that day.

Then it was evening and I was staying there and I was thinking that I would start for home the next morning. But the next morning before I started, I was thinking whether to go home or go back. I had two sandwiches, as I said, and I ate one of them that morning and I had one left. So I stayed there that day. Then I thought that I would not go any further for fear that I might get lost, or that something might harm me. This came to my mind, and so I stayed there; I drank my water and then in the evening I ate my sandwich—the last one I had. I had just a little more water and so I drank it and I was staying there. I was thinking, of course, what to do. I feared that if I went back that I would get a strict strapping from the disciplinarian, as he usually did that when children ran away from school. I feared that, and so I stayed there that day and I was out of grub. I had nothing to eat. There were many rabbits around there that I saw and I was chasing them trying to catch some. Finally, I was chasing one and it went in a hole in a flat rock. I could see the back part of the rabbit and I looked for a stick and I found a cactus stick. I took the stick and I got the rabbit out by twisting the fur of the rabbit. When I took him out, I peeked in and saw there was another one. So I went around to the other side and put my cap where the hole was. It was shallow. Then I went back to where I took out that first one and reached in and got the second one. I peeked in again and there was another one there and so I took it out too. There was still another one there. There were four rabbits in that hole, in that flat rock, and so I had four rabbits. Then I went back to my place in Camel's Back, where I stayed. It was just a little way from there, at the valley of Camel's Back.

Well, I cooked those rabbits that I got, for food, but the next day my water was gone. Before I ran away, it rained down at Phoenix and around that valley, and so I looked for water. I found water on a flat rock where it was shallow. I got my water again and I took it back to where I camped. I was staying there and that was the fourth day.

I made up my mind that night that I would go back, but still I hated to go back to get a strapping. So I stayed another day and I was living on those rabbits. On the sixth day I made up my mind to go back to the school, and so I left.

They didn't know I returned until the next morning when they came out of the dining room. One of the sergeants took me to our disciplinarian, Mr. Green. That was his name. When he brought me in the room, Mr. Green was gazing at me, looking at me. He said, "Why, Irving, where have you been all this time? We've been looking for you day after day." I said, "I was at Camel's Back." "What were you doing at Camel's Back?" "I got so lonesome here and so I ran away." "And that's where you were staying?" "Yes." Then I said I was staying there and I carved on a rock the time I came there. It was September 25, 1900. I carved that on the rock where I was staying—in that cave. I was looking at him, and he kind of smiled. Then he said to me, "Irving, do you see this?" I looked up and there was a razor strap hanging there. "Do you know what this is for?" "Yes, I think I know," I said. "Well, since you have come back yourself to school, I am not going to use it on you. But you must never run away again." Then I said, "I won't; I won't ever run away anymore."

So I continued to stay there at the school and I had another chum that I got acquainted with, and so I was doing all right. At the Phoenix school our teacher used to tell us about whiskey. Of course, we didn't know anything about whiskey. They told us never to touch it. The Hopis call it "fire water." They used to tell us not to be bothering or drinking that. They used to tell us all about how to get along, not to be mean and to respect people, and all that advice. My teacher was an Indian, an Oklahoma Indian. Her name was Miss Beaver.

My older sister, Effie, was in the Phoenix school too, in 1900. Her Tewa name was Petsan. It means "nice root." She was a little older than me. I had a younger sister named Isabel. She was in school at Keams Canyon, but she passed away when she was about seventeen. Her Tewa name was Hompooviy. It means "mistletoe." She was the youngest sister. My oldest sister, Oyegi, went to Haskell school.

In 1904 I was in a band. My instrument was first B-flat cornet. We went to California in April and stayed there one month, and stayed at a place they call a "shoots park." There were many animals there at that park. We were staying around there close to the park and we were giving concerts every night. We stayed until May and we were going to come home. Our bandmaster told us one night that we were going to go to the Hopi reservation, and so we started from there in the month of May.

When we came to Gallup, there were three mule teams of the Navajo people waiting for us. We stayed overnight at Gallup and the next day we went on to Fort Defiance, and there we stayed overnight. The next morning we started again, and went on until we came to Ganado, where we gave a concert. The next day we arrived at Keams Canyon about four o'clock, and there was a group of boys that met us who were also learning music. Before we got there, they were fooling the people, telling them that they were the Phoenix band. But we met them and went on to the school in Keams Canyon. That was in May 1904 that I returned to the reservation. We played two concerts at Keams Canyon, and then went to First Mesa, where we played again. There at Tewa Village they asked me to give a solo. My bandmaster, Mr. Schefner, asked me to do so, as I was a boy from that village.

The next day we started again for Second Mesa. We stayed there overnight, and went on to Munkapi, and then came back to Keams Canyon. When we came to Keams Canyon, my uncle, Talasoyo, happened to be there. He said that I would not go back to the school with them, so we sneaked off and he brought me back home. The next day the band boys missed me and one of them came out to Polacca to look for me.

When my uncle brought me to Polacca, he hid me away among some rocks, so they didn't find me. On the following morning, the next morning, the band boys started for Holbrook, to go back to Phoenix, and I was hidden away among the rocks. In the morning my uncle brought me a can of water and some piki. I stayed there during the day and in the evening he came after me.

I was then staying at home and no one ever came again. I thought I would be doing something, and I went to Keams Canyon to ask for a job. I came there and they gave me a job as a night watchman. That was in 1905. Then they promoted me to be a fireman, and I worked in the basement where the furnaces were, keeping the buildings warm. I worked there two years and came home to Polacca. When I came home, there was nothing much to do. That was in 1907. So in 1908 I went to Winslow. I asked for a job there and they gave me a job as a fireman, at the Old Run House, which is now the Harvey House.[5] That's where I worked in 1908. The next year, in 1909, in about the middle of the month, some men came down from Polacca selling potteries. They came to where I was working and brought me a letter.

I opened the letter and read it, and it was from a girl whom I was talking with when I was in Keams Canyon. She said in the letter that we were going to be married. I showed the letter to my boss and he read it and said, "So you are going to be married. You can go and get married but be sure and come back to work. I want to keep you here on the job."

I went and looked for those men who brought that letter, and I told them that when they were going to go back home I would go with them. They said, "Tomorrow; we haven't sold our potteries yet. Some of it we didn't sell yet and so we are going to stay here today, tomorrow we are going to go home," they said. That night, I stayed overnight at their camp, but before I started from there I went to the store and bought me a suit of clothes and I also bought me a wedding ring. Then we started off. So that's how I came back from Winslow. It was in 1909.

When I got home, I went and saw that girl whom I was talking with before I went to Holbrook, and she said she's willing to take me. On the 19th of June I went to Keams Canyon to get a license. I wanted to be married with a license and so they gave a license, which was number 1. When I came back, we set up a date when to be married.

At that time she was working at the Polacca Day School, as a seamstress, and two of my uncles were also working there. The superintendent set a date: the 22nd day of June we were to be married. He sent for a missionary who was living near Lower Orayvi, Kiqötsmovi. His name was Mr. Epp. He came to Polacca and we were ready to be married. He married us at Polacca Day School with license number 1. We still have that license framed, and my daughters are keeping it. I was a married man then.

In those days the people used to depend on their sons-in-law or whoever was married to their daughters to work for them. As that was the custom of the tribe, I had to stay with them to help them with their work. They had cattle and they had sheep, and the custom of the Hopi tribe is whenever you are married to people that have cattle and sheep, they usually give you part of the herd. I was waiting for that in the year 1909, but nothing of the kind was done for me.

In 1910 a man named Mr. [Matthew] Murphy and his son Dick Murphy were out here to survey the region which is now called the 1882 area [the area established as the Hopi reservation].[6] They were surveying that land for farmland. They got some cedar trees and cut them about three feet long which they used to mark off the farm lands. I was working with them and with three others. Their names were Clifton Gala and Duke Pahona—Paynele, they called him. The other man was Gus Honiy. None of them are living at this time, but I remember they were the ones that were working there. At night when we came back from our work, Mr. Murphy used to visit our camp to tell us what was coming in the future. He said to us, "Now we are working on this area, which is Hopi land, and I'm going to tell you men to get away from the mesa and build your homes away from there. Sometime the land is going to be scarce." That's what he used to tell us in the evenings when he visited us. After the allotments was made, we were done setting up posts; it was an individual allotment at that time. Because of the lack of water it didn't go through, and in 1912 windmills were set up. And so that's how come the land was allotted but it didn't take effect because of the lack of water. I know this from Mr. Murphy when I worked for him as a surveyor and a flagman.

One night I called my wife's brother. His name was Grover Ova—he's not living now—and I told him what Mr. Murphy had been saying to us. He happened to take interest in what I told him and he made up his mind that we would build a ranch on his farm lands, near the windmill north of Wepo. That's the area where they kept their cattle and sheep. We went out there and we worked to build a ranch. We stayed there two weeks. First we worked on the rocks to put up a wall and three of us put up the wall. The wall was pretty close to the windmill, about two hundred yards away. Of course, we didn't know that it might be against the law to build it so close to the windmill. After the wall was finished I put a long rock above the doorway and I rubbed it and made it smooth and clear. Then I carved out on that rock above the doorway, "March 25, 1914." That's when the ranch was completed for them.

I and my other cousin went to where they call Greasewood Point, where there is a spring. I told him that we will build another ranch there which will be for our people—our relations. So we went there and in two weeks we put up the walls. As there was no way of getting anything for roofing, we didn't finish it, but the walls were finished. I told him to go up to the other windmill; that's the third windmill, north up the valley from Polacca. At that time it was just a windmill, not an artesian well. We took our grub and our crowbars and our stone hammers and started to build another home. There were three families of Navajos that were living close by. We worked on the rocks for three days and we had the wall from the foundation built about two feet high and our grub was gone. So we came home.

We stayed at home for two days so our folks could make some piki so we could take it and other food back with us. On the third day we went back again, and when we came there our foundation was all broken up. There were some Hopis from First Mesa and some Navajos who

21

were up there building, too, and I said we'll go back and report it to Keams Canyon, and so we came back home. The next day we went to Keams Canyon and reported to the superintendent, Mr. Crane. He said, "Where about is that place?" I said, "At the third windmill from Polacca, up towards Taylor's ranch." "Do you know who broke the foundation up?" "No," I answered. "Well, I'll send the Navajo police to find out who did the damage and you wait for my answer." And so we came back to First Mesa.

We waited for an answer, but no answer came back to us, and we went back to Keams Canyon and spoke to the superintendent again. "Well," he said, "I don't know what can be done," but he didn't send the Navajo police to find out. Afterwards we found out who the people were that destroyed our foundation. That's how come we didn't have that place built. Then from there, as we had no way of getting any help from anyone, we didn't try to find another place to build a home off the mesa. After this had happened, we didn't build it; we gave up until 1940, when we started again.

A Trip to Zuni and
Other Adventures

I guess I might mention what I have done before 1940. In past years, I and my uncle George Kochesi planned to go to Zuni when they were going to have a Shalako dance, which they give in the middle of the month of December, every year. That was in 1913. We heard about it, that they were going to have a Shalako dance, and so my uncle George came to me and said that we would go to Zuni. I said, "All right," but we were still in Walpi kiva.

It was pretty near the end of November, and we were still in the kiva there, as I belonged to the Hopi religion, and so I was there.[1] I told my uncle George and then he said, "When will you folks be through?" I said, "Tonight will be the last time that we will be in the kiva, so we will go up tomorrow." The next morning when the doings were over at the kiva at Walpi, I came home to my wife's place. Then I said to her that I was going to Zuni to see the Shalako dance, and she said, "Who are you going with?" I said, "My uncle George." "Okay." And so after we had our breakfast then I went to my uncle George Kochesi.

He was living on top of the mesa at that time, at Middle Village [Sitsomovi]. He had two horses ready when I came to them. There was a big gray pony that had been saddle-broke, but not much, and that was for me to ride. He had another horse, a bay horse, that he was going to ride on. And so we got ready, and from there we came down [from the top of the mesa]. We bid them goodbye and then we came down. George said to me that we would try to go as far as we could that day. We got to Greasewood Springs about four o'clock, and we didn't stop there but we went on. Finally, we got to the place they call Coyote Springs. It was late then, about sundown, when we got there. There was a Navajo living around there and so he [George] said we will stay overnight here and then start out early tomorrow. We went around and came to a Navajo man. A little ways where he was sitting there was a hogan burning and we just wondered why that hogan was burning. The man said that one of his sons had died and that's why they were burning the hogan; that is what they do when anyone dies in their family. We went over to another hogan where they were living and there were a few other people there and they made supper for us.

So the next morning we got up early and we went on. We went on until we came to where they call Yellow Bush Hill. It might be about twenty miles from Zuni. We stopped and took a rest there under a cedar tree. The Navajo were going by on the road near us.

Then we asked them when the Shalako was going to be, and they said, "Tonight." We were resting there for a while and we started to go on again. We came to Zuni late, it must have been about eight when we got there, and we went to our friend's house, Flora's house. The dance was not yet going on; those Zunis who were taking part in the Shalako dance were still talking. They were talking about the history of where the Shalako came from. It was a long speech that they always made so we were waiting there and then after they were through with their talking they were starting to have the dance. Flora asked me to go up to the other room, and there were some boys and girls and women there. They were cutting up meat, mutton. As that was my first time being in Zuni, I couldn't understand any Zuni. However, I talked a little English all right, but not very many of them talk English and so I was sitting there and they were talking among themselves. One of them young girls told me to come and work on the meat with them and so I went over there and we were cutting up the meat. There was a lot of mutton they were cutting to be boiled.

As we were cutting the mutton, they were laughing. I just wondered why they were laughing, and after a while I went back to the other room where Flora was. I came in there and she said, "You folks finished cutting up the meat?" "Well, yes, but they were talking among themselves and laughing and so I thought I would come back." Then she went over to them and when she came back she was laughing, and then she told me what they were laughing about. "They were saying that whoever that is cutting meat with you will be your girlfriend; that's what they were saying and they were laughing at you." "Oh, is that so," I said.

The next morning, after the Shalako dance was over, that girl took me to her house and her mother and other folks were making soapsuds. Then they told me to come over to the bowl. So I went there and they washed my hair. That was the way they do when a girl gets a boyfriend. They washed my hair and then took me back to Flora's place.

Of course, it was my first time going to Zuni. I didn't have anything

24

along in the way of selling anything to them. We stayed there four days until the Shalakos go back home. They had dances every night of those four days. The next day we told Flora that we were going home. When we were ready to leave, Flora gave us—me and George—two shirts that she had made for us. We started home and they gave us a lot of Zuni bread which they make in the ovens. It took us two days to get home as we were just taking our time. My uncle said to me that we will go again the next December, when they're going to have Shalako.

When he told me that, I went among the people to buy some black dresses, what they call *manta*, and Hopi belts. I bought some and had it put away until when we go back to Zuni the following December. And so, when we heard about when they were going to have the dance, then we went early so that we will get there before they have the dance. We came there to the same place, to Flora. She is a daughter of one of my uncles who is a Zuni man. He was a Bear clan man, and so by clan, he's our uncle.

The next morning I went to take what I had brought from home for my friend. I brought her a *manta* and two Hopi belts. And so at that time I went to Zuni two times and then as I had a friend down there, afterwards I sometimes go there where they were having some doings. My friend is now old and her husband is also now kind of an old man. His name is Ka'asti. I went to the Shalako one more time after that and that was my last doing at Zuni. The Hopis also have a Shalako dance. Something like the Corn Maiden dancers. They have a headdress made way up [about twelve feet high] and there's a lot of nice designs painted on them. That's the way the Hopi Shalakos were. We don't have that Shalako very often, but sometimes when someone wanted to have the Shalako, then they always have it here [First Mesa]. We have different songs for the Hopi Shalako dance, and the Zunis also have different songs for the Shalako. The Hopi have their songs in Hopi, but us Tewa people have our songs in the Navajo language. When we first had Shalako dance years past, we didn't have any songs; you see, we don't have any Shalakos. So myself and some others, we went among Navajos. Of course, these songs are medicine songs of the Navajos which they sang to us. And that's what we got from the Navajos, so it's all in Navajo language. There are a lot of those songs because the Shalakos dance all night, see, until sunrise, and so there are a lot of songs that we have.

I also used to go among the Navajo when they had their Yebechai[2] and Nit-a' dance. That's a round dance. That's how my brother and I

25

The Life of Irving Pabanale

learned their language; we were talking to them in their language as they couldn't understand ours. The first time I went among the Navajos was after I was married, when they were having a Fire Dance at Piñon. It was a little different from the Yebechai and Nit-a' dances. The Navajos were always kind to us as they have been our neighbors, making their homes in that 1882 area. They also used to come to Walpi when we were having the Niman Katsina Dance [the Home Dance, celebrating the departure of the Katsinas from the villages and their return to their home in the San Francisco Mountains]. Now days they don't come around very often—just once in a while, to bring some mutton to trade. I couldn't say why they don't come anymore, but a lot of the Navajos know me because we always go among them, see. I got a lot of Navajo friends.

In the early days we used to go rabbit hunting with the young girls and boys. Whenever any of them killed a rabbit—a jackrabbit or a cottontail—then the young girls would run over and get it. That's the way they do it when they are hunting with the girls. The girls are supposed to get the rabbit, which they kill. After they have gotten the rabbits, the girls would make food the next day. They made *somiviki* [sweetened cornmeal cakes boiled in the husks] and then they took that over to the boy from whom they got the rabbit. That was the custom of rabbit hunting of the Hopis. But now days no one ever has rabbit hunting parties. That has been past; no one has given anything like that anymore. When they are going out rabbit hunting with the girls, they usually call out in the evening that there will be a rabbit hunt with the girls the next day. Anything that the Hopi do, they always notify the people by making an announcement before they do it.

Lots of other things are gone now that was the Hopi life, see. All those things which they have been doing with the girls and the boys. The boys used to go to get wood, too, and when they were coming home the girls would be on the road to meet them. When a girl meets a boy bringing wood, she gives him some *somiviki* and then takes him to her home. That is what they used to do when they went after wood. As I have stated, there are many things that we have been doing that are now gone, perished.

In 1915 I went to San Diego with some of my relations, as they were having a world fair there, which they called Panama Exposition. I was working there as janitor and guide. My wife and our little child came down from Grand Canyon to San Diego and we stayed there until we were transferred to San Francisco, where there was another fair. Then in May a letter came to us from home. My wife's sister's husband was dead. They were branding calves and a cow threw him off a cliff and he was dead. The letter said this and so she wanted to go back home. I said, "They already have buried him and why should we go? We are here working and I don't think we should go back there." But she wanted to go, and so we came back to the mesa.

When we returned from San Francisco in 1915, I had some jewelry made in San Francisco by a Navajo silversmith—beads, silver beads, silver belts, silver bracelets. That is what I brought home. Then in August, I and my brother Nelson went to a man by the name of Chi'na'chinee, a Navajo man. We were at the Yebechai dance and I had three strands of red beads and at the bottom of the red beads there were earrings. I had that around my neck when we came to the Yebechai dance. He asked me for those beads and said he would give me some cattle. So I gave that to him. Later he moved down to above Red Lake, down below Tuba City, where Red Lake is. And so, as I had that silverware, my brother said that we would go and collect those cattle that the man owed me. And also we might buy a few more cattle.

We went down to Munkapi where they were having a Butterfly Dance. After about three o'clock, two men came to us; they were Navajo police. They told us to come to the office of the agent. My brother asked them why. "Well," they said, "we'll go over there and you'll find out why; they want you at the agency." And so they took us to the agent there at Tuba City. When we came in there, the superintendent said to us, "Are you the men I wanted here? I sent these police after you. Are you from Walpi?" "Yes," I said, "we are from Walpi." "I will tell you," he said. "A letter came from Walpi village to me, that I should stop you two men here. Do not go any further." That's what this superintendent, or whoever he was, said to us. Then I asked him, "Who was the man that wrote the letter?" "A man by the name of Maho." "Okay, will you read the letter to us?" I asked. And so he read us the letter. It said for us not to go any further than Tuba City to buy any cattle. That's what he was reading. So I said to the superintendent, "Why is it that he stops us to buy any cattle? This is a reservation, Hopi reservation, and there is no law right now that says we can't go among the people that are living within the Hopi reservation—our neighbors, Navajos and Hopis. And these Navajos, they come to our home for something and we go among them for whatever we want. This is the way we are getting along at the present time, and I don't see why we should be deprived of getting any cattle from this district." "Well, that's what the letter said, but it's up to you, if you want to go up there." "Yes, we are going up there, because

27

The Life of Irving Pabanale

we are going to collect some cattle from a man that owes me some." That's all he said to us.

There were a lot of people there [at Munkapi] as there was a Butterfly Dance going on. And so about four o'clock we started on down to Red Lake. As we were going, my brother happened to look back and said that there were two men coming behind us, and they were following us. He said, "I suspicion that those two men are going to do something, the way they are together and talking to one another. In case they come after us or stop us, you must try to be a man." And so we went on. Before we got to Red Lake store, they came running—they were on horseback— they came running behind us, then they passed us, and each of them got our bridle reins. These men had rabbit skins coiled around their braids, on both sides. They were Paiute Indians.[3] When they caught our bridle reins, they whipped us with their quirt. As soon as one whipped me with the quirt, then I also used my quirt on him, the one that was close to me. I whipped him on the face and around the eye and I got a hold of his braid. I got a hold of his braid and I wrapped it on my saddle horn. Then I jerked my horse and it jumped. I threw him from his horse and then I got off. And there we were: he was trying to fight me, but I throwed him down. I turned around and my brother also was on the ground. That Paiute man was a big man that was fighting my brother, and so I left that man that was fighting me and went over to my brother to help him. I turned that Paiute man that was on top of him and then I went back. Just about at this time when we were having this trouble, we heard a noise, like horses coming fast towards us. Finally, when they got to us, there were three men. One was a white man and the others were Navajo Indians; they were policemen. That white man was a storekeeper. They got a hold of us and they said, "What's the matter?" I just told them in brief, "These men came; they were following us. They came behind us, then they got a hold of us, and they were whipping us; that was the trouble. I don't know for what, but that was where the trouble started." They caught those Paiute Indians, and the white man told us to come on to the store to talk the matter over, over there. So we went to the trading post and those policemen took those two Paiutes there. There I told what happened and so they took those two Paiutes back down to the agent at Tuba City. That storekeeper told us to stay there overnight until the next morning.

We hobbled our horses and the next morning we got up early. We asked the storekeeper where that Navajo man was living and he told us it was about two miles from the store. We went there early in the

28

morning, as the sun was just coming up. That man came out from the hogan and saw us, then went back in. We got off our horses and went inside the hogan. They had a fire going there. As is the custom of the Navajo tribe, they already knew why we came there. When a Navajo owes anyone anything and the person comes to them at sunrise, early in the morning, it means that they have come to collect from the Navajos. That was the custom, so they knew what we came there for. We had our breakfast and then the man that owed me the cattle said to us, "I know what you came for." And I said, "Yes." "I know," he said, "so we will go and round up the cattle." He and two other boys of his went to round up cattle. It was not very far where the cattle ranged, and we went over to the corral. That man gave me two head of cattle and he asked me if I had anything else to sell. I had that silverware with me and so I showed him the silver beads and silver belts and bracelets. That man's wife wanted the silver beads and she asked me what I want for them. Well, I said, "I want some cattle for them." "How many?" she asked. "Well, it's up to you to say how many you'll give me." She offered me two. I said, "Okay." That man got the silver belt and gave it to his boy, and he gave me another two head of cattle for it. And so we had six then, six cattle that we got. After we got those cattle, we started to come home. It was about noon when we left and we tried to make it as short as we could. We came to the place they call Cow Springs and stayed overnight with the cattle. We drove them into a little draw and we built two fires. Then we went to sleep. That fire kept the cattle from getting out. The next morning we started on again. It was before noon when we got to Hotvela. We had some relations living there so we corralled the cattle and went up to visit them. It was evening when we got home with those cattle.

When we came back home in 1915, in the fall, there was a cowboy that came from Gallup to buy cattle. At that time I had a few head of cattle. He was buying the cattle over at Wepo and I sold two steers to him. Then he said that he wanted someone to help a Navajo to take those cattle to Gallup and he asked me if I would go. I said, "When are we going to start?" "Well, the cattle are going to stay here overnight and tomorrow you can start." I said, "Okay, I'll go back home and go after my horses." So I went home and after I had my dinner, I came back and went after my two horses. I packed up my clothes and my little suitcase and went to Wepo where the cattle were corralled. When I got there, there was a Navajo man there already and the next day we started driving those cattle. We went three nights before we got to Gallup. When

The Life of Irving Pabanale

we got there, he told us to take them to a big lake, northwest from Gallup. That's where we had those cattle. We stayed there a week before we sold the cattle. After we sold the cattle, that man told us that we were through now.

That evening I went around downtown and there were some Indians camping there. I came over to them and they were Zunis. I asked them if they wanted to buy a horse; I had two horses to sell and so I sold those two horses. Then I made up my mind that I would go on to New Mexico, to the Tewa Pueblos. So I went to that cowboy who we were working for and told him that I was going to New Mexico. "What are you going to do with your saddle?" he asked. "Well, I'll take it along if it's packed." "And when are you coming back?" he asked. "I might come back in about two or three weeks." "All right, when you come back, be sure and come to me, here." "Yes, I will," I said. And so, after my saddle was packed, he took it for me to the depot.

When we came to the depot, I went in and there were some Navajos there. As I was sitting there waiting for the train to come, they were looking at me. Finally, they got up and came direct to me. I had turquoise earrings on and that was what they were interested in when they came over. They asked me where I got those earrings. I said from San Francisco, California. They asked me if I had any more. I said, "Yes, I got three strands, one two-strand, and one one-strand." "Let us see," they said—they were a couple. I got my suitcase open and I showed them my beads. They were sure interested and they had money because they had been selling cattle. I suppose they had quite a bit of money. So they asked me what I wanted for those beads. I said, "Two hundred dollars." "All right," the man said, "that is two strands." "Have you got any more?" the man's wife asked. "I got one more strand," and I showed it to them again. They asked me how much I wanted for that. "I want sixty dollars for that." There was just one strand. That is how I got some money. So, on I went when the train came. I came to Santa Fe and stayed overnight at the Indian school.

The next day I went on. There was a little car running across to Santa Clara Pueblo. Before I came to San Ildefonso, the whistle blew and then I got busy. I pulled the emergency line to stop the train and I got off; it was still two miles before I got to Buckman. However, my saddle was taken off at Buckman, at the depot. I came there and there was a Mexican there, and he was talking to me. As I had learned a little Mexican when I was in school, I knew what he said, and I told him I was going to San Ildefonso. He said, "That's where I live—that's San

Ildefonso Pueblo—that's where I live. I'll take you there." He had come after some lumber and after we loaded it on, we got on top of the lumber and went on to San Ildefonso.

I stayed there about four days when a Tewa man, who was married over in Santa Clara, came down there to get me, and from there they took me to Santa Clara in a buggy. That's where I was staying that month of November and then a letter came to me from Keams Canyon office for me to return home. That man I was staying with was a policeman. That evening when we finished our supper, I was sitting there and he seemed to be thinking something, but he didn't say anything. After a while he spoke. "We call one another uncle," he said to me. "Uncle?" I said, "Yes, what is it?" "A letter came to me from Santa Fe. The superintendent at Keams Canyon had wrote a letter. Your wife was there at the office and he wrote a letter to you, to return back there. I hate to tell you, but that's what the letter says." "All right, I'll return back the day after tomorrow." So I started from there back to the reservation. When I came to Gallup there was a big snow on the ground. I went to my friend the cowboy—Tom was his name—and asked him if he had any horses to sell. "Yes, I have a pasture of horses. You want horses?" "Yes, I want horses to go back home. I'm going home now."

The next morning we went to the pasture and he told me to pick out the horses I wanted, and I picked two of them. Both of them were gray; one was broke already but the other one was not. I picked those out and we came back to his home. I had brought my saddle back on the train and my chaps and my grip and everything, so I was ready to go.

So from there I started home on those two horses—riding one for a while and then the other. When I came to St. Michael it was about sundown; it was cloudy and a big snow was on the ground. I was riding the horse that was broke already and I thought that he was kind of tired, so I made up my mind that I would put the saddle on the other one. I came to a cedar tree and I stopped there thinking what to do because that horse was not broke yet. They both had halters on so I tied the halters to the tree where I could get a hold of him, then I commenced to start again. I saddled that other horse right there and, of course, when I got on him he bucked a little. But I happened to get a hold of the line that was on the halter and that's how I got the horse, and from there I was leading.

I got off the road as there was no road showing. There was no road showing and I didn't know where I was going. It was evening already, too, and the sun had gone down. The snow was about a foot and a half

The Life of Irving Pabanale

deep. I was leading my other horse along and I thought I was on the right road, but I was going wrong. Finally, I heard a dog barking and I was coming direct to a hogan where some Navajos were living. So I came there and got off my horse and tied him to a pine tree. The Navajos were about to go to sleep when I came there, and they were looking at me, and were talking Zuni to me, since they thought I was a Zuni. I told them I was a Hopi; I had come from the Hopi reservation. "And where have you been that you are coming here so late?" they asked. "Well, I'm coming back from Gallup. I took some cattle to Gallup, and from there I went to San Ildefonso Pueblo and now I'm going back home." "Oh, is that so." So they built a fire and they asked, "What clan are you?" I told him Bear clan, and he said to his wife, "He is your brother."[4] There were two boys there, and he told them to take my horses to the corral, and told them to feed them hay and grain. So that's where I stayed overnight. The next day I asked them where the road to Cross Canyon is. "It's just about a mile from here, but this is the south road you are going on." They showed me the road and I came on. I stayed overnight at the place called White Rocks.

When I got home in December there were a lot of feathers at the plaza. They were having their ceremonies at Tewa that night.[5] That was in 1915.

Becoming a Policeman

The next year I became a policeman. It was in 1916. My brother was a policeman at the time and as there was a lot of trouble going on among the Navajos, the superintendent wanted more police. He asked my brother Nelson who he thinks would be a help to him, as he was a policeman.[1] My brother said that I might do the work as I was his brother. There were just three police on the reservation, at that time: my brother and two Navajos. My brother told me about it and we went to see the superintendent at Keams Canyon.

And so when they called me in the office, he got a paper out of his desk and he asked me, "Are you the one whom Nelson selected to be a help to him as a police?" "Yes," I said. "All right; I will read this form to you." And so he read the form to me. There was a question there: "Are you willing to be a police?" I answered, "Yes." "Okay. When you become a police you must do the work according to what is written on this form. It says that as a police your work is to do according to what you are ordered by the superintendent. Will you do that?" "Yes, I will try to do it." "Okay. Whenever there is any trouble and you're going to the people who are in trouble, you go there to arrest them and bring them to the office. That will be your duty." That's what it said on the form.

"I'm going to tell you. Whenever you are going to any man, do not take any chances if he has a rifle or a pistol. When he has that ready to use it on you, you must defend yourself right away. Try to use your rifle at the foot of that person, not on the body, up from the feet." I said, "Okay." "And you must remember all the things which is written on this form." "All right," I said. That was about all he said. "Your orders is to be given by the superintendent." And so he told me to stand up and he pinned a badge on my breast and he handed me that billy [club], then the handcuffs, then the last, the rifle. "Now this is the equipments that you are going to use," he said to me. "All right," I said. "Do you understand what I have said to you and what I have read to you on the form?" "Yes, I think I understand." "When you go to people, you must go to them in a right way. You should be a help to the people, not an enemy. Then if you come to a person and he objects coming with you, then you use your handcuffs. After you handcuff him, don't hit him with this billy because he's already arrested. This is going to be your work and so you must listen to what I am advising you, so you get to understand what your work will be." And then he said, "I have a white policeman here now, and in extreme cases he will help you. His name is Mr. Hoffman."

That was the time he hired that white policeman, Mr. Hoffman. The [Hopi Agency] superintendent at that time was a man by the name of Mr. [Leo] Crane. That was in 1916. This is what he said to me, and then he gave me all that equipment and then I came home with my brother.

The next day Nelson went back, as in those days the police were stationed over there at Keams Canyon. We had a corral there where we keep horses. We ride the horses, at that time, to go among the people. As I was then a police, I was staying on the reservation, at Polacca, and my brother Nelson, who was staying at Keams Canyon at that time, came out and he told me that we were going to the Navajo. A Navajo man had shot his wife, shot his wife dead. This was reported to the office, and my brother came out and told me about it. That was at Tsaihaskai.[2]

We came to the office and Mr. Hoffman, the white policeman, was with us, as it was a serious case. Before we got to that Navajo's hogan, we came to a farm a little ways from there. Mr. Hoffman said, "Wait, boys," so we waited. "Do you see what's on the fence there?" he said. We looked down toward the field and there was a bone—a head of a sheep—on a post there. "I want to know how you can shoot," he said. "You can shoot first," I said, "and then afterwards we can try." He was good in shooting, that Mr. Hoffman. He got a pistol out and got it on his finger and then went like this—turned it like this—and off he shot. He hit that head of a sheep. "Now you try," he said. And I said to my brother, "You shoot first and see how you do."

He fired that pistol and he pretty near hit the bone. Mr. Hoffman just laughed. "Ah, you're pretty good in shooting." Then I tried. I nearly hit the bone. It was about three inches below the bone, but my brother, where he shot, was about four inches below the bone.

They must have been watching us when we were doing that. Then on we went and Mr. Hoffman said, "You must be careful and watch them and I'll be watching them close, too. It is dangerous," he said, "he might have a gun or a rifle, because he is in a serious trouble." And so we went toward the hogan. We came there but no one came out.

They must have heard the sounds of the shots that we were doing. "I will be out here, outside, and you go in and get him," that white policeman said to my brother, "and you go with him, behind your brother." This was the order he gave to us. And so we went in and the Navajo was laying on a sheep pelt, and sure enough, he had a rifle by the side of him. That rifle must have been a 30-30. Well, my brother and I were in there and he said, "We come to get you." He didn't say a word. Then he said to him again, "All right, get ready and we will take you up to Keams Canyon." So he got up, but he didn't touch his rifle. He didn't handcuff him; he was willing to come, so we took him out and got him on the horse.

We were bringing him to Keams Canyon, and there was a straight road to Keams Canyon from the place where those people were living at Tsaihaskai, they call it, north along the Polacca valley, near Piñon. And so we brought him in, but we didn't know what was done with him. He was not detained in the jail at Keams Canyon, as it was a serious offense. This happened when I was a police.

Another time when the Navajos were having their Yebechai Dance over at Low Mountain [about fifteen miles north of Keams Canyon], right at the little trading post there, my nephew and myself took some watermelons and muskmelons over in our wagon. My old lady, my wife, was with me too. I was going there on horseback and we were bringing the watermelons and muskmelons to sell to the Navajos. We came to the place at Low Mountain and there were Navajo police there. This time my brother was not with us but we had a stockman with us. We were selling melons, muskmelons, to the Navajos and finally it got late; the sun was going down. We pretty near sold all the melons we had, with my nephew Clifford. Then they began to have their dance and I was ordered as a police to look out for the drinks. There were three Navajo police there, too.

Well, after when they were dancing, a man came to me, a Hopi man, that was Preston Masa. He came to me and he said that he was ordered to come there by the superintendent to watch for the liquor, if they had any liquor, and any drinking. "I am sent here by the office to help you," he said. "Okay," I said. While they were dancing, he was sneaking around to find any bottles.

In a few minutes he came to me and he said that they had some wine.

35

I asked him if he was sure they have it. "Yes." "All right, let's go." And so we started towards where those Navajos were having that wine, selling the wine. We came to them, and sure enough, they had it. I got a hold of the bottle that one of them had. They were ready to sell it to other Navajos. I took that bottle away and then we came over to where the fire was. When we left that place where the Navajos were, they followed us, and when I came to where the fire was, I was standing there and they jumped on me. Just at that time my nephew Clifford came to help me but that Hopi, Preston Masa, didn't show up, and the stockman didn't show up either, and they took that bottle away from me. There were about three men that jumped on me and they got that bottle, then they throw it on the rock and it was all busted.

After a while a shot was heard, either a rifle shot or a pistol shot. They shot at me, I don't know which way, but they just want to scare me, I suppose. I didn't get scared, but we called for help, but none of those Navajo police came to us. That stockman went away, too. This is what happened at that time, too.[3]

Another time, I had my sheep about five miles away from the mesa, where they call Religious Springs; that's where I was having my sheep. At that time my son-in-law, Herman, had his sheep with mine. We had our sheep together and also Clifford's. We found out that some sheep were always missing. So one time we went there when Clifford was going to herd the sheep, and looked around to find the tracks. We examined the sheep and one was gone again. We looked for the tracks and about fifty yards from the corral we found the tracks of a horse, and I said, "All right, Clifford, we are going to herd the sheep and we will track them to where they are taking them." The horse track was easy to follow because the horse must have crooked feet. That way we could easily tell the track of the horse. And so we followed it. We followed the track and it was going up towards Tsaihaskai again. There were just a few Navajos there at Tsaihaskai, and we tracked it clear to the place where that Navajo was living. When we came there, we asked them, "Who came here?" They didn't answer. And then a lady said, "What you want to know for?" "We want to know because someone came over to our corral and got a sheep; one sheep was missing, and so that's why we followed the track up to here."

That man was gone, the man that took the sheep. Well, they didn't tell us what they done with the meat; however, we searched around the hogan and we found the skin of that sheep but we didn't find any meat. That meat was taken to a high rock for butchering. There was a trail that that man used whenever he butchered the sheep that he took from the Hopi. And that's where that meat had been hidden but we didn't find the meat there. We came back and reported that to the superintendent. The Navajo police went after that man at that time, and then we were called to the office. As we had tracked him clear to his home and then from there up to that trail, he owned up to what he had done. His name was Cha'nayogisi. That's the Navajo man's name who stole the sheep. Okay, when he was brought to Keams Canyon, to the superintendent, again we were called in, and we testified against him at the office; he was sentenced to so many days. We didn't know how many, but he stayed there at Keams Canyon jail.

When I was ordered to go and get any people, I never had any trouble because I go to them in a nice way. I never had any trouble when I was a policeman, especially when I came to Hopi people. They never argued with me or anything but were always willing to go. And so I can say that I didn't have much trouble when I was a police. The people know it.

One time [ca. 1918], the Hopi people and other people, as I have heard, were having sickness [influenza], and the sickness got worse among the Hopi and we were ordered to get the Hopi to come to Keams Canyon to be bathed with some medicine. It was the agent that sent this notice out by the police for the people to come to get that bath. It was a liquid made with tobacco; I don't know what sickness it was, but it was bad. They were bathing the Polacca people down at the Polacca day school. They didn't object to it, and all of them came down there to have a bath. Then at Second Mesa, at Musangnuvi, after the Polacca people were through with their bathing, we went over there to bathe the people and they were willing to have their bath. Then over at Songoopavi they had their bath there and from there we went to Orayvi, to the lower village, where the people were bathed. We tried to get the Hotvela people to have their bath, but they object to it. In the next few days we were ordered down there to bathe them, us policemen. There were two others that were deputized. One, Conner Kylily, he's still living, and Travers Mali. They were all with us. So we came there and we called the leaders of Hotvela to come to the day school to talk with us. They came over there and they were talking about why they objected. My brother, of course, could talk Hopi and he was telling them that it wouldn't hurt them; it would protect the children from the sickness. But they still object to that; they don't want to have a bath.

We stayed there till about twelve o'clock trying to get them to agree,

37

but they said that they will not take the bath which we were after. There were three Navajo police with us and so, after twelve o'clock, those Hotvela leaders went back to their homes. We were talking among ourselves and the principal came into our room where we were and he brought some wagon spokes and then gave it to us. "If they objected, then we should use the spokes on them," he said. But my brother, Nelson, said to us Hopi police—myself and those two others that were deputized—"We must not take these spokes tomorrow for fear we might hurt them seriously. We are all Hopis and I don't think it would be right to use the spokes on them, and so we won't take them along."

Then he asked the Navajo police and they said, "Okay, we won't take the spokes. We can do some wrestling with the men, to bring them away; maybe in that way they might come with us." So the next morning when we had our breakfast, we went to Hotvela Village. And there was a buckboard there at that time, at the day school. The principal said to Conner to take the buckboard down to the village, to bring the old people to where they're going to have the bath. And so we went over to Hotvela. First, we gathered them all at the plaza, then we asked them again to come with us. It was in midsummer, in hot July. They said that they wouldn't do it. All right. Then we began to get hold of those men and we were wrestling them, in that way to bring them out from that village. After that we would go again for some others. Two of those police there were guarding those men. The womenfolks also object; however, finally they had to come too; the womenfolks had to come by force. We got them all together away from the village and then they were taken to where they were going to have their bath.

Then we were looking among the people and there was one man gone. They asked me to go and see where he was. I went to the village again and went around and finally I found a track—it was a man's track. I followed the track towards the south. He had gone down off the mesa and it was sandy all the way I tracked him; he was about two miles from the village. I didn't overtake him but I was still on the trail. Then when I came to as far as he went, as far as the tracks went, I looked around. There were no tracks from there on. So, as I looked around and couldn't find any tracks, I saw there was a flat rock—two flat rocks were leaning together. He had buried himself in a cave and put some stones on top. I noted there was a stick at that place, stuck at that place, and I know that's the way the Hopi bury the people and they put the stick on top. So I peeked in and there was that man. He was my clan relation, my uncle, and he was laughing at me and he said, "My nephew, you are the one that came after me?" "Yes," I said, "it wouldn't hurt you to go and get your bath. Why did you run away?" "Well, because I was going to work on my feathers; a religious ceremony of mine is at hand and so I was going to work on my feathers. That's why I didn't want to go where you are bathing the people."

I said to him, "Let's go; it won't hurt you, and as soon as you bathe you can come back to the village." And so I took him. When we came up on top of that mesa, there was my brother waiting for me. Then from there we took him and we were talking to him, but he didn't say much, and that's how we got him to be bathing.

When we came to the place where they were bathing the womenfolks, there were two Navajo police there at the doorway. When those women first came out, of course, they had long hair and they all got their hair and then shove it up to the Navajos. That's what they were doing. So they had their bath and we were done with all of them. I was a policeman until 1927, when I retired.

"Blossom Bride"

A DRAMATIZATION OF A
TRADITIONAL HOPI WEDDING

In 1927 a woman by the name of Miss Anita Baldwin came to the reservation to get some Hopis to go to Los Angeles with her, to put on a play called "Blossom Bride–*naasomi*." At that time, you know, I was yet a police.[1]

She was a well-off lady and she went around the villages to find the people that would go. After she found some who were willing to go, she asked me to take them people.

So I went to Keams Canyon to ask the superintendent [Edgar Miller] and he said it would be all right to take them. So we went to Los Angeles and we Hopis were up there, acting at the theater. It was a play about how the Hopis get married. It [the stage] was built like Walpi village, where we were acting.

There were nine people from First Mesa, from Polacca, and seven from Orayvi. I had an eagle feather headdress on like the way our people used to dress.[2]

A man came to us there, when we were putting on that play, and asked me if I would like to go down to Long Beach with him. I said, "How will I get there?" "I will take you down in a car," he said. Then I asked him, "Why should I go down to Long Beach?" He said, "To see all the things that are going on down there." I said, "Okay." "First, you will see what is going on down there and then after that your people here will go down to Long Beach too." And so I agreed. Then he took me in a car and when we came there, he took me around to see a carnival there. They were having some machines that you ride on, called Jack Rabbits. It's a machine that goes around in all different directions when coming down to earth. They start from above. They have some fortune tellers there, too.

Then he said he was going to give me a ride in an airplane with that headdress on and with the way I was dressed. I said, "Well, I've never been in an airplane and it might be hard on me." He said, "I think it will be all right for you to get into an airplane." So I agreed to go. I got in with him and he tied a belt across my chest, like I been tied to the airplane. And so we flew and I went clear up. I don't know how many feet we went up; then he said we were going to make loops. "No," I said, "don't do that, I can't stand it," I said, but he made the loops. He went down and then up again and down and then all of my headdress—my feathers—all came off. Then I said, "That's enough; let's go down, go back down." So he got me down and nothing was left of my headdress but an old hat on which the feathers were put. That was the only thing on my head when I came back down. The next day they took the others down to Long Beach and I went along with them. That man that was with us asked them to get in the airplane and have a ride and as I had lost my headdress, they feared to get in, but the man said, "I will not make the loops, but I'll just take you for a ride in this airplane." Two of our people got in the airplane. They had a story about that in the newspaper.

I came back from there in 1928 and I thought I would make use of that check that I had, and I still had some cattle and sheep. I got my cousins together and was talking with them about wanting to put up a little trading post, but I wanted someone to take care of the sheep and cattle. They agreed to it and so I put up a little store there. That was in 1928; I opened my store on First Mesa, in Middle Village.[3] I sold groceries, some clothing, and other things. Lots of people came. It was in one of my niece's homes because I hadn't any house yet and I had my grocery and stuff in her home. I had that store there for one year, and in 1929 I had a store built—it is where my daughter Edith lives. I took my stuff there and was selling my things until 1940. That's when I closed my store. It was wartime and everything was rationed and it was hard for me to get much stuff and I couldn't make any money during those days. As I was also a farmer, I had to go to take care of my farm and I also had some stock, so I closed the store. Whatever was left in there, we used it up.

When I had that store there, someone had been breaking in and one time I didn't take my cashbox along when I went home at night and the next morning when I came back, it was gone. I was wondering who took it and I examined my windows and one window was open at the top, you know where you turn the little hook that they have there. It was open and that's how come I knew that someone had been there in the night. I was wondering how to find out, or how to get the fellow that had gone in. Right then, there were some Katsinas going to Paaqavi, to dance, and they asked me to be a clown there. Those dancers were Long Hair Katsinas. So I went with them to be a clown.

Before I started for home, I went to a young man by the name of Oyala and asked him to watch my store and see if he can catch anyone that breaks in my store. This is what I said to him before I went to be a clown at Paaqavi. When we came back, sure enough, he caught a boy stealing in the store and he told me who it was. Then I said that I'll talk to his father and see what he says. So I told his father what his son had done—breaking in my store and he was caught at last. You know, those parents, they don't realize anything when a fellow does wrong, but they don't like it; they get mad.

The FBI man from Holbrook came out and he examined the window to get the thumbprints. Then he asked me who my partner was, or who was working with me at my store. I told him that my nephew was working with me but I don't think he was the one and later he found out who it was. That FBI man asked me what to do with this boy. "Well," I said, "he could be sent away to school." We went to Keams Canyon and the superintendent sent him to school down around Tucson.

He broke in my store three times. The second time when he broke in, I had four hundred dollars and that was gone. I just got two dollars that day because that four hundred dollars was in the cashbox at the store. However, I continued to have the store until 1940.

Becoming a Medicine Man

In years past—I don't quite remember when—my brother Nelson went to Santa Clara Pueblo to visit the Tewa people. He went to Santa Clara and he stayed there one year with them and then a letter came from him. They wrote a letter from him to us, and it said that he was going to be initiated as a medicine man and he wanted our advice about it.

We were in the kiva, on First Mesa. It was wintertime, in the middle of December, and we were about to work on our feathers for the Soyal ceremony.[1] I told the people in my kiva that I received a letter from my brother Nelson, from Santa Clara, and it asks their advice, and I read them the letter. Two brothers were the head of that kiva, the Corn clan kiva, where I belonged. Travers Mali's father and his brother, Harvey. They were the head of that kiva. I read the letter to them and they said it will be all right "because we haven't got any medicine man out here and it will be all right with us," they said. Then they asked the other people that were in there, what they think of it. "Well," they said, "it will be all right because you are the head of the kiva and you have given your opinion of what you have in mind; it will be all right with us," they said.

So the next morning I wrote a letter to Nelson and answered him right away, before he was to be initiated as a medicine man. I told him what the people had said here and after a year when he was staying there, he became a medicine man, in the middle of winter. He learned all the songs that the medicine men sing and they showed him all kinds of herbs and what they were used for, in the way of curing the people who are not in their usual health.

After he was initiated, he stayed there another few months, which made it two years. He came back home then and no one but us Tewa people knew that he had been initiated as a medicine man. But after he was here a while, the other people found out that he was a medicine man and they came to him and he gave them the medicine of what he has for different sickness.

From then on he was known as a medicine man and he showed me all kinds of medicine that grew here on the reservation and he usually took me around to show me how it was used. That's how I knew some medicine and how to use it among the people.

I don't give people these medicines unless they come to me themselves and ask for help. That's the only time I give them. This is how come I and my brother knew about those herbs and what they are for. I can't say that I can cure people, but I try to help them. I used to try to cure rheumatism. There are some herbs that I use for that, which I steam. Sometimes people would have swollen arms or legs. When they are swollen up, then I would use the herb, see. I'd boil it, then put it in a clean rag, and then put it on where it is swollen. I also had some medicine for tuberculosis.

One thing I know from my brother, and I have the medicine also, is for the people that get crazy. You know, young girls or young boys, they sometimes get out of their minds and get crazy, and I have the medicine for that, too. It works sometimes. There are some people living that I have cured.

I have said that we use herbs. We got to know the herbs, the medicine that we have. We also have songs for that sickness, you know, when a person gets crazy. Sometimes, they say, they get crazy, get the sickness from the deer. When they are hunting and killing deer not in the right way, that cause them, their women and girlfolks, to get that disease, or get sick like that. I don't know if it's true or not, but that's what the old people say. I worked on some people back home when they got that way, and they got better. I worked on one lady at Orayvi when she was in that kind of condition. When they get very crazy, they chew rags and any kind of weeds, just like those deer and antelopes and any other kinds of animals that are living on grass. But we cured them people. Of course, we prayed for them too, in Hopi, when we are giving them the medicine and performing on them when they get sick in that condition.

While I am talking about this, I will say that one time a woman from Winslow was sick and, you know, when they have heart trouble, their mouths will be twisted. Their mouths will either twist this way or to the left and the Hopi medicine man knows the songs for that, to cure the person.

A white woman came out here because someone had told her that the Hopis knew how to cure that disease. So she came out to First Mesa and went to Walpi to see the man who knew how to cure that. They had that curing ceremony in the wintertime, see. They had songs for it. They took her down to Winslow to perform the ceremony, down there, on account of her being in that condition. After they performed the ceremony in the way that they knew how, that lady got well. When she got well, she came back to First Mesa and wanted to give a reward to that man that performed on her when she was in that condition.

It is also done by praying. When we pray, we say, "Our Father in Heaven." You see, we pray up to heaven too. But that man to whom we are praying to, his name is Sootukwnangwu to whom we pray to.[2] Some people, you know, make fun of the way that the Hopi pray, coming to the prayer stone with cornmeal. They stand there and they say, "Our Father who is above," then say their prayers. Those prayer stones are just like the churches the white people have. They are not really praying to the stone, but that is where they go to make their prayer, see, and some white people make fun of that. But that's their way of praying. I said this to some white people once before. They have all kinds of churches that they go to on Sundays, to pray.

I still have people come to me today, especially the Navajos. Most of the Navajos come to the Hopi medicine man. When they go to white hospitals and they are not cured in the hospitals, then they come out to the Hopi medicine man for medicine. We first try to find what is wrong with them. They state what is wrong with them and then we give them certain kinds of medicine, those herbs. I don't keep them very long to find out about what they came for, or what they asked for, and so I don't know much about their cases; I just give them the medicine, that's all. I used some white man's medicine too. Those Navajos would have some of the same kinds of sickness that the Hopi people have—rheumatism, heart trouble, tuberculosis. They know that I have medicine for that crazy sickness, too.

One year, two white men came out to inspect our Hopi medicine. They may have been sent by the office, and they came over to the sheep camp where I was at the time. They knew I had some medicine. They had a book with them and they opened the book for me, and there were pictures of those herbs. Then they asked me if I knew what plants they were. "Yes," I said. "What is it for?" Then I told them what those medicines were for, and what kinds of sickness they cured. Then they went to Preston Masa, who knew a lot about medicines, and they went down to Second Mesa where there are two medicine men, too. They went to Songoopavi and on down to other villages.

The Indian
Reorganization Act

In 1932 the Howard Bill [Wheeler-Howard Act] came from the office in Washington and it said that the Hopi people could organize and have a constitution. The old chiefs were called to Keams Canyon and were told about the bill, as interpreted by Albert Yava, but they didn't accept it. After 1932 another bill came to the agent's office in Keams Canyon and a man by the name of [Oliver] La Farge came out from Washington. The chiefs of the Hopis were called in again. There the bill was read to them and it was something like what the Hopi life was like and so they agreed to it, then. They came back home and had a meeting—all those Hopi chiefs—and they were asked by the agency to get four men from each village to represent their people.

So the next day they were going to tell whom they selected to talk with the chiefs. That evening, when my wife and I had just finished our supper and she was cleaning the table, she peeked out and saw a man coming. She said, "Someone is coming to our place." So we waited a while and then he came in. He was the Hopi chief from Walpi—Tuno'a was his name. He was my friend and he came into our room and was smiling. Of course, he was one of the big men and I was wondering why he came here. I told him, "You can sit there; we just had our supper; do you want to have a little something to eat?" "No, I had my supper already," he said. "All right, sit down," I said, so he sat down and he said to me, "My friend," he said, "I came to you." "Okay, what can I do for you; what do you want of me?" Then he told me of being called to Keams Canyon by the superintendent. He said, "We were over there and there was a man who came from Washington [La Farge]. They said there were some papers to be made for our tribe. We were talking this over last night. The superintendent told us that we were to select four men to help us to draft these papers." Of course, he didn't know of that constitution, but he said we will have a paper of our own, as the Hopi tribe. "And my friend, I select you," he said to me, "to represent this

Tewa Village." There was also Herbert Seeni from Walpi Village and Jackson Lomakima selected from Middle Village, Sitsomovi. (This name means "rainbow sign"; the sun has a good house—said when it is going to rain.) From down below [Polacca], Tom Pavatea was asked.

"Four of you are to come down tomorrow and we will meet with that man [La Farge] over at the day school." "Well, I will go," I said. "As you really want me to represent this village, I will go." Then he said, "Your chief will be down there to listen but what we are going to talk about is the Hopi beliefs and religion that we have. You having been initiated in the Hopi religion and you knowing all about the Hopi life, you will be representative." "My friend, I wouldn't know all of it," I said, "but I was initiated to the Hopi way of living and I know of the religion." I asked who was going to interpret. "Your nephew, Albert Yava, is going to interpret. But you four men can help us because you know the Hopi way of life," and so I agreed.

The next day I went down and our [Tewa Village] chief Sapele went down and three of those chiefs: Tuno'a—he's the head chief of the Hopis, and his partner 'Inik Kutka. He was the Bear clan chief of the Hopis [at Walpi]. And the other one was Hongyi—they called him Hongyi. He was chief of the [Walpi] Snake clan and he announced the religious ceremonies; he was the announcer. And so these three went down and the other one didn't show up. His name was Maho; that's the way they called him, but he didn't appear. And so the three chiefs were there.

Well, we came down there, you see, and those chiefs were first talking among themselves of what they know of the Hopi life. They asked the head chief, Tuno'a, of the Antelope clan, "Where will we begin our talk?" Then Tuno'a said to Hongyi, the Snake chief, that he will be the spokesman, "as we all know our history and our life."

And so Hongyi said, "Where will I begin to talk about our life? It is one that we know; all three of us know how the Hopi have come here, and from where they came," and so Tuno'a said to them, "It's up to you to speak of what I said we know. We three know about our Hopi life"; and so they talked about it. They first talked about the Hopi land—how far they claim their land is, and then they were talking about the eagle nests—that is the sign that tells how far the Hopi land exists.[1] Those eagle nests tell us how far the Hopi land lies. Some nests are on one of those buttes near Winslow—the last western mountain. Beginning from there and west of Bita Hochee is another. Then out to Steamboat. This was all before the 1882 Executive Order. The Hopi land went out beyond that order. It is really Hopi land up to Steamboat. From there, up to Kayenta, and from Kayenta, down to Blue Canyon. From there, south to Dinnebito, and to that mountain near Tsaibitakai. Wherever they [the eagles] were living was considered Hopi country. That is our reservation, they said.[2]

After that they talked about farming land, how far the farming land of the Hopi is. And they said that it goes as far as "Five Houses";[3] that's about two miles from the village and then up towards north, the same distance—two miles. Two miles in all directions there's just two miles of the farming land, land which is considered as the farming land. Beyond that was the grazing land. That was what they talked about. La Farge was asking them about that—how far the farming lands were. Then they said no one has any right to plant on a different clan's land, without the clan's consent, because it is dangerous. It is dangerous for them to be planting on the land that don't belong to them by their clan. When they said that, Mr. La Farge asked, "Will you tell me why it is dangerous?" Then they paused for a while, those three chiefs, and the spokesman, Hongyi, said, "I will tell you why it is dangerous. Because it don't belong to them and they will be at fault if they plant on land that don't belong to them." Then again La Farge asked, "What is the danger?" "Well, I will tell you: the time when the Hopi, you might say, were allotted the farm lands, they asked the men to make it so it will be considered clan land, so that no other clan will use it. But the men didn't agree to it and so a woman said, 'If you don't want to do it, I will do it'—that she would make it so it will be considered clan land." That is what Hongyi said. Then she said, "If we don't do anything about that, there will be trouble all the time." Then she told the men to get all the grass and all the things growing on the land. And so they gathered that up and put it between two flat rocks and she built a fire. Then they took the ashes of all the grass and all the things that grow on the land and then buried it in different places where the clan owns land. So the meaning of doing this is this: whenever anyone plants in another's clan land, he would disappear. That is the reason the men didn't want to do it, but that woman said that she would do it. She was one of the women who belonged to the clan of the Hopi chief—the Deer clan. She said, "We have to do it as there will be trouble all the time." So this is why this has been done, to consider the land as belonging to a certain clan. This is the story those old chiefs told.[4]

And then Mr. La Farge said, "Oh, is this why it's dangerous?" "Yes, this is why." "We understand why," he said. Then after this had been understood by Mr. La Farge, he asked them to speak of other things about the way of Hopi life. Tuno'a, the head chief, asked, "What do you mean by that?" And he said, "I'm asking this because a Hopi has a different way of life, giving their prayers, and a white man has a different kind of life, giving his prayers, and that will have to go on the paper that is going to be the Hopi paper." That's what he said to the chiefs.

"Oh, is that what you mean? All right," Hongyi said. "I will talk about that. At the time when the Hopi were created on earth, they met with some people who are called white people. They met one another, also other Indians, Navajos, and there they stated that they have a way of praying. The Hopis stated that they make their prayers by getting cornmeal and going to their shrines. The white man, of course, he makes his prayers in a different way, which we know now, as they have churches. That will have to be printed in our paper."

And this is what they were talking about. They talked about the kind of religion they have. They have religious dances which are different from other dances which they call sociable dances. This will have to be in that paper, so that they will be allowed to have these dances. And so these things have been said there by those chiefs.

Towards the last they again said, "Two miles in different directions is considered farm lands. Beyond that is considered grazing lands." This is what they stated towards the last, and then they talked about another thing; that was adoption. The Hopi said that those other Pueblo Indians who were living a life like a Hopi would be welcomed on the reservation. But first they must come to the Hopi chief. Hongyi said that the Hopi are waiting for others to come on the reservation whose lives are like his life. He didn't mention just what people, but he meant those other Pueblo people. Then when they come here they will be adopted by the Hopi tribe. This is what they said there, down at Polacca Day School, where we met. We worked on the constitution a whole week. After we finished the constitution, the way these Hopi chiefs talked, we sent it to the other mesas for inspection and to have amendments made to it. It went to all the villages, clear over to Tuba City, and then it came back. Then we got together again. There were no amendments made to what had been written by the chiefs at First Mesa. So then it went to the Washington office [Bureau of Indian Affairs] and became law. When it came back again, the superintendent told the people to select their delegates. They chose Tom Pavatea, myself, John Makiwa, Jackson Lomakima. These were the first delegates when this constitution was adopted. It was voted on by the people and it became the law of the

49

tribe. That was in 1934. We served four years as delegates of the Hopi tribe.

At the other villages, they also selected their people, and so there were altogether nine people who were the first delegates. We resigned after four years and then there were some others that were selected by the people to be delegates.

Becoming a Judge

Three years after I resigned as a delegate, the council was going to establish a court, a tribal court. All the people got together at First Mesa; the
three consolidated villages got together—Walpi, Sitsomovi, and Tewa.
The council asked them to recommend two names to run for judge. A
man by the name of Andrew Sichoma and myself were written on a
paper. Then the people [council] voted for us two. I had the most votes,
therefore I became a judge. That was in 1940.[1]

Mr. Seth Wilson was superintendent at that time. I was called in the
office and he said, "You have been elected by the people to be a tribal
judge." "Yes," I said. "I heard I had the most votes, but as it is going to
be for the tribe, I won't deny; I'll try," I said. And so he got out a book.
It was about two inches thick—it was the Federal Code. Then he said to
me, "Here is the code. You read this code when you have your court and
use your judgment in rendering decisions, as you are a judge of the Hopi
tribe. This man Albert [Yava], here, he is the official interpreter. He will
help you in case you don't understand." "Okay," I said. And so I took
that book and went home. I was reading it that night, studying it. After
a week I went back to Keams Canyon, to the superintendent, and said
to him, "I have read the book and I know it is going to be new to the
people, and so I will try my best in rendering my judgment until they
learn." This is what I said to Seth Wilson. "It might take about two or
three years before they will learn what 'court' is. Is that all right?"
"That's all right, but there's a provision how to render your judgment
when you're just beginning."

"Yes," I said, "It is provisioned. I read that." Then I said to him, "It
is somewhat like the Hopi people when their children are bad. The
Soyokos come to them, to tell them not to be mean and all other things
that the child should not do.[2] It's just the same as that," I said.[3]

So then I had court the coming Monday. Seth Wilson said, "Monday
you are going to have your court. That's when you will open your

court." I had a Ford car, the first car I had. Then I asked him, "How about transportation? Of course, I have a car, but as I'm not working anywhere, I haven't got the money to be coming when I have court."

"We'll help you on that. Whenever your court day is at hand, we'll furnish you the gas to go back and forth," he said. "All right," I said, "I appreciate that." And that is how I became a judge in 1940. After I became a judge, we had a new superintendent named Mr. Bert Ladd.

The very first case I had as a judge was that of a boy who was under influence of liquor and he was brought to the court at Keams Canyon. That was the first case that I had. He must be now about thirty years old, but he was a boy when this happened.

He was from Middle Village, Sitsomovi, and he was caught drinking on the reservation. I asked him where he got his liquor, but he wouldn't tell. He wouldn't tell who he got it from. As that was his first offense, I put that boy on probation. That was what I rendered judgment in that first case. I put him on two months' probation. After he had done the first offense—it was about a month later—when he was brought in again for drinking. He was still on probation. Well, he was brought in again to the office by the police, and as he was on probation yet, and done that again, I said to him, "You have done the same thing again, drinking, which I advised you the first time not to do. It's not right for you to be drinking and as you were on probation yet, I will have to sentence you." That's what I said to him. And so I asked him again if he would not do it again. Well, he didn't answer me on that. Then I again asked him where he got the liquor, but he wouldn't say.

"All right," I said, "Because you have done this the second time while you were on probation, I will sentence you to twenty dollars' fine," and so I fined him twenty dollars. That was the first time I had fined a person for what he had done again while he was on probation.

I didn't have any trouble from the people whose boys came to court. They liked what I was doing because they say it was fair the way that I render my judgment.

It is very hard to remember all the things which I have done when I was a judge; however, when thinking it over, it comes to me and so I will talk about the Munkapi people. When I was on my second year as a judge, in 1942, they called from Munkapi to Keams Canyon, to the superintendent, for me to go down to Munkapi. And so when I got the call from Keams Canyon I thought I would go down. There was a quarrel down there among themselves. There are two groups down at Munkapi, one lower and one upper group. The Navajo judge tried to

52

settle the matter, but he couldn't and that's how come that they wanted me down there. When I came down there, there was a white man there. I don't know who he was, but the man was there waiting for me, and he called the Navajo police to get those Hopi men to come to court. And so I was taken over to where we were going to have the court. I sat there as the people came in. They came there from two groups, the lower group and the upper group. I said the court will be in session, and I asked them what trouble they had. They stated that they couldn't get along. I said to them, "Why can't you get along?" "Well, we're always saying things against one another." That was the answer that the lower group people said. "Will you state what kind of trouble you had down there?" I said to them. "Well," the lower group said, "we can't say just how come we had that trouble, but we can't get along."

Then I asked the upper group for them to tell their side of the story, why they had that trouble, and when it started. They said that two men were fighting after quarreling with one another, and they came to a fight—the men from lower and upper Munkapi.

I said to them, "Did you talk to anyone about this?" They said, "Yes, the Navajo judge was talking to us, but he's a Navajo and we don't know just how to talk with him, as we don't talk very much Navajo." "Yes," I said, "that's why the people called for me to come down. All right. As you have stated that you have been fighting with each other, I'm going to try to talk to you, and try to settle the problem that you have." Then I said to both parties, "You are all Hopis; I don't see why you can't get along; you talk the Hopi language. I just can't say to you that you shouldn't have troubles, but I'm going to tell you, do not have any more trouble. Both of you are living down here—the lower village and the upper village are all Orayvi people. You are Hopi people. If there was another tribe here with you, that might be different, I think, and so I'm going to ask you if the fight you had is serious." They said yes. "Who was the one that started the fighting?" They said the lower village. "Did anyone get seriously hurt?" I said. "No, we had a fight, but no one was seriously hurt." And I said, "Who was the first one who laid hands on the other?" And they said that the upper village man did so. "You start the fighting then?" I asked. "Yes, I tried to stop him from talking and saying all kinds of unbecoming words to me and that's why I laid my hands upon him." That's what he said. "As you have said that no one was seriously hurt, I think both of you must forget the trouble that you had. How do you both think about this, you two men?" "Well, I don't think we'll ever get along," they said. "All right, as you have laid

53

your hands upon this other man, I think you ought to give him a little something to forget the trouble. This is what I think," I said to them. And the upper village man said, "All right, I'll do that. I'll give him a little something, but we must not ever more be quarreling; he must not ever come to quarrel with me again."

"I think that's all right," I said. "And so both of you parties must forget this trouble that you had, and this will be the record of the court. There's not much to say now as you have agreed to give a little something of your own will." And so I didn't make any definite judgment on this but just told that man to do whatever he wants to do, to give the other man something that will end this trouble.

That was the last thing I said to them, to make up between themselves so they won't quarrel anymore, and told them, "You both have a right to be living here and as to my knowledge, you should both agree with one another to not have any more trouble."

I came back home and reported to the superintendent what I had done, and so that was the end of this matter, in 1942.

There were many different cases brought to my court. In 1943, I reckon, there were two young girls that altered a government check. They were working for the government; one was from Second Mesa and one was from Polacca. They were brought to my court, but I didn't know that until the FBI man came from the office when this happened. I went to my court at Keams Canyon and I was waiting for those two girls. They came there about two o'clock, and so I had my court with them then.

After they came in the courtroom, the FBI man came in also. He asked me if I was the judge of the Hopi tribe. I said yes. Then he said, "Do you know why these young girls are brought here?" "I really don't know why they are brought here," I said. Then he told me why they came there; they had done wrong. "But as you are a Hopi tribal judge," he said, "I will ask you to render your judgment the best you can on this matter. This is a serious matter," he said to me. And so I said okay. I asked those two young girls some questions, but they said they didn't know that it was against the law what they had done. Both of them said that they were very sorry that they had done so. They said, "It's up to you, whatever you decide to do, as you are the judge; we will take it." "Is this your first time being in court?" I said to them. They both said that it was their first time that they had committed an offense. So then I explained to them that it was wrong to do that; never add any more to the check that they get for their work; it is wrong to do that. "That's a government offense," I told them. "You can't get out of that, but as you two are young and this man has given me to think this matter over, to render a judgment, I will put both of you on probation as this is your first offense. But be sure and do right hereafter as I have explained to you the wrong way which you have done. I put you on probation for six months, to remember and to try to do right."

And so the FBI man said to me, "It's okay with me what they have said, that they would never do that anymore. It's okay with me the judgment you have rendered." Then the FBI man asked those girls how far they came on foot. It was fifteen miles to Keams Canyon which they had walked on foot to come to court. That's how come I had my court late. I usually open my court in the morning at ten o'clock, but because of having them to come late, I had my court late in the afternoon.

I had a stenographer there and I also had to have an interpreter at the court and Albert Yava was the interpreter. I also had police to attend the court. That was the way the court was organized.

At times I had some Navajo cases. Once a Navajo man murdered his wife, shot his wife, and was brought to my court. As it was a federal offense, I said I'd rather have it taken to the federal court and so they transferred that to the federal court down to Holbrook and then from there down to Tucson. Afterwards I heard that he was given four years to serve for the wrong that he had done. He served about a year down at Tucson; then he was transferred to Texas. There he was put into the penitentiary again. I knew that he served his term there for four years, then he returned back. That was one Navajo case I had. Another case that was brought to my court was that of a Navajo who broke into the home of Sikwi [a Hopi man] down at Jeddito. And so he was brought to the court and I asked him why he broke into the house of Sikwi. He said, because they don't want any Hopis at that place; it was below Jeddito where the home of Sikwi was. That's where they broke in and that was his answer. They didn't want any Hopis to live there on their land, which is in District 7.[4] And so I said to them, "Okay," and I asked my niece, Edna, Sikwi's wife, what they took from the house. She said that she didn't know just what they took, but they broke in through the window, but nothing had been taken. However, as he had done wrong, I put him to hard labor for a month and a half. That's what I gave that Navajo man. I had jurisdiction over the Navajos who were our neighbors, who were living in District 7.

I once had a case that involved a *pahana* [white man]. That was about 1942, as far as I can remember. There was some drinking going on at

55

Keams Canyon, and so those police filed a complaint against a man, a federal employee. He was a coal miner and it was brought to my court. And those police at that time were two brothers, Hale Adams and Bob Adams. They were two brothers but they had different mothers, both of them.

And so I opened my court; it was on Monday. They came in there, in the courtroom, and Albert, my nephew, was there, of course, as my interpreter. There was a lady that worked there in the office as my stenographer; she was present. And those two brothers, Bob Adams and Hale Adams, they were the police, and they came in, too. Then the coal miner they had filed against came in. I asked the clerk of the court to read the complaint and she read the complaint—it was for drinking. Then I said to those police, "Are you positive in filing a complaint against this man for drinking? How did you know that he was drinking?" And they said, "The people say this." "What people?" I asked, but they didn't mention what people.

Then I said to those police, "Of course, you have brought this case to our Hopi tribal court but I will tell you that I don't have that authority to convict a federal employee. And so you are wrong. I can't do much about it as I don't have that much authority as the Hopi tribal judge. And so you must be careful. Maybe, you don't know, but I will tell you; you must be careful in the way of arresting people. For the Hopi people and Navajo people who are not federal employees, the Hopi court has a right to render judgment, but in this matter here at this time, it is up to the superintendent whom he is working under."

Then again I said, "You police must be careful; just because you are police, do you think you can do what you think of yourself?" This is what I said to the police. "And so this will be all in this matter."

Other things happened that I think would be important, in that same year, 1942. These two police were following three men, from Keams Canyon up to Polacca. When those men got to Polacca, they went up to the Gap and down to the other valley, away from the mesa. Then those two police went after them. They were about three miles towards Wepo when they overtook them. And so they had a little fight there. One of those men got away and there were just two left. They were arrested and taken to Keams Canyon. As it was a federal offense, they were taken down to Holbrook; then from there they were taken down to Tucson. They served a time down at Tucson; then they were transferred down to Prescott. As they were serving there, a call came to me from Prescott, and so I went. When I came there, I was called by the judge to the court-

56

room, and so I went upstairs to the courtroom. Of course I didn't know why they had called me, and then they said that those two men who had resisted the officers are here at Prescott. "Okay," I said, "and what about it?" "We heard that you Hopis had a tribal judge." "Yes, I am, I am the tribal judge." "These two men that were brought here lately were very nice; they behaved themselves. And so I would rather have them to come to your court. They will be released from here and so you may take them."

And so I brought them. I took them out from the jail there and I brought them home. Then afterwards I had a court; I had them to come to court. So they came, and I was talking to them. "Of course, it's wrong to resist an officer," I told them. "You shouldn't have done anything to them, as they were officers, federal officers." They were listening there and I was talking to them, and so I said to them, "I will do the best I can in this matter as it has been transferred to my courtroom, here. I'm going to first ask you if you feel sad about what you had done." And they said yes, they were sorry that they had done that.

Then I said to them, "I'm going to put you on parole for two years as you have been convicted by the court already and have served some days for the wrongs which you have done. So I will give you two years to be on parole." And so they said, "Okay, we will try our best not to do anything like that; we will try to behave." And so that was the judgment I rendered afterwards, after they had been taken to federal court.

It was in 1944, on a Monday, my court day. There were a couple of people that had filed complaints. There was an Orayvi woman that had filed a complaint against her husband. I asked the defendant to come to the witness chair, so he sat down, and I asked him, "Why did your wife file against you; why did you leave her?" He didn't say anything for quite a while. Then I said to him, "Will you express yourself, either if you're having trouble with your wife or what caused you to leave her without being divorced?"

Then he said, "She's too mean to me." "Why was she too mean to you?" "I don't know," he said. His wife was there and I asked her, "What have you been doing to him, getting him mad?"

"I have heard and I found out that he was living with another girl, and he left me," she said. "I'm not mean to him but he left me." "Oh, is that so," I said. "Did you hear what she said?" I asked the defendant. And he said yes. "It seems to me that there is no good reason for you leaving her. There isn't any serious trouble. But she wants that you should not go around with other women," I said to him. "If you intend to do that, why didn't you get your divorce?" He didn't say anything.

"Okay," I said, "you can sit there for a while and I'll talk to the other witness here." I called the girl who he was living with, and I said to her, "You have heard all what these two have spoken. What kind of work are you doing here at Keams Canyon?" "Matron." "Oh, you're a matron. At the girls' or the boys' house?" "The girls'."

"Well, if you are a matron working for the government and also living at the girls' building, why were you doing this without being married? This man is a married man that you are living with." And then she said, "Well, I just don't know what to say, but I like him, that's why."

"Sarah, you have done wrong doing those things at the government building. You should be an example to the girls, not to be doing those things. You ought to be telling them not to be like that; instead of that you went ahead and done it yourself in the government building." She didn't say anything then. Then I said, "Is that all you want to say?" "Yes," she said.

"Okay," I said, "you both haven't got much reason to be living together. He's a married man and you should know that, whether you like it or not. As you have already answered what I have asked you, all of you, I'm going to render my judgment. You both haven't got much reason so I will render my judgment by alimony—$250. That will be the alimony you will give to this lady who has been deserted by you," I said to him. "So that will be the report on this case; however, I will say that she is under the jurisdiction of the superintendent. It is up to him. I render this judgment and let him either talk to you or do whatever he wants to."

In 1943 they brought a man in for running sheep without a permit. I asked the defendant to come to the chair and he came to the chair. I asked him to state his name and he said, "Cecil." "Your full name," I said. "Well, that's what they call me; they don't call me by my Hopi name," he said. "Okay, so your name is Cecil."

"Is it true that you are running some sheep without having a permit?" He said yes. "Who is the man who you are running your sheep with?" He said, "A Musangnuvi man, Chacha." "Don't you know, Cecil, that you have to have a permit, at least a temporary permit, to run your sheep?" And then he said, "Well, I didn't know I needed one. I thought I was running those sheep the right way." "No, we are having permits to run stock and so you are running your sheep without a permit. If you wish to have any sheep or get into sheep business, you can apply for a permit. The stockman is here, listening here," I said to him. "All of us

58

should have a permit to run our sheep and cattle. And so either you get a permit or dispose of your sheep. How many have you got in your herd?" "I got about twenty-four head." "How long have you been keeping them?" "Just this last year." "Okay, that's all I'll say to you now. I'll call the complaining witness now."

I asked the complaining witness to sit in the witness chair and so he sat down and I asked why he filed a complaint against Cecil. He said, "Because he is running those sheep on my permit. I have a permit, but he is running his sheep on my permit." That's what he stated. I said to him, "All right, will you let me have your permit?" He said he didn't bring it. "Why didn't you bring that permit?" "Well, I didn't know I had to bring it." "What number of sheep have you got on your permit?" "Twenty-three head." "Okay, so that's your permit, but you haven't got it." "No," he said. "All right, I will have to look into this on the next court day. Then you bring your permit and we will see what it says there, and maybe you will have to have a new permit. That will be all today for you," I said, "but come the next court day, that will be on Friday." "All right," he said.

There was another complaint that had been filed against another man sitting there, and I asked him to come to the witness chair. He couldn't talk English, so I asked my nephew, Albert Yava, to interpret for him what I was saying. He sat down on the chair and I said to him, "Will you state your full name to the court?" My nephew interpreted for him. He said, "My name is Bruce Nuvanganiwa."

"Is that your full name?" "Yes." "A complaint has been filed against you by the stockman, for having five black bucks. He is here in court. That is what the complaint reads here." And he said yes. Then I said, "Don't you know that the council has brought improved bucks so that the Hopi sheep will be improved? And you having five of those black bucks, you should try to get rid of them or give them to people who need mutton. In that way you can use those bucks that the tribal council bought to improve your stock." He was looking at my nephew, Albert Yava, all this time. Then he said, "Let this fellow say something." He was looking at Albert. "It's his father who wanted me to get as many black sheep as I can; he said that he was going to buy some bucks for me. We people that are weaving black dresses for the womenfolks want as much black wool as we can get." And then Albert, my cousin [nephew], said to him, "We have already explained to you that there are some other bucks that you will use to breed your sheep with." And I said to him, "I'm going to again say to you, either give them away to people who need mutton or castrate them." Then he said, "If I castrate them and some die, what's going to be done with them?" "Well, I can't say what will be done, but all what I have said to you is that we are trying to improve our Hopi stock. I'm going to go this far on this matter; I'm going to give you eight days to get rid of those black bucks. Then get the bucks from the council." He said, "I don't know whether I can get rid of them or not." "Well, if you don't get rid of them in eight days, something else will be done," I said. "So I give you eight days. This will be all for this complaint."

After that the clerk of the court handed me the next complaint. I asked my interpreter to read the complaint before the witness, and it, too, was filed by the stockman. On it, it said that Clifford Nahoyva branded a horse that didn't belong to him. I asked him to come to the witness chair, and he sat down. Then I said, "Clifford, as you are my close relation, I'm going to ask you to listen, and then I'll let someone else take up this matter of yours. You are my close relation and I am not qualified to take this case," I said. "My associate judge, John Makiwa, will sit in my chair." So he came and sat down. I said, "John, as this man is my close relation, I rather have you take up this matter." John said to Clifford, "The complaint has been read to you; do you understand the complaint?" "Yes," he said. Of course, all this time we had an interpreter, and the interpreter asked him again if he understood the complaint. "Yes," he said. Then the associate judge said to him, "Why did you do that when it's not your horse?" "It is not my horse," he answered. "That horse looks just like my uncle's horse; he's black. And so when we were branding them at the buck pasture, I branded him, as they were branding all the unbranded horses and burros there."

"Okay, so you didn't know it was not your horse, or someone else's?" "No, I didn't know." Then he said to him, "What brand did you put on that horse?" "MP." "Is that your brand?" "Well, that's the brand we are using; that's my uncle's brand. The judge [Pabanale], that's his brand, 'MP,' but we are using it on our horses." That's what Clifford said. Then the associate judge said, "Is that the only brand you put on, or is there some other brand you used?" "Well, the stockman, Mr. Lowry, he branded that horse, too."[5] "What did he brand the horse with?" "H-6." "And whose brand is that?" John asked. "I think that's the Hopi brand. All the Hopis brand their horses, burros, and cattle with H-6." "Oh, is that so. All right, you sit over there for a while and I'll speak to the complaining witness." So he sat on the other chair and then the associate judge called the complaining witness and said to him, "Will you state your name to the court?" "George, my name is George Numayesva." "That's your full name, is it?" "Yes." "Are you the one who filed a complaint against Clifford?" "Yes."

"Is the stockman here in the room?" "Yes, I'm here," he said. "What is your name?" "Mr. Lowry." "You are the stockman here on the Hopi reservation, are you?" "Yes." "Did you really put that brand H-6 on that horse when they were branding the horses down at the buck pasture?" "Yes, but I didn't know that it didn't belong to Clifford, and so as we are branding all the horses there, I branded it." Then John said to him, "You have heard what he has stated; this was done by mistake. He didn't intend to brand that horse, but it was a mistake. He thought that it was a horse belonging to his uncle Norris; that's what he stated." "Well, that was a mistake," the associate judge said. "It won't be right to convict a person for a mistake that he had done, and so that will be all."

Then George Numayesva said, "Aren't you going to give him anything for what he has done?" John said, "No. You have heard that it was a mistake." So this was the end of that case. Now the next court day was at hand, it was on Friday, when I told those people to appear in court again. I had seen them on Monday and as that case was not completed yet, I told that lady to sit in the witness chair. She was from Second Mesa, the daughter of Bruce Nuvangayniwa. "All right, have you got the stock permit?" Then she answered in Hopi, "*Puhinqawu?*" "What did he say?" she said to Albert. "He asked if you have the permit." Then I said to them, "I will have to talk English on these matters as much as I can for the record; however, we have an interpreter here to explain it to those who are uneducated." So she sat at the table where I was sitting, and she was looking for that permit in her handbag, and her handkerchief fell. Then her father, Bruce, said, "When are you going to take that permit out? Your handkerchief fell." Finally, she got the permit out. "Here is the permit," she said. "This is all we have that the mice have not yet eaten up and it is just part of the permit." I said to her, "Where were you keeping this permit?" She said, "In the corn stack." We Hopis, you know, always have corn stacked up when we harvest and that was where that permit was. "Well, I'll see if that number is on there," and I tried to find the number. She was lucky! The number was on there—twenty-three head.

That was what Hastings, her husband, was allowed. And so I said, "Well, it is true that you have a permit, but I think that you should have a new one and it will be copied from this permit." So I gave it to the stockman, Mr. Lowry, to get her another permit. That closed the case.

The Life of Irving Pabanale

I had another case that happened on the reservation in 1945, but I didn't file any report on it. There were three men around here on top; two of them were my cousins and one of them was a Hopi man. They were in a car here and two police followed them on the way to Polacca. They didn't overtake them, but they were just following them. Then they went far to the Gap and went on to the other side of the mesa, and still they were following them. It was about two miles when they overtook them. They were signaled to stop and they turned off the right side of the road and stopped. As soon as they stopped, one of them got out, that was my cousin, and the other two were in the car. So those two police went over and got a hold of them, took them out of the car, jerking them out. That got them mad. The police took out their billies and handcuffs and as the men didn't like that, they had a little fight there. But the driver had gone off, ran away. I didn't have any report of that, at that time. Then they were brought here and taken down to the federal court at Holbrook and from there they were transferred to Tucson. They stayed there a while; then they were transferred to Prescott.

Now, it was in August and I was going on Saturday morning to the Gallup Ceremonial. I went there with one of my boys who was working with me at my little store. We took some potteries and went to Gallup and the parade was just over when we got there. We went to the grounds and all of those Indians and other people were over at the grandstand. So we went to the grandstand and were sitting there when the loud-speaker was speaking. It said, "A call has been received from Prescott for the Hopi judge. If he is here, he must go over right away." We just wondered why, and I said to that boy, "Well, let us go." It was just a little while before the dancers were performing, and we left to go to Prescott. We got to Prescott late and so I said, "Let's get a room somewhere close to the court so we can get there by eight or nine." The next morning we went up to the courtroom and someone asked, "Are you from Hopi?" He asked me my name, and I said, "Irving Pabanale." "Oh, you are the Hopi judge, are you?" "Yes, I am the Hopi judge." "Yes, we called you to come out here because those two boys that were transferred from Tucson are here, but we don't know why they were brought up from the federal court, and we would like to make a report on it." So I explained to them that I was not notified that they were taken to Holbrook, to the federal court. "Well, you can take them back now; they have been good boys; they have behaved themselves and do what we tell them to do. That's why I called you to take them and maybe you can make a report on the case." "All right," I said, "I will do that."

And the next morning I brought them home. We came home about three-thirty as we had an early start from Prescott and I said to them, "You both must come to my court a week from today, and I will have a report made on what you have done."

One week later they came into court and I asked them, "Were you taken down to Holbrook federal court, right direct down, or were you here at Keams Canyon court?" "No, they took us down there." So I asked them, "For what reason were you taken in?" Then they told me what happened. "Yes," I said, "it is a federal offense, that's why they didn't notify the court here at Keams Canyon; however, now you are both back." They said, "If those police didn't jerk us and hit us with their billies, we wouldn't do anything. A fellow will get mad when someone is doing that." They said, "You have been a police; did you ever do that to anyone?" I said, "No. I come to a person that has made a mistake, in a right way. I tell them I came here to get you in a right way. Of course, sometimes they won't answer for quite a while, but I am free to say I never did use my billy or my handcuff on any people."

"In order to make a report of this case," I told them, "I will put you on parole, as you have already been convicted. I will put you on parole for two years and a half. You behave yourselves up to that length of time that I am giving you and report to me every month. That will be all," I said to them, "but remember, do not do anything out of the way in that length of time. If you do, you are breaking the order of the judge here."

You see, those men were under the influence of liquor when the police stopped them, but they weren't very intoxicated. I don't know why the police used their billies right away instead of talking to them in a right way. I never did that when I was a police, and the Hopis know that. That's why they say that I was always kind when I had to come to the people. In those days, way back in the past, I served eleven years as a police.

I didn't have much Navajo cases because, as they have their own court, I always transfer them to Fort Defiance or Window Rock. But when the Navajos are butchering Hopi sheep or Hopi cattle, I always have those cases come to my court because it happened in my jurisdiction.

I had a case one time in 1946 where a Navajo tried to hang that old man Sikwi. They had trouble at Lizzie [Lee Zee],[6] and of course, they didn't want those Hopi to live down there and they were against them all the time. We had trouble with that man, that Navajo man. That man that tried to hang Sikwi asked two other Navajos to help him. But those other Navajos, they didn't want to do that—to hang him—but that one man said that he was going to do it. And those other two said, "We will be in trouble if you do that; if he dies we will be in trouble." They said that. But he didn't mind them. Sikwi was in the hogan there and they were arguing. Then he got a rope around Sikwi. He threw the rope at one of those logs and then hung Sikwi. Those other two Navajos were against him when he had done that. Then those two men went in there and got him down from the rope.

That case was filed in Keams Canyon. Of course, he would have killed him that day, but because of those two men not taking up with that one Navajo, Sikwi didn't die at that time.

And so that case was brought to my court and those police brought those three men in. Only one man did that, but those other two were involved and so all three Navajos were brought in along with Sikwi and his wife, Edna.

They came to court and the clerk of the court read the complaint to me. I asked them three men, "What was the trouble that you have hung this man, roped him and hung him at the hogan at Lizzie?" The two men said, "We were telling him not to do it but he was so mad and so he rope him."

"And why didn't you go to that man and take the rope away from him before he roped Sikwi?" I asked. They didn't answer that. "If you were really not thinking to do that, you should have gotten the rope right away before he roped Sikwi," I said. "You pretty near killed this man and I want to ask you why you don't like them [the Hopi] to be down there? What was your reason for doing that?" Well, that man who roped him said, "He was always quarreling with us. Whenever we tell him not to be grazing his sheep around here, he gets mad; that's why he's always arguing with us, and we don't want any Hopis living down here where we are living." "Well," I said, "he has a right to have his sheep wherever he wishes to." "Yes, but this is our land," he said. "You are wrong. This is not your land; this is Hopi land but you fellows are living here," I said to him. Of course, it is in District 7 but it's still Hopi land. Then I told them the Hopi land goes way up towards Piñon, beyond Piñon—"that far it's Hopi land. It's not Navajo land; it's the Hopi land but you are against them." That's what I said to them.

"And how did you do it?" Then he took his rope and he threw it to the interpreter, roped him, the way he done it; he just showed the way he done it. "Who was there when you were doing that?" I asked him. "These two Navajos that are here." "Did they help you do that?" "No,

64

they didn't help me." "How long did you hang him?" "Not very long." "And what did these two Navajos say when you was doing that?" "They told me not to do it, but I was angry of course, and so I done it." "Did any one of those Navajos help you?" "No, they didn't help me but they was telling me not to do that." "But they didn't help you?" "No." "All right, I will talk to them after I get through with you," I said.

Then I said I'd hear from the complaining witness and I asked him to come to the witness chair. I asked him to state his name and he said it was Sikwi; that was the only name he went by.

"Have you got anything to say?" I asked Sikwi. "Why did they do this to you?" So he stated his side of the story. He said they were quarreling about him herding his sheep there. "I always herd my sheep around there and they are always barking at me to herd my sheep somewhere else. They say it's their grass but I think I have a right to herd my sheep on this land."

Then he said that while they were quarreling, "That man got the rope and he roped me, and right away when he roped me he put the rope through one of those logs and pulled it down, and hung me. That's all I know," said Sikwi. Then I said to him, "All right, that's all I want to say to you at this time." I got the defendant on the chair again. "You have heard what Sikwi has said?" "Yes." "You have done wrong," I said to him. "He won't live very long; you have ruined him." And he didn't answer me. "All right, now I want to talk to these other two who are here." And so I ask the other two Navajos, "Is it true what this man has said and what Sikwi has said?" "Yes," they said. "Is it true that you didn't stop him?" "It is true we tried to tell him not to do that or we would be in serious trouble if he dies. That's what we tell him, but he won't listen to us." "Why didn't you take that rope off of him before he was hung on the hogan?" "Oh, because he was mad and might hurt one of us." "You were two men there, but you didn't try to defend Sikwi."

"Well, I'm gonna render my judgment now. I will give you, Situ, three months at hard labor at Keams Canyon, and these two men that were with you I'll give them two months for doing this. Now this is going to be written in the record; if you ever do anything similar to what you folks have done, it will be different from what I have rendered judgment here today, so that will be the end."

Then Sikwi's wife, Edna, said, "Judge, may I speak?" "Okay," I said. "We have been having trouble with them all these years when we were down there. In 1916 we made a home down there when our old folks tell us to go away from the mesa and make our homes away from mesa,

The Life of Irving Pabanale

so that will hold our land. Our uncle said this; that's why we went down there. And you know what they used to tell us." "Yes," I said.

"Whenever we are planting, they come and break up our planting sticks and scatter our corn around. All these things have been happening. And another thing; they been butchering our sheep." "How far is your corral from your home?" "It's not very far, but they come around in the night and do that." "Okay, this will be all, as I have already made my judgment and they will be brought here to serve their term."

Not long after those Navajos served their term, that one Navajo, Situ, died, and Sikwi died about four years ago. Our Navajo neighbors living within the 1882 area, which is the Hopi land, are the ones causing the trouble. There are many good Navajos, but some of those in that area are making the trouble.

When anything happened in that jurisdiction of District 7 with our Navajo neighbors, I usually hold the court with them; but when they are found drunk or doing other things out from that district, I usually transfer it to the Navajo court. But I handle those that are living within the Hopi reservation in my court.

You know, I was retired as a judge in 1949,[7] and two years after that, the Hopi councilmen got together and wanted to get me back on the judge position. I said, "I don't think I will take it, as I have retired from that position and I'd rather have someone else to be a judge." They asked me back because the new judge, Pisatsmo—Sandpile—was his name, was not agreeable to the people who came to the court. Sometimes he used unbecoming words, see, and they didn't like that. He was dismissed after a while and then there were other judges before Judge Emory Sekaquaptewa.

Before I became a judge, the superintendent had the authority to bring them [cases] to Keams Canyon office. In those days when I was not yet a judge he was the man that was handling the matters that the people were doing which is wrong. The police, of course, they bring the people to Keams Canyon, to the superintendent, and that's where they were corrected. The superintendent was the one that rendered judgment. He gave those people so many days at hard labor. That's the way he was doing it. They don't appeal because they know he is superintendent and that he has the right to correct them. The court which was had by the Hopi tribe was new to them, and so I made my best judgments on the cases brought to my court.

In 1945, I reckon, the Hopi stock—the sheep—were to be reduced and we were told that we will have to reduce our herds. They said it was on account of the range; there was erosion starting and there wouldn't be much grass in the future, and there are too many stock on the range. And so, Mr. Ladd, the superintendent, told the people to select some men that will work on the stock reduction, because they know the people and how much stock they had. The stock was going to be reduced according to how many sheep they had and how big a family they had. Four men were selected to work on it. So they went among the people and, of course, at First Mesa they didn't object to it. At First Mesa they reduced the stock and it was also done at Second Mesa. At Third Mesa, at Hotvela, the people objected to having their stock reduced and there was trouble there at that time; they didn't want to have them reduced. The Hotvela people objected because they said they used a lot of mutton for religious ceremonies and in other things; it was very important for the Hopis to have stock. That was the reason they object to it. Mr. Lowry, who was a stockman at that time, filed a complaint against them and brought it to Keams Canyon, to my attention, at the tribal court. When it was time for me to hold court on that matter, those people who had objected to having their sheep reduced, they came in by the order of the Keams Canyon office.

I told them that it was a federal offense, and that I had no jurisdiction to take that matter up. I told this to Superintendent Ladd and told him I would transfer it down to Holbrook, to the federal court. So I didn't handle that part. Those Hotvela people have never reduced their stock.

Where there is a government offense on the reservation, I transferred it to the federal court at Holbrook. But in civil matters it was pretty hard to render a judgment that would be satisfactory. Where there were criminal cases, every offense had a penalty written, and so I rendered my judgment according to what had been written in the book.

One of the men at First Mesa wrote to the office that I was too severe in my judgment. When he wrote that, to the office, a man came from the main office and he looked over my court records. Then he said, "There is nothing that I can find that is unjust in how you rendered your judgment, so you go right ahead." That's what the FBI man told me. So therefore, I went on and served until 1949. That was the last work I did that was connected with the federal government. I worked eleven years as a police. Then I served six different departments in civil service.

Stock Improvement
on the Reservation

It was in 1936, after the Hopi constitution was adopted by the tribe, that I was selected to be a councilman. In 1936 the ones who were first appointed as councilmen for the Hopi had some meetings to discuss what should be done for the Hopi tribe. At that time we had all kinds of sheep—black, brown, white, spotted—all kinds of sheep we had. Then we decided to try to improve the Hopi sheep. The tribe didn't have any money and so we went to Keams Canyon to borrow some money on loan. We got the money from the agency on loan and we bought some young rams—improved rams, from Colorado. The following spring there weren't many new lambs from those young bucks, so the next years we bought some two-year-old bucks, and the people had some lambs in the spring. At first, all the sheep owners gave ten dollars to pay for the loan which we got from the office, but it hardly worked; we were not catching up on our account and so the following years we decided to have the sheep owners donate two lambs each, to pay off what we owed. This was done and it helped. In three years we met our account. After about six years the Hopis raised good lambs. The Hopi wool is good wool, when it was sold and sent to the factory; it was first-class wool. The buyers always come for the wool and the lambs because the Hopis had good stock. As I have said, we always help our people to improve their stock. The cattle owners also bought registered bulls for their herds. Therefore they have good cattle now. This was done when we were councilmen. We also bought cattle—improved cattle at Springerville. The Hopi stock was tested and considered to be the best stock—both the sheep and the cattle.

Now at the present time we are in lack of water, over at the place called Wildcat Butte [near Wepo Wash farming area, part of the Tewa region], where most of the Hopi stock range. Last year [1970], many of that stock died on account of not having any water. There's a windmill there but it doesn't produce enough for those cattle that range in that area. I am thinking, as we are yet with the government, to ask if there will be an artesian well built there. This is what the Hopi stockmen have in mind, but some are afraid to speak and they were talking to me about this. It won't hurt if we ask. I'm saying this in reference to what it reads in the Hopi constitution. Whenever anything could benefit the tribe, it says we should negotiate with the federal government. We are very much in need of water for the cattle and other stock. That's about the main thing that I have in mind. Of course, the land is dry on account of not having any rain and not having any snow in the wintertime. But we can't help that. But what the water problem is, we are thinking of. We really want an artesian well to be built to not lose the stock.

A Trip to Taos with Nelson

NELSON'S ILLNESS

It was in 1943. I and my brother and two other people planned to go up to New Mexico, to the Taos Indians. My brother Nelson had some jewelry—rings, bracelets, and other things that he wanted to take along to sell. We started to go two days later, and went in a car that belongs to Tom Pavatea's outfit.

We came to Gallup about noon, so we stopped there to have our dinner in a restaurant called Eagle Cafe. When we got out from the car, my brother was kind of shaken. I asked him what the matter was, if he feels all right or not, but his jaw seemed to be stiff. He tried to talk but couldn't very much and I know he was in a bad condition. So after we had our dinner, I said to him, "Let us not go. You don't feel well. We will go back home." He said to me, "I think I will be all right. I might be just tired from the car." "Yes, but I know you are not in your usual health." But he wanted to go and so we started on again.

It was about four-thirty when we came to Paquate [Laguna Pueblo]. We know some people from Paquate and we stayed at their place but I noticed that he still didn't feel right. When we got there, the womenfolks got busy making food and so we had our supper there. We stayed up for a while talking with them and then we went to bed, but I was still thinking of him being like that when I laid down. I didn't go to sleep; I was just thinking about him. It must have been daylight when I heard a noise in the room. I was reaching with my hands where he must be. I said to him, "You know I told you that we would go back from Gallup, but you didn't want to." Then he didn't answer me. I touched my brother; he was crawling around. I waked up those other two people; they were with us. My brother said—he seemed to say like he want to go out, and just motioned, and so we took him out. Two of us got hold of his arms from both sides and we took him out in the air. After being there for a while, we went back in the room and it was daylight. So we were sitting there and the folks got up and were making breakfast. After we ate I asked those people where a hospital might be around there. They said there is no hospital around here. They said it would be best to take him to Albuquerque. I said, "All right." I told those two people to drive a little faster, to get there soon. So we went.

When we came to the Albuquerque Indian School I took him upstairs where they have their office. I told them that my brother was in very bad condition and I said he is a government employee. "He is our policeman at home, and I brought him here to the Indian School."

Then the man who was in charge of that place, he must be the boys' adviser that were in the school, he said, "We will keep him here, try our best. We'll take him to the hospital." So we left him there and told him that we would be at Santa Clara today, and we would wait to hear what condition he may be in. "If he's in very serious condition, let us know," I said to him. They agreed that they would let us know, and so we went on to Santa Clara Pueblo. We didn't hear anything about him and the next morning we went on going up to Taos. We came to Taos about three o'clock and we were selling some things that we took along. I sold some silverware that my brother had and we bought some buckskins there; they had a lot of buckskins at Taos. I bought one buckskin shirt with beadwork on it. So we stayed there overnight and we started back to Santa Clara the next morning.

When we got there we went right on to Albuquerque, and his [Nelson's] wife was there. They must have called her to come there. My brother couldn't talk much. He just made motions and I said we better go on home and take him to Fort Defiance Hospital. We got to Fort Defiance and left him there. We told the people in what condition he was in. As he was a government employee, they were willing to take care of him. We left him there and we returned to Keams Canyon. After about four days his wife went back to Fort Defiance and she brought him back home. He could talk a little but not very much when he came back. He was all right for a while but not very well. He didn't live very long and he died soon after. He had been a policeman, working for the government for many years.

Trouble with the Navajos

THE LAND DISPUTE

I can't say exactly what year it started, but the dispute of land rights now with the Navajos is still at hand. That 1882 area was designated for the Hopi people by the authorities but still the Navajos want that land. Right at the present time they are talking about that, all the time. So it is not yet exclusive Hopi, because within that 1882 area there are many of our Navajo neighbors living there, and we don't know how to kick them out because they were born in that area. The Hopi didn't go away from the mesa to live in District 7 because it is Hopi land. On account of that, they [the Navajos] are still living there. All the others that were living in District 6 were taken out of District 6. That was about eleven years ago [ca. 1958] but the Navajos are still living on top of Keams Canyon not in District 7. District 7 is the land that was called Hopi land in 1882. So this is the big question yet: how can they kick them out and we are thinking of how it can be done, but my idea is still this: they can live with us but there must be a law made, a strict law, that if they bother the Hopis again, like butchering our cattle or stealing our sheep, stealing our crops, that they must immediately be taken out of District 7. That's my idea.

They might call us again sometime to meet with the Navajos. Those that were down at Prescott have testified about the way the Navajos were treating the Hopis. That's the reason why they didn't start working on the oil wells. We have oil, as those people who have gone through the reservation know. We have oil and other minerals.

The coal is plentiful, but beneath the ground we have many minerals like oil, gas, and zinc, whatever they call that. They know we have that because the man who used to stay here had a map made of what kind of land we have. He says we are rich people but we haven't got the money yet because they haven't drilled wells yet to get the oil, to get the gas, and it is on account of this that the Navajos want this 1882 area [see Appendix 2].

Becoming a Mormon

FAITH IN A PUPPY

I was first initiated to the Hopi religion; then when I got in this condition [became blind] and couldn't go to the kiva when they were having their ceremonies, I made up my mind to become a member of a church because our fathers and old uncles used to tell us about the white people who are to come in the future. Their [the Hopis'] belief is that they are brothers with the Mormon people, and so knowing this from the old folks, I became a member of the LDS church. Not because I don't want to believe in the Hopi religion, but that was said by the Hopi chiefs when we were drafting the constitution. That was brought up by them, that religion will be up to the person himself. If he wants to be a member of any church, that's up to him or her. That is what the chiefs said. That was their belief. There are many things that those chiefs brought up at the time they were drafting the constitution and I was selected to help them. So I know all these things. And so the Hopis don't say anything against the churches. And the white people, if they want to be right, should not be making fun of the Hopi way of praying, because we pray to someone we don't see but we still say "up above," which is heaven, see?

Before 1950, I was acquainted with the people of Snowflake [Arizona] who are Mormons. They gave me the LDS book and I was reading it very often to find out what it contains—that *Book of Mormon*. Finally, I found out it is somewhat like our history and our belief. That is the Tewa people I'm speaking of. And so in 1952 I went to Gallup with one of the elders who was here on the Hopi reservation. They first asked me here at the church if I will have someone go with me so that he will baptize me, and a man by the name of Cliff McGee took me.

We went over to Gallup and we directly came to a church there and it was on Sunday. We had a little session there and some of them were speaking of this church. Then Cliff McGee said to them that we came there to be baptized. When our church session was over, they took me in a room and there they baptized me. First they asked me of my father, mother, and how old they were and all that and what their names were. And so I told them the names of my father and mother, that's when I was baptized. Then I became a member of the church.

I think it is a very interesting book, the *Book of Mormon*. Comparing it to the Bible, I will say that it is a record that has been translated from the Bible in English by the Mormons.

The Mormon book which I was reading was similar to our belief, the way that our forefathers and older people told us about our life and how come that we do not belong to any church. That is what we found out in the book and that is why I myself wanted to be a member of the church. After I got in this condition [became blind], I was thinking of what it said in the Hopi constitution that it will be up to a person to be a member of any church. This is what I was thinking about, and I rather be coming to a place where I can have my prayer heard or can be asking in prayer. And that is my reason for becoming a member of the Mormon church.

I will say that because I had an interest in that church, I have many things that have proved to me that there is a living God. How I can prove that there is a living God? I will state. Five years ago [1964] I was living with my niece and her husband, down below Jeddito. One day they went to town—she and her husband, Harrington—and I was alone. However, they fixed me lunch to have in the afternoon. When they left, I came outdoors and I was sitting there and I thought of washing my handkerchiefs—three handkerchiefs I had. And so I got a wash pan and got some water and I went outside. There's a little porch there and I sat there and I was washing my handkerchiefs and dried them in the air. I stood up and walked across to throw the water out. When I was going to throw that water, I counted the steps that I made going. There were seven steps that I made and then I threw the water there away from the house. After I done that I turned to come back to the house. I counted seven steps but I was not there, so I felt around with my cane which I had, but I couldn't touch anything.

I stood there wondering which way to go and I thought I would make my steps again towards right and then towards left, and see if I could find the house. I did that but still I couldn't get to the house. I again made wrong steps, then I didn't touch anything. As I was standing there I was thinking of what to do as I was alone. Then I happened to think of a paper that I read in the past. It was in a California paper where I read that dogs could lead a person. I thought of that as I was standing there and then I called the dog that was there. We called her Puppy. She was a small dog and she had some little ones and so I said, "Puppy, come on," I said several times, and she came to me. I said, "Puppy, I want you to lead me to the house," and I took one of my handkerchiefs and put it around her neck and then tied the other two that I had to the handkerchief that was tied around her neck. Then I said, "Puppy, now let's go; let's go to the house; you'll lead me to the house." She came to me and she was wiggling her tail and I said, "Let us go." And so she started and I walked after the little puppy to take me to the house; then she stopped. She stopped there and I stopped and felt around, and it was where she had her little pups. When we stopped there, both of us, I took the two handkerchiefs that were tied to her and I took them off, but I still had the other one around her neck and she went in where the little pups were. She must have been missing them. It was under a tree and under a box where she had those little pups. Then I felt around; I didn't know where that tree was, and I came back to where she went into where the little pups were and I stood there.

Then I said to Puppy, "Puppy, come out and let's go to the house," I again said. Then I was standing there and I prayed; I prayed to our Heavenly Father to help me and to help the little puppy to take me to the house. And so I tied those two handkerchiefs again to her neck and then I said to her, "Puppy, let us go." So she started to walk again and I followed her. She was going and I still was following her. Finally, we got to a place and she stopped. I also stopped and felt around. She brought me to the corner of the house. I said to her, "Thank you, Puppy. Now I can go into the house." And so I felt around to find the door and then I said to Puppy, "You come with me and we will have our lunch." But as soon as she brought me there, she went back to her pups, I suppose. I found the door of that house and I went in. Then I went to where my lunch was and there were two sandwiches for me and some meat stuff. As I was eating I was thinking how to give that little puppy some of my lunch. And so I ate one sandwich and half of the other one. Then I took the half and went to the door and went out. I went out and I sat there on that porch and I called the puppy again. She came there, and I fed her that other half sandwich that I had for her.

It was late, it must have been about four o'clock, and I was sitting there waiting for them to come, those folks that went to town. They didn't come. I was waiting for them and I got cold. I got cold and I went inside the house and there was some coal near the heater. I touched the

75

heater and it was still warm and so I felt around for a poker and for some wood but I couldn't find the poker. So I again felt around for something to poke the heater as it was still warm. There was a piece of wood about two feet long that was near where the other wood was. I used that to poke the stove. There was some coal in that heater yet and that piece of wood that I was using, I suppose, caught on fire, and I took it out and threw it back in the wood box. There was some wood in there, and there must have been some paper, too, and it caught on fire. I didn't know what to do, because the wood box was a cardboard wood box and so it caught on fire, too. I felt the blaze and smoke around me and I stood up and got my quilt and felt around for that box and put it outside; then I went in again. It was all smoking and it was blazing hot. I came to that davenport where I was sitting and it caught on fire right then; it was burning. I had a little water which I usually keep in daytime and it was right beside the davenport which I was sitting on. So I felt around and got it. It was a little can that I had and there was some water in it yet. So I took that and I threwed the water to where the blaze was. I must have thrown the water to the right place where the blaze was.

Then I thought of getting more water but I couldn't find the other room where the water was. I kneeled down there and I prayed again. I got up; then I searched around and came to the place where the water was, and there was a dipper there on top. So I got the dipper and got some water and then went back to where the blazing fire was. I threw the water towards where the blaze was. I was standing there and the fire seemed to be out; the blazing seemed to be out, and I went to the heater and sure enough there wasn't any blaze anymore. However, the smoke was bad inside that room and so I again went and I got some more water, and threw it around. Just when I was through putting out that fire, they came—the people who went to town.

Of course, there was a lot of smoke and they said, "What's the matter? There's a lot of smoke." "Yes," I said. "The quilts are outside here." I caught on fire, I told them. They opened the door wide and the windows, to try to get the smoke out. Finally all the smoke was out.

This happened down there, and because of that little puppy and because of me praying, helped me. And that's how come the whole room didn't caught on fire. This is why I believe that there is a living God. This happened in 1964.

To my knowledge, the Mormon church is a good church and we are trying to have a Mormon church built here at Polacca, but some of the people object to it and that is why we are having our services at my nephew's garage, down below, before you come to the hills. Our Mormon members now are eighty-nine. Most of them are Tewa people and there are some Hopis.

When people belong to any religion, and the head of the religion dies and no one takes his place, then the religion is dying out. Now, you see, right now, we have no Antelope priest here, but just the Snake chief, so that [the Antelope Ceremony] is going to die out, I suppose, if no one takes the place of the Antelope priest, who died recently.

In other villages there are young people now who are the head of the religious ceremonies, and so they will continue because they are young. But on First Mesa the young people didn't want to take up the old religion, and no one can force them. It don't belong to other people. Those who belong to the religion are the ones that don't want to take it and continue it. The old chiefs spoke about this. They said that the religion of the Hopi is going to die out someday.

Alcohol Problems

I would like to say that it is a great and considerable problem that permits me to speak in behalf of my Hopi people concerning liquor. What is good in liquor? This question requires an answer. The Hopi are a very small tribe compared with any other Indian tribe, and so we are worried about what is going on. Some of our young men and women have passed away on account of being under the influence of liquor when driving. Accidents have happened. Some of them have ruined their health by their drink as the doctors report.

Who shall we depend on for help in this matter? Who shall we go to for help to prevent this trouble on the Hopi reservation? A Hopi has never been in favor of having liquor on his reservation, but it is coming in. We are having a big problem on this matter. Our young boys and young girls are shouting and disturbing the peace, going around at night, keeping the people from their sleep. We are all worried and so some of us have met on this matter. I know a big problem is hard for any individual to stop; however, they have a full right to express their opinion as to what they think that is bad and wrong that is going on.

We have about six young Hopi men on the Hopi police force, yet the liquor is coming on the reservation. Some of us think that if some different men would be put in their place, it may help to prevent this trouble. As I am saying this, I don't take myself as a perfect man; I might have done some wrong in the past. No one is perfect in the world. I am free to say that I have never been in jail, for any misdemeanor. This is why I am speaking. The only thing that we have in mind is to ask our nearby town people who are running bars, selling liquor to people, and who are manufacturing the liquor. We ask that if any Hopi couple should be in those nearby towns, do not sell them those drinks for them to bring out onto the Hopi reservation, as it is trouble. If nothing is done for this trouble, there won't be very many Hopis in the future. I am saying this because the young couples are doing most of this, those who are expected to increase the population. We old people are going on our way; there is no increase of population from us old people. This is what some of us have in mind. I am not speaking as an individual. As I have said, we have met on this matter with some other people. I don't know what else to say but to ask those townspeople, do not sell the liquor to those young couples. That may be a good help to us.

I have asked our council to have this considered, but they haven't done anything—either express their opinion, or anything. They read the note that I had written by my daughter, and we presented that to the council about two years ago, for their opinion and their help. It was read when they were having a meeting down at Orayvi, but they didn't do anything about it—even express their opinion. Right at the present time the tribal council does not ask the people anything before they pass anything, so I continued to try to get this to be known. Now, if there's anything I have said that doesn't sound right to anyone, I'll be glad to be corrected.

Like now, we're having trouble on the mesa having a church to be built. As to my knowledge, it is all right for a church to be built, but what I had in mind is to not have them to take too much land. And I have heard, the people have agreed to give them forty acres, which is a big part of Indian land to be used. But the day before yesterday I heard that it was four acres. A church can be built on two acres as to my knowledge. Those people that agreed and donated their land, I know they are ignorant of what an acre is by the white man. But I know because I worked with [white] people in the past allotting the Hopi area.

I think it is all right to have a church as the way we are living; see, that might help for the people to live peacefully. Of course, we are not all alike; some don't have this in mind, to live right and it might help. We have already got two churches on the reservation. A Baptist church which has been built first in years past, and there's another church across the wash, which they call Holy Roller. There's a church that has been built with a lot of trouble. And some of us who belong to Mormon church, one of us donated his farming land. He's a Katsina clan. But of course, we are not all in belief. That's why there was trouble about that. Choyo is the one who donated that land, a little ways from the foot of the mesa. But there was trouble over that, and as our people are renting that church, at the foot of the mesa, they want a church to be built without any trouble. That's why they didn't do anything at that time. That was in 1952 that old man Choyo donated his farmland. The people of the Mormon church didn't want any church to be built or any trouble

79

and that's why they stopped at that time—until now and the church is now up across the wash. And it is my clan land is where the church is built, but I have no objection to have it built; it's already built. The council has already passed it and so we don't have anything to do about it; not to have it fenced up as they say they are going to do. Why should it be fenced up when it's a church to welcome people to their church?

I think that the church will help some of our young people with their liquor problem. Of course, we are doing our best, talking to our young people, but it's a very hard thing to prevent anything like that after it has gone so far. So it might help some of them to quit the drinking.

Now we have some Hopi young men on police force but they are not honest in their work. Whenever any one person is found in disorderly conduct, the first thing the police thinks of is relations, and best friends, then they overlook them. They don't report that to the agency. And this is how come it is going on yet. Some of them have been appointed by the former superintendent Herman O'Hara, who was stationed at Keams Canyon. He appointed those men regardless of having the people [the tribal council] to decide who would be eligible for that job. In the past, a superintendent usually came out on the mesas and mentions it—whether a police is needed. Then the leaders get together and find a man who they think would be eligible for that job. And this is why they are not honest in their work. When they are called upon, they don't answer the calls; when there are troubles, whoever call the police they don't answer the calls. There is no fear in those who are related to police. This is what is going on, on the Hopi reservation.

Some of these police are not treating the people right. I know myself. Once, when a fellow was arrested by the police, he was handcuffed and thrown in the panel [truck]. Then he beat him up, which is not right to do as he is already handcuffed and can't do anything. Why should he beat him up? This complaint has gone into the office and so they dismissed him right away. I think that I have said that I have served as a police for eleven years. I have never had any trouble with anyone, because I go to them in the right way. That's what some of those police are doing; they don't have no pity on no one. A police should be a help to the people, not an enemy. This is what I learned when they put me on the police job.

I don't know just when they started drinking, but in the past when Arizona state was dry there wasn't any trouble on the Hopi reservation, but when liquor was open to the public, that was about the time when they got to drinking and doing wrong. In the past there wasn't any trouble at all among the Hopis; they were happy. I can't very well state just when they started doing so, but they learned it from the whites.

The Hopi lack power to stop any big problem like this. That is why we are asking for others to consider this, as it is wrong, and it's getting the Hopi people wild. We ask for others to consider this.

They also learn it from the Navajo, but the Navajo, of course, get it from the whites, too. Navajo laws are also against this—their tribal council, their judges, and the police, they are talking about this, too. A big thing like this, one man can't stop.

There are many Navajos and some of them don't care about this because there are a lot of them. But we Hopis are a small tribe; that's why we are worried over it.

I would say that drinking is a habit. When these boys first start to drink, then they want to drink some more. Wherever they find liquor, they want to drink. Not all of the Hopis are doing that, but these young folks are doing it right along. I don't know why they like the drinking, but when they get drinking, they get talking and they get laughing and all that, you see. Maybe that's what they want to drink for. It's a habit and you can't stop that. Sometimes there are just two or three that will be drinking but they don't go in a group; just two or three get together for drinking.

As I stated before, anything that is a big problem is hard to have it stopped. But the thing which I myself and others are thinking of is how to stop it so that young couples that come to town would not get the liquor, because in many ways this is hard on our people. When they go to town and they get drunk there, and the cops get them and they fine them, it's a serious thing. Their families have to pay the fine. Right now we are having big trouble and the people are thinking about how this trouble is to be avoided.

Why was a person called a Hopi in the past? Because he was a good person, a decent person. That is what Hopi means. But now we are not living according to what that Hopi name means.

Our young ladies and young girls are now drinking liquor. I will say it is serious to my knowledge what they are doing on the Hopi reservation. Not on one mesa but all over those Hopi mesas, they are doing this.

We have police, Hopi policemen. But they can't talk Navajo. To my knowledge none of them can talk Navajo and so they can't go among the Navajos to avoid this trouble. That's where they are getting the liquor, on top of Keams Canyon. Who is to blame? The Hopis don't

81

make the liquor but we all know who makes it and who sells the liquor. They are the ones to blame. If they are not making the liquor, there won't be much trouble on the Hopi reservation. Many of our Hopi young couples have passed away on account of liquor, having accidents. I don't know how it can be stopped, but that is what some of us are thinking, that there should be some kind of advice that could be given by anyone, as we are in serious trouble right now. I am not the only one that is speaking of this; there are others that are thinking just what I am thinking.

The people ask, Why don't they give us the grapes as they pick them from the vines without decaying the grapes, and other things that they make liquor of? Why don't they give us the corn when the corn is fresh, without having it decayed for drink? If they want to give us grapes, they can give us the ones they pick from the vine; this we will appreciate.

Speech to the Crowd at Walpi Snake Dance

In 1965 the Snake and Antelope chiefs made arrangements for me to make a speech to the crowd at the plaza of Walpi where the Snake Dance was going to be held. And so about two o'clock a man by the name of Conner Kylily took me to Walpi, to the plaza. We came there to Walpi and we were sitting by that Snake rock waiting for someone to take me to the middle of the plaza to make this speech. As we were waiting there, we could hear the crowd and so I said to Conner, "There must be a big crowd." And he said, "Yes, there's a big crowd here today."

And so about two-thirty a policeman came to me. His name was Maho. He took me to the middle of the plaza, then said to the crowd, "This man is Irving Pabanale. He is going to make a speech to the crowd here today." Then he went back to where we were sitting and I was there in the middle of the plaza. First I said,

Our white brothers and others who are here today, I have been asked by the Snake chief and Antelope chief to make a speech to the crowd here today. This dance is a religious dance that is given by the Snake Society every other year. This year we are having a dance here and also at Second Mesa, at Musangnuvi. We are very glad that you, our white brothers and friends, have come here to see the original Hopi Snake Dance, to see with your own eyes. I supposed some of you have seen a snake dance down at Prescott [Smoki dances] where the white people are painting up themselves to look somewhat like Hopi Indians when they are having a snake dance. They were singing but no one knows the meaning of their songs and this is the way they sang as it was told to us: "Hi-a wa wa." That's all there is to their song, but of course we don't know what that "Hi-a wa wa" means. The Snake Dance song here has meaning and so it don't look right to the Hopi people what they are doing at Prescott. That is the reason why I mentioned this. I don't think it is right to be making fun of anyone's religion. There are different nationalities in the United States. You have different churches and you have respect for your churches. So this dance here, the Snake Dance, is respected by the people. It is not a sociable dance; it is a religious dance.

Now, my friends, as I have said, it don't look right for anyone to be dancing or making fun of any religious dance. I will tell you now. One time I was down at Flagstaff. I happened to be standing nearby a bus station. As I was standing there, a Greyhound bus came from the east. The bus stopped there and the driver said to the people who were on the bus, "Thirty minutes before the bus will start again, and so if any of you wish to have lunch you can do so." The bus driver said that to the people who were on the bus and so they were getting off the bus, rushing over to a little restroom. So about half of them came off the bus and there were two couples got off from the bus also. They just got off from the bus and stepped a few steps and then they were standing there, whispering to themselves, looking at me, where I was standing. Then they started to come to me, direct to me. They came to me and said, "Hello, Chief." And as I know when a white man meets an Indian, he's always called a chief, I said, "Hello." Then the man said to me, "Chief, where are you from?" "I came here from Hopi reservation." "Oh, is that so; so you are one of the Snake Dancers." Then I said to them, "My friends, you are wrong. Just because I was from the Hopi reservation you take me as a Snake Dancer. Of course, the Snake clan and those that were initiated to that religion take part in the dance, in the Snake Dance, but no others. So you are wrong." Then they said, "Oh, now, we have learned something." Then I said to them, "Yes, you may have learned something from me. I will tell you," I said. "When a white man writes a book about Indians and about Hopis, they add a lot of stuff that is untrue. I have read those books myself. In order to have the book to be selling rapidly, to be interesting, is why they add a lot of stuff that is untrue of that tribe." And so I will say again, that it don't look right for us Hopi people having that dance down at Prescott. This was asked of me to speak of today, by these two chiefs—Snake chief and the Antelope chief. And so my friends, I am glad that you are here to see this dance. So I will say at this time I hope you'll have good luck going back to your homes and I will thank you for listening to my speech. This is about all I will say to you today, here at this Walpi plaza. So I say good-bye to you.

The next day after the Snake Dance was over, one of my—I might call her sisters, because she was born to the Tobacco clan and I had been born to Tobacco clan; my father was also Tobacco clan—told to me what the white people had said to her when I was making my speech. She said that the people asked, "Who is that man that had made a speech; what is his name?" "That man is Irving Pabanale," she said. "It was a very good speech that he made. Where had he been to school?" they asked. "He went to Phoenix Indian School." "Is that where he got his education?" "Yes." "We appreciate to hear what he has said. Everything what he has said is all right; we know that making fun of any religion is not right as he has spoken." This is what those white people said to her.

PART TWO

FOLKTALES

I am now going to tell some
stories which we people tell to
our children in the middle of
December. It is known to tell
stories in wintertime when
there's snow on the ground.
Then we tell these stories to our
children.

I like to tell these stories to
children, but these fairy tales are
hard to believe. But it was said
that once upon a time all the
creatures used to talk. That was
what the old people used to say.

When I used to see, before I was
blind, I read white people's
stories in a book. So I know
that they have some stories, too.

The Boy Who
Became a Girl

(HOPI)

There once was living at Walpi, down below (that's where the people were living once upon a time), an old lady with two little boys. There were three in the family. These two little boys were usually trapping rats—kangaroo rats, field mice, and other little animals—to have food. One morning, they were trapping around again and the older brother of these two said, "Let us go up on top a little higher where we can trap." So they went on up to where we call Walpi.

It used to be a sandhill, sloping down from both sides of that point, that mesa. And so they went up there and were looking around where to trap. They found a place, and as they were putting up their trap, they heard a noise like someone grinding. And so they stopped for a while and were listening and they said to one another, who it might be.

As they were saying that, they heard a voice. Someone said, "What are you doing?" Then they looked up and there was a girl. She was the one that they heard grinding corn. Then they said, "We are up here trying to trap—put up our trap to get some food." Then the girl laughed and said, "I don't think you will ever get anything in your trap, but if you do catch anything, I will go with you boys to your home." That is what the girl said to them. It was a Hopi girl and the boys were also Hopis, living down below. And so they put up their trap; the younger boy was the one that put up the trap and then they said to one another, "Let's go back right away and tell our grandmother what she has said to us."

Then they went down and went direct to their grandmother. When they came in, the grandmother said, "Why are you coming back so soon?" And the older boy told the younger one to tell what the girl had said to them. But the younger boy wanted his brother to tell what the girl had said to them, and so the older boy told their grandmother what the girl had said to them. He said, "If we get anything in our trap, the girl will come down here, to us. This is what the girl said to us and we came to let you know," they said. "Are you sure the girl said that?" "Yes." "All right," she said, "we must tell my sister." And the little boys said, "Grandma, who is your sister?" "I'll tell you where she lives because when you get something in your trap, tomorrow, the girl is going to come to be married to one of you, and so you must go and tell my sister to come and we will all be here when the girl comes." Then the old lady said to one of them, "You are older than this boy and so you go and tell my sister to come."

But the older boy didn't want to. He said that he didn't want to go, and wanted to stay there. Then she said again, "Well, you must go tomorrow, either one of you. If you don't want to go today, you will go tomorrow. One of you has to tell my sister to come, and so you stay right here and don't go away today."

The little boy brought some sand in a sack; he put it on the floor of their home.

She said to them to wait there until she comes back. Then she went in another room and the boys were sitting there waiting for her.

It was quite a while when she came out and they noticed that she had been washing her hair, as her hair was wet yet when she came out, and she had something in her hand. She brought that out and put it by the side of the sand, which she poured on the floor. Then she went in again. She brought out a bag with something in it. She put it there and she went in the other room again and brought something else out. She untied the last bag she brought out and it was cornmeal. So she spread cornmeal on top of the sand; then she said, "You boys must watch carefully what I am going to make." Then she got the thing she brought out at first. She was making something out of what she got off of her body. She had been rubbing her body and she made a little antelope, out of what she got off. The two boys were watching her. When she made that little antelope, she set it on top of where the cornmeal was spread, on top of the sand. Then she said, "I forgot something," and she went into the other room again and brought out another bag. She put it by the side of the other things, where the little figure of the antelope was standing. Then she said to the little boys, "We will try to make this come alive and you watch this little antelope. If he comes alive, watch this garment which I will be holding over it. When it begins to move, one of you must have a rope ready. So you get ready with the rope and as soon as it stands up, you put the rope around his neck. Then one of you get a hold of his front legs and you watch; I'm going to do a little singing," she said.

And so they were all ready and were watching when the old lady

90

began to sing. She sang the first song and stopped. The little boys were watching the *atö ö* [robe], they call it, that was over the antelope, and the *atö ö* was moving. Then the younger boy said to his brother, "It's moving now." And the older boy had a hair rope ready. Then the old lady sang another song. She was singing there with a little gourd that she was rattling and soon the *atö ö* that covered the antelope which she had made fell off and the antelope was standing there. As soon as the antelope came alive and was standing there, the older boy put his rope around his neck. It had two horns and it was an antelope. Then the grandmother said, "Now you take this over to your trap. Take him over there and put him under your trap." She told them to go up before it gets too dark.

From there they took that antelope up—one was leading it and the other was pushing from behind. It was sundown when they got up on top. Then they put that antelope's head in the trap where they had set it. The old lady also gave them some kind of medicine, herbs, to chew and sprinkle on the trap so that the trap would hold the antelope. It was a little after sundown when they did that, and no one saw it, and they came back down. Then the old lady asked them, "Who put up the trap?" They said it was the older boy that put it up. "All right," the old lady said to them, "tomorrow you must get up early and go to your trap—right straight to where you put the antelope in." Then she said, "Let us go to bed so you can get up early tomorrow to go to your trap." They went to bed and were sleeping that night.

The next morning, early in the morning, the old lady got up and told them to go to their trap, to see if the antelope was yet in that trap. So they got up and went there. It was about sunrise when they got up on top, and the antelope was gone. It was not in the trap. They were standing there and looking for the tracks, when that girl that was grinding corn peeked out and said, "We already got it up here and skinned the antelope. My brothers and uncles already got it up here and skinned the antelope. This is what I said to you two boys yesterday." And so they said, "Let us go down and tell our grandmother what she said."

They went down to their grandmother and they said to her, "We got the antelope all right but when we got there that girl told us that they had already taken it up to their home and skinned it, and she told us she was going to come tomorrow."

Then the old lady said, "Now one of you must go and tell my sister to come right now. When a girl is coming to your home, you have to have something ready for her to eat and we must all be here today," she said. Again she asked them who had set up the trap, and the older boy said, "I was the one." "So she is coming to you and so you go and tell my sister," she said to the younger boy. But he didn't want to. He'd rather stay there to meet the girl when she comes to their home. Again she said to the older boy, "Go and tell her to come with you and we'll be waiting for that girl to come to our home." "Where does she live, the one you call your sister?" the older boy asked. "It is south from here after you pass that big point and right around where that sandhill is—that's where she lives." This is what she said to him. So he got up and went but the older boy did not go and was staying there.

When that young boy came to the place where he was told to go, he looked around there and he heard a voice saying, "Come in." He looked to see who had said that and the voice said, "I am the one talking to you," and it was the sister of the old lady. She said, "Come in." "How can I come in?" the boy said. "As soon as you step on that hole it will become bigger and you can come in," she said. And so he did that and sure enough, there was a ladder coming up on top to the surface of the ground. So he went in and the old lady said, "You are around so early," and then the little boy said, "Yes, our grandmother told me to come and tell you a girl is going to come to our place this evening and said you must come and we will all wait for her." "Oh, is that so," she said, "all right." Then she said to the little boy, "Go down and get two of those greasewood sticks; get them and bring them right back." The boy went right off to where those greasewoods were and he got two of them that were straight and he took them to the old lady. When he brought them there, she said, "Lay them down here and I will boil some water." So he was sitting there and the old lady poured some water in an earthware bowl and set it on top of the fire to boil. After she did that, she went and picked those two sticks that he brought and was taking the bark off them and she was sharpening them, both of them. After she did that, she laid them aside and went in to get a big food bowl. So she poured the water in that bowl and told the boy to come there. The little boy went to her and she told him to step in that bowl. He was standing in that bowl where that warm water was and she bathed him.

After she bathed him, she took one of those sticks that she sharpened and put it at the middle of his head and was twisting his head. Pretty soon the skin was coming off that little boy when she was twisting that stick. She got the skin off from that little boy and told him to get out of that bowl and to sit by her until she was ready to do something else. So the little boy was sitting there by her side and she took that other stick and used it on him where his hair was, and tamping it down. Pretty soon, she had long hair clear down, pretty near to the ankles, and then she said, "Now I got what I want." Then she put cornmeal all over the little boy's face and all over his body. When his skin was taken off, the boy looked like a girl, so when his hair was dried then she told him to sit down and she would work on his hair—he became a girl then. He looked exactly like the girl that was going to come to their house.

After she had done this the old lady said, "We must be hurrying to get to your home." She said this to the little boy who had become a girl. He didn't know that he became a girl. She worked on his hair first and made it into what they call squash blossoms, which the young girls wore at that time. Then she untied the other sack in which she had some things and took out a black *manta* [dress] and put it on that little girl. Then she took out another thing from that bag and that was a *kweewa* [belt], which the girls put around their waist after putting on the *manta*. Then she took another thing out of the bag and it was moccasins, already made. And so she was fixing that little boy there and dressed him up like a girl. The last thing she put on him was a robe. It was a red embroidered *atö ö*, they call it, and she put that around him, as that's the way the girls dress when they come to a boy's home.

When they were ready to go, she got some cornmeal out that she had and put it in a plaque. Then she told that little boy, who was a little girl now, to go up on top of that girl's house and stay on top of their doorway and wait for the boy to come after her. Then the old lady went to her sister's house, and there was some meat boiling there; it was venison, deer meat. She was getting it ready for the girl when she comes to the house. So that boy (who was now a girl) was waiting for his brother to come to get that girl, but it was not the girl that was grinding corn. It was the younger brother that the old lady fixed to be a girl who was waiting for his brother to come. Soon his brother came up on top there and she told him that she was waiting for him, and he said, "Yes, I didn't want to come but the old lady told me to come up after sundown and that's why I came now, so let us go." He said this to that girl, who looked like that girl that lived there. Then he brought her down to his home.

When they came down to the foot of that mesa, he asked that girl to love him, to put her arms around him, but the girl said, "No! We are going to your home and when we get there, then you can love me," she said. So they started again toward his home. Before they came to the place, he asked her again, but she said, "No, we are now at your home and we are about to get on top on the ladder." And so they got on top where the old ladies were waiting for them. When she came in, she had some cornmeal on a plaque that she had ground, and the old lady that lived there took it from the girl and told her to sit down. Then she got the meat ready to eat and they were having supper that night with that girl that the older brother brought. She was eating the meat and throwing the bones down—nothing like a girl would be doing. After they ate, the old ladies said that they would go to bed. And so the old lady that lived there got some corn ready for the girl to grind early in the morning, as that was the custom of the people. She had it ready where the metates were, on which they grind. And so they set their beds, put down their bedding, and she had a buffalo skin, a tanned buffalo skin, which they used for blankets, and she made their beds right close to the metate so the girl would get up early in the morning to grind. So the old ladies made their bed and were ready to go to sleep, and that girl and boy went over where she made a bed for that girl. They were lying there and he was bothering her. She got tired of him bothering her so she yelled out that the boy was bothering her.

But now the older brother knew that the girl was his own brother who was fixed like a girl and so they didn't have a chance to sleep together. The old ladies got up and one said to the girl, "You can go back to your place." So right then she left the place. Then the grandmother yelled out, and that little girl became a boy again and it was the boy's own brother. The older brother was supposed to go after that girl because he was the one that had that antelope in his trap which the girl's brothers and uncles took up to her. This had happened at that time. And so this is the advice to boys when they are young: Not to want the same girl when you are two brothers. Because those two brothers wanted that girl and were fussing over her, the old lady had power to change the little boy into a girl. So that's how come they were not married, because that girl was his own younger brother. This is the end of this story.

How the Red Eagle
Got a Bellyache

(TEWA)

This is a story I learned from my father, when I was a boy.

Once upon a time there lived some little field mice down at Coyote Springs, below Walpi. They had brown skin but they were very small. They were living below Tewa Village, and above them lived a red eagle who was always on the lookout for rabbits in the early morning. And these little field mice always danced in the morning. They joined their hands together and they usually danced a round dance while one of them was drumming. They were doing this and the eagle was sitting on top of the high rock right above them. The eagle said, "These field mice are bothering me, and on account of their making too much noise, I can't get my breakfast. I am here on top of this high rock to get some rabbits, but they are making too much noise." So she said, "If they dance again I am going to fly down and get all of them." And the field mice danced and then went home to rest. After a while they came out again and they were again dancing in a big circle. As they were dancing, the red eagle got mad and flew down to get them. Of course, when they saw her coming down to get them, all the mice went in their little holes and the drummer happened to be the last one to try to get in his hole. But he was too late and the red eagle got him. He had a drum in front of him that was tied with a string of yucca plant. The drum was fastened with that around his shoulder.

And so the red eagle ate the drummer and then flew up to where she was sitting and pretty soon she got a stomachache. Then she was talking to herself and said, "I wonder why I have a stomachache." She said, "I will go down on the other side of this mesa where the old medicine man lives, the anteater."

So from there she flew up to that gap on First Mesa and she sat on the rock there looking down where the old man was living. So she flew down and he was lying on top of his home, on a flat rock. He was kind of an old man. The eagle came down there and the old man was lying there on top of his home, and she called to him. She said, "Grandpa!" But he didn't hear. And then she said again, "I'm calling you, Grandpa." When the third time she called him then the old man heard her voice and he was getting up and he said, "Someone seems to be calling me. Who is it?" "It is I that am calling you." "All right, what do you want?" he said to the red eagle. "This morning I was sitting on a rock trying to get my breakfast where I can get some rabbits, but I got a stomachache and it's hurting me very much. Why do I have a stomachache?" she said to the doctor. "Well, lay down and I will feel your stomach," he said to her. So she lay down and the old man was feeling her stomach and he laughed and said, "What have you eaten that caused you a stomachache? There is something alive there; I can hear a drum beating in your stomach." And then the red eagle said, "Will you take it out for me so I will be cured and won't have any more stomachache?" "Well, I hate to open your body, but I have to open it before I can take out what is hurting you." And she said, "Take it out of me because I am having a hard time." That's what the eagle said. Then the old medicine man said to her, "Are you willing for me to open your breast?" And she said yes. "Now sometimes when you open a person at the breast, they don't come back to life." "Well, it is all right since I am having a pain that is serious." "All right, you lay still there and I will go and get my knife."

So he went under that flat rock where his home was and got a long flint which he uses for a knife, and a bone awl and he had something in his mouth when he came back to her. He was chewing. He said, "You must lay still until I am ready. I'll tell you," he said. He was chewing something and pretty soon he took it out from his mouth and was rubbing it on his lap and it was sinew which he had in his mouth. And then he was drying it and made three strands, strings, of that sinew and was drying them and told her to wait until those sinew dried out. And she said, "Hurry and open me." Then again the old man said to her, "Do you mean what you have said? Do you really mean for me to open you at the breast? You might not come back alive." "It's all right," she said. "I will be very glad if the thing that is in my stomach is taken out. It's bothering me." "All right," he says, "you must lay still." So the eagle was laying on her back, and the old man used his knife on her and opened her at the breast. As soon as he opened the eagle at the breast, the little field mouse jumped out. He still had a drum fastened on him which he was beating; he was still alive. And so when the field mouse got out, off he was going, back to where he was living. And the eagle didn't come back to life for quite a while. After she came back alive, she said thank you to the old man. "Now I am well," she said. And she was sewed back where she was opened by that old man, with sinew.

Then she said, "What shall I give you in reward? What do you want? I am now cured and would like to give you something as a reward." The old man said, "No, it is all right, but I am going to tell you, you must never eat anything without chewing it for fear you might get a stomach-ache again. If you eat anything without chewing it, it will be alive in your stomach. And so you must never do it again." "All right, but I want to ask you again, what will I give you for taking that out from my stomach, it was aching pretty bad." "Well do you really want to give me something?" "Yes, I want to give you anything you ask for me to give you." "Well, if it is so, you can bring me some of those red ants. That's what I like. I like the red ants." And that's the food the old anteater wanted. And so the eagle said, "Yes, I know where to get them." Then he said to her again, "Don't you ever eat anything without first chewing it." So from there she flew back on top of that gap where her home was.

The next day she was up again early and was watching for some rabbits and she got one rabbit that morning. She took it up on the high rock and then she was working on it with her bill to get off the skin. She had time to fix it so that the rabbit was really dead, and when she took the skin off, she commenced eating it. And so she ate the rabbit. Then she said to herself, "Now I am going to get the red ants that the old man wants in reward for what he has done for me yesterday." And there were some ants living right near where she was sitting.

So she got a little bag. It was a little bag made of buckskin. So she took this bag and went to these red ants and they were already up on top of their home. She was taking them one by one and putting them in the little sack. She got the sack full of little red ants. So she got a hold of the bag and flew from there, taking it to the old man. She again flew to the gap and stayed there watching if he was at his place and she knew that he was lying there on top of his home again. And so she flew down and came to him and the old man was lying there again, and she said, "Grandpa, I'm here," she said. Again the old man didn't answer until the third time he said, "Someone seems to be talking to me. Who are you?" he said. "I am calling you. I was here yesterday when I had a stomachache and you cured me and so now I brought you what you wanted." "All right, bring it here," the old man said. And so she untied the little bag where she had the little ants. As soon as she poured out the little bag of ants, he commenced eating them. He ate them all and he said, "Thank you. I will live on this for some days," he said, "and so I

97

thank you very much." And so then she flew back and came back to her home.

This is the reason why we tell you children, Do not swallow anything without chewing or it might come alive in your stomach. First, chew your food before you swallow, so you won't have any stomachache like the red eagle. She suffered and if it was not for the old man, the eagle would have died. This is the end of this story.

How the Coyote Cubs Became Spotted

(TEWA)

Once upon a time there were some deer living where it is called Deertrail. There is a draw there, where the deers were living. One morning the mother deer took her little ones over across the wash where there was plenty of grass, and while they were there, someone was coming. The mother said, "Someone is coming," and then she told the little ones that it might be the "going around lady." That's what they called the female coyote. That's what she is called, and so she said that "going around lady" is coming and told her little ones to come to her, close to her, so that the she may not do anything to them.

So they were standing there when the coyote was coming to them. She came there and said, "Good morning." The coyote lady stood to the side of them and she was watching those little deers. Then she said, "Your little ones look cute," and the deer mother said, "Yes." "How come that they are spotted?" the coyote lady asked. "Do you want to know?" said the deer mother. "Yes, I would like to know; I have two little ones too, two puppies, and I want to get them to be like your little ones." "Okay," she said, "I will tell you how I got them to be spotted." "All right," said Mrs. Coyote. Then the deer mother asked, "What kind of place are you living at?" "I'm living under a flat rock and my puppies are there and I'm going around to look for food for them, as I usually do every day." "Well, if you are looking for food, you can go wherever you want to." "No, I'd rather have you tell me how to get my little ones to be spotted."

And so the deer mother said, "I will tell you. When you go back to your place where you have your two little ones, you go and look for some pitch from the piñon trees. There is pitch on the piñon trees. Get some of that and bring it to your place. Then gather up some wood. After you gather up some wood, then you build a fire and put this pitch on the fire to make the smoke. You must not let the smoke out, but close all the holes so that the smoke will be closed in that room. And then you put your little ones in there and just have a little opening place to watch them and hear them." This is what the deer mother said to the old coyote.

"All right, I will do that," and so she went back to her home and got some pitch and some wood, and then made a fire and closed the holes under the rocks and left just one place to listen from. She was sitting there listening to them and asking them if they had become spotted yet. First they said no. Then again she asked them and again they said, "No, we are not spotted yet." She asked them several times and there was no answer. She asked them if they were spotted but there was no answer and so she opened the holes and took away the rocks that were piled there and put them all away. Then she went in and they were dead. The two puppies, little coyotes, were dead, both of them.

So she got mad and said, "I'm going after those deer. I'm going to eat them before they get away," she said. Thinking that they might be over at the place where she met them, she got very mad and she came down where those deers were. When she came down, there were no deer there—they were gone. So she went around to look for their tracks. Then she found the tracks and followed them to where they went. When she came to where they said they were living, they were not there either. So she looked around again and came to the trail that was going up from that place where they were living. She went on following those tracks. They went up on top of the mesa and when she got on top, there were only rocks on top and she looked around for tracks but she couldn't find them. So she came back down and then looked for them again where they were living, but there was no one there. Those deer and the little fawns went away, about three to four miles away from that place, and the coyote didn't have any tracks to look for because of the rocks.

So the coyote came back to her home where her little pups lay dead and said that she would go away from there. She couldn't live there anymore. So from there she started to come down to the south. She came to what they call Owl Hill, and Owl Draw, and that's where she stopped and made her home. She found a new place to live and she may be living there yet, they say. The advice of this story is, Don't ever get fooled by what someone tells you. Because the coyote believes everything that anyone tells her, she made a mistake and she lost her pups. This is the way they tell this story.

Sunflower Girl

(HOPI)

Once upon a time, when the Hopis were living on the other side of First Mesa, down below from where they are living now, below Walpi, there was a Hopi girl living there. The boys were always coming to visit her but she didn't talk to any of them. There was one boy, however, who didn't go around at night like the others did, and he had a chum— another boy—and they both belonged to the same kiva.

One time, when they were sleeping on top of this boy's home, his chum said to him, "Why don't you go and see that girl?" The other boy said, "No, I don't think I'll do that because I'm a poor boy," he said, "and I don't think she would have any interest in me." "Well, you can't tell; maybe she might take interest in you. Let us go over there and I'll stay around close by and you can go and talk to her," his chum said to him. Then he finally agreed and said, "Let's go," and they went to that girl's home.

In those days, the girls were busy grinding corn in the evenings, and so when they came there she was grinding corn. This girl was a Sunflower clan girl, so she was a sunflower girl. When they got there, his chum went a little ways away from there, and the boy went to where the girl was grinding corn. She stopped grinding and he was talking to her. She asked his name, and he told her who he was. Then she said to the boy, "Do you have interest in me? Is this why you came to me?" "Yes," he said. "All right, but I will have to tell my mother and father tomorrow." That's what the girl said to him. "You can go back home and you also tell your father and mother that you have been here to see me. Then come and tell me what they have said to you and I will also tell you what my mother and father have said." So the boy said, "All right," and he went back to where his chum was standing, and his chum said, "You see, she talked to you. What did she say?" he asked. "Well, she said that I am to tell my father and mother that I have been there to see her and she will also tell her mother and father." "Now, you see, you have talked with her. When are you going back to tell her what your father and mother said?" "She said to come tomorrow; tomorrow evening I will go over and tell her." And so they came to where they were sleeping on top of that boy's home and went to sleep.

The next morning, after he had his breakfast, the boy told his mother and father what that Sunflower girl said to him. Then the father and mother of the boy said it would be all right. "You are a poor boy and we are poor, but maybe she is interested in you and that's why she talked to you," they said. "So you go back in the evening and tell her that it will be all right with us."

After he had eaten, his chum came to him and told him that they will go out rabbit hunting and so they both got ready to go. In those days they always went around hunting rabbits as that's how they got their meat.

They came back with some rabbits, and when evening came, he and his chum went over to tell the girl what his father and mother had said, and told the girl that it will be all right. She also said that her father and mother are willing to have him. The girl told him that she will come over to his house the day after tomorrow. "I'll come to your house." "All right," the boy said. And so he went home again with his chum, and his chum asked him what she had said, and he told him that she was going to come to his house in two days.

The next day when the sun was up, the chum went down to the kiva where they both belonged and he told those people down in the kiva what that girl had said to the boy that he was with. As I have said from the beginning, the boys were trying to get that girl and those who were in the kiva didn't like it when that boy's chum came to the kiva and told them that the girl was coming over to see him in two days. Those kiva people, they didn't like it. When they had their breakfast those other boys and men met together in the kiva. There they met together and they asked, What can be done? They didn't want that boy to marry that girl and they were mad about it. So they talked among themselves about what could be done so that he wouldn't live with her. They talked for quite a while and one of them said, "Well, I'll try to get rid of him," and then the others said, "How are you going to get rid of him?" "They will be going hunting again and I will go where they are hunting." The others said, "All right, you can do that." Then they asked him, "How are you going to go to him?" "I will go to him as a rabbit, fix myself as a jackrabbit," and they said, "Okay."

So that boy went hunting again with his chum. His chum knew about

102

what had been said in the kiva but he didn't tell his friend. They went out in the morning after they had their breakfast, and were hunting across the wash—Wepo wash, near Walpi. They went across that wash and were hunting. Since it was wintertime, the snow was on the ground and they found jackrabbit tracks there and they followed the tracks.

Finally, a jackrabbit jumped out from a bush, a rabbit bush, they call it. Then they followed the tracks and it went clear up to the other mesa, north of Walpi. There another jackrabbit jumped out and so they went on and his chum said, "I guess I will go back; I will go back and you can go after this jackrabbit and when you overtake him, then you can come back."

So that boy went on to track the rabbits, but there were two tracks now where the other jackrabbit had jumped out, and he didn't know which one to take. Finally, he took one track, and it was deep. He knew that this might be the one that he saw first, so he followed the deep track of the jackrabbit.

When it got to the foot of the other mesa, the jackrabbit track was going eastward from the mesa, and so he followed the track there. After a while he could see the jackrabbit and he went after it. When he came near, the jackrabbit ran and stopped again. He thought that the jack-rabbit was "all in," and that he might get him, so he continued to follow it until he came to a hill, a little hill.. The jackrabbit went over the hill and so he went over the hill also. It was late and there was snow on the ground. After he got over the hill, he tracked him again and the tracks went as far as a hole there; that's as far as the jackrabbit's tracks went and he knew that he went in that hole—it was a badger hole. Then he went after the jackrabbit and he could see him in the hole. He took off his blankets which he was wearing, as it was winter, and then he stooped down and reached in and got a hold of the jackrabbit.

When he got a hold of the jackrabbit, the jackrabbit caught him on the right hand, at the wrist. They boy tried to pull himself out, but the jackrabbit had turned into a human; it was not a jackrabbit then, but human that had got hold of him, and he was trying to get away. Then someone whispered in his ear while he was being held there, "You have something around your waist you can depend on; take it out and use it." That was the Spider Woman who said that. Then he felt around his waist, on the other side of his arms, and he took out a little stone animal; it was a mountain lion. He put that stone animal on the side of his right arm that was being held, and pretty soon he heard someone crying. That stone mountain lion had got that jackrabbit and it was crying like a human. After it was killed, the boy pulled it out of the hole, and it became a jackrabbit again. It was one of those boys from that kiva that turned himself into a jackrabbit. Then he said to himself, I wonder why this has been done to me. It was late then so he again covered himself with his blanket and he went back along there.

Before he got to the wash, there was another jackrabbit that ran out of the bushes. The boy had a rabbit stick which he used to catch rabbits with, and he threw it and killed that rabbit.

He started from there again and another rabbit, a cottontail, ran out in front of him. He threw that stick again and he got that rabbit too. So he tied them altogether there where he killed those two jackrabbits, but he knew which was the first jackrabbit that he killed. And so after he tied them together he came on.

It was about sundown then, and he crossed that wash and he heard someone calling his name. It was his father coming to look for him. He was going to look for him because it was late. So he met him before he got at the foot of Walpi Village, and he came along with his father back home. When they got on top where they were living, he said, "Father, let us stop." So they stopped and he untied the rabbits and gave the jackrabbit and cottontail to him. "You can take these to our house and I am going to take this other one to the kiva," he said. So he took that jackrabbit that he first got out from that badger hole and went to the kiva, and it was already sundown. Those people were in the kiva, and when he got on top of the kiva he said, "You can have this and do whatever you want to with it." He threw that jackrabbit down in the kiva. No one said anything when he did that and then he went back to his home. This happened the first time when they went hunting, before the girl was going to come to his home.

The kiva people met again and their chief said to them, "We must not do anything anymore for fear that all of us may be gone if we try to get rid of that boy; soon we will be gone," he said. Those other men and boys in the kiva said, "No! We will not give up," they said. The kiva chief answered, "I said to you do not bother him anymore; the girl is over at his house now." But they said that they were going to try again to get rid of that boy so he wouldn't marry that girl. He didn't say any more, the kiva chief, as the others were planning to try again.

In those days when a boy got married, he has to go hunting for four days before the girl went back to her home, and so those kiva people met again and they knew that he was going to hunt again the next day and they decided to try again to get rid of him. "I am going to try again."

"And what are you going to do?" one of them said. "Well, we know he is going to be hunting tomorrow again. I'll meet him somewhere," one of them said. The chum of that boy heard this again, but he didn't tell the boy what they said. His chum was a witch and that kiva had lots of witches there, and this boy's chum was a witch, and so he didn't tell the boy what they had said that night.

All right, the next morning the boy got up and got ready to go hunting again, this was his second day to hunt, and his father asked him, "Which way are you going to hunt today?" "I'm going to hunt north, towards Wepo and beyond Wepo." "All right," he said. Then his father told him to go to his grandma and get advice from her, and so he went over to his grandma, the Spider Woman, again. When he came there, of course the Spider Woman already knew that the girl was at his home. Then she said to him, "Which direction are you going to hunt today?" "Up north, towards Wepo." "All right." Then she gave him some medicine, some herbs, to take along, as she knew that the first hunting day they had tried to get rid of him and that's why she gave him that medicine. Then the Spider Woman told him, "When you are tracking a deer, and you come to where the deer is, you must watch yourself." That's what she said to him. "And so I'm going to give you this." She gave him an arrow which was made with parrot feathers and said, "When you come to him watch yourself carefully. When he begins to run towards you, you be sure and use this arrow." This is what the Spider Woman told that boy.

And so he came back to his home and then told his father and mother he was going on his way, and so he went. This time his chum didn't go with him when he went towards Wepo. He got to Wepo and went clear up the trail on the other mesa. He went along and finally he saw some tracks, deer tracks. So he followed the tracks. He followed the tracks about half a mile, tracking those deers, and one of the tracks went away from the others, and it was a big track. He thought that he might track that one that has big tracks. He knew that it would be a buck and so he was tracking it. Finally, he overtook the buck and it was standing under a cedar tree when he came near him.

As the Spider Woman had told him to be careful and watch the buck when he came near him, he did that, and he had his arrow that was given to him by the Spider Woman. As soon as that buck jumped towards him, he shot him with the bow and arrow. He shot the buck right at the throat and he knocked him down. When he came over to that buck he was dead, and it was a big buck. He was standing there thinking of what to do and then he happened to remember what the Spider Woman had told him and the medicine she gave him. So he took out that medicine and chewed it and then sprinkled it on the buck. It got small, the buck got small when he put that medicine on him after he chewed it. After that, he tied the buck up and he thought he would go back. He didn't hunt anymore from there and he started home.

That buck got small and so it was not heavy when he tied him up and carried him on his back. He was coming home and it was getting late. He came down beyond Wepo, coming down towards Bean Spring, near his home. Then his father met him so from there they both came home. When they got to their home the boy said, "I'm going to take this to the kiva," and his father said, "All right." He didn't kill any other thing that day but the big buck and he was taking it over to the kiva and it was about sundown when he arrived.

As soon as he put that buck on top of the kiva it became a big buck again; it was no more a small buck. Then he said to the kiva people, "You can do whatever you please, you people. I brought this for you." And so he threw that buck in the kiva. There was not a word said after he threw it down. In a few minutes the man that was the head of the kiva again said to them, "I told you that we might be all gone soon if you don't quit doing these things and so I don't want you to do it anymore." He again said that to the people who were in the kiva. That boy's chum was also in the kiva as he was one of the witches.

Well, for quite a while they didn't say anything and then the chief again said to them, "If you don't quit doing this we will soon be gone, and besides he is already married and what can we do? It has been shown that he is not alone. Someone is helping him, someone is with him, and so we must not do it anymore," he said. No one said anything then. Of course, that chum of the boy heard this but he didn't tell the boy anything.

The next day they were going to hunt again and that night, after they had their supper, the boy's father said to him, "Tomorrow is your last day to hunt and I will go with you; we will both go this time, tomorrow is your last day to hunt, and you keep that arrow that your grand-mother gave you."

106   Now that girl was at his home and so he didn't sleep on top of his roof anymore and that chum of his didn't come anymore to him. The next day he got ready to go hunting with his father. They got ready but they didn't take any lunch along because the father said that they would come back early before sundown. This time they were going to hunt in

a southward direction. The boy still had that arrow that the Spider Woman gave him.

He and his father left early and they went south. This time they were going to be looking for antelopes. They knew where the antelopes were and so they went southward to where they call Flower Spring. In those days of course the Hopi were good runners, and so they were running to get there early, to where the antelopes were. While they were running the father said to his son, "When we come to them, they will all get in a bunch for that is the way that antelopes do before they run. When they get together then one will lead the crowd and then they will run. That is the way that antelopes do. When we find them, you must be on the other side and I will be on this side, and they can run through to where we are. When they run through there, be sure and aim at the leader. It will be a buck, for that's the way that the antelope do. The buck always leads the crowd when they are running." This is what he said to his son. "Then I will try my best to get another antelope when they are running."

And so they went and finally they got to where the antelopes were. You could see that last butte, that mountain, from Walpi; you could see that mountain. That's where they went. When they came there, they saw them. They got in a bunch, and all the antelopes followed the buck. Then the boy and his father ran towards them from both sides, and the antelopes ran right between them. So the boy used his arrow which the Spider Woman had given him and he got the leader; he brought down a big buck and then his father throwed another one down, so they killed two of them. As they didn't have any lunch, they wanted to come back right away and so they butchered the animals, packed the meat, and tied it up; from there they went back.

When they came to the foot of Walpi on this side, on the south side there were some people living there, some Hopis. They saw those two carrying the antelopes on their backs and they knew that someone had got married for that was the custom at that time. They went hunting and brought in the game. They knew that someone had been married on the other side of Walpi.

They came home before sundown, and the sun was up yet when they brought those antelopes in. Then they cut up the meat—all of the meat of both of those antelopes.

Then the father called out for everyone to come there to eat. That was what they did when they had a new bride at their home. So they did that and everyone who was there, on the other side of Walpi, came and ate there. And those kiva people came there too, to eat. After they had their

107

supper, then the girl was going back to her home, taking the boy then to her home. And so they went to the girl's home.

The chief of that kiva spoke to his people again. "Now you see we can benefit by this boy; that's why I told you not to do anything anymore." The crowd agreed not to do anything anymore to that boy, and so they were living there again. This girl was called sunflower girl. Their children may be living somewhere around here. This is the end of this story.

How the Coyote
Got Fooled

(TEWA)

I will tell a story that I learned many years ago from one of our old Hopi men. His name is Mi-nhti'iy, my niece's father, Edna Sikwi's father. I learned this story from him, and so I will tell the story the way it was told to me.

Once upon a time, there lived a coyote northwest from the Walpi village, at the foot of the mesa. They called that place Many Waters because there is plenty of water there. That's where a coyote was living with two little coyotes—pups. One was a boy pup and the other was a little girl pup. The coyote always went around to look for food for them. One morning she said, "I am going to look for some food for you and so you must stay right here and don't go away. The people living on top might see you and harm you, so you must stay right here until I come back." She said that to the young pups. So she went north from there, among the rocks, chasing rabbits, but she didn't get any rabbits. Pretty soon she got kind of tired chasing them around among the rocks, and so she made up her mind that she would go up north where there are no rocks and look for jackrabbits. So she went. She went clear to the place they call Bean Water. She came there and she chased jackrabbits. She was chasing them around but couldn't get any.

Then she came on down, chasing them, and she came to a place they call Crow Point. She was very tired and she sat down on a little hill to rest. As she was sitting there, she heard some noise from a bird. She wondered where that noise was and so she looked above and there were high rocks, standing in a row, and a little bird was on top of the middle rock. So Mrs. Coyote saw the little bird, and the bird saw the coyote. It was just a little way from there that bird was sitting on top of the rock, and Mrs. Coyote was sitting down on a little hill. Then the little brown bird said to the coyote, "What are you doing there?" She said, "I am very tired and I am sitting here to rest. I'm looking for food for my little ones." Then the brown bird said to the coyote, "Come up to us." And the coyote said, "How can I get up there? It's too high." The bird said, "You go around the other side and it's not steep and you'll get here where we are living." And so the coyote went around the row of rocks that were standing there and sure enough, when she got on top it wasn't steep and so she got to them. And there was a little hole in the rock in which the brown bird was sitting and singing. The brown bird said "Come in" to the coyote. And Mrs. Coyote said, "How can I go in? Your home is too small to go in." "Well, step over to the hole; it will grow big enough so you can come in." And so she did what the brown bird told her to do. All of a sudden the hole got bigger, and so she went in. There were two little birds there also. There she met the birds and they were talking for a while and the coyote was telling them what she had been doing all that morning, chasing rabbits, but couldn't get any.

Then the brown bird said to Mrs. Coyote, "You take your rest and I'll get something for us to eat. I will build a fire and cook something for us to eat," said the brown bird. And so Mrs. Coyote was sitting there watching the bird to see what she was going to do. And so the bird went into another room and brought out a little bowl in which she cooked things. She built a fire and put the bowl on the fire and then she poured some water in the bowl. Mrs. Coyote was watching what she did. After the water boiled, she said to her young ones, "Come here, my little ones." She first told the little boy-bird to come to her, and the little bird went hopping toward his mother. She got hold of that little bird and put him in the boiling water. Then she told the other little bird, "You come here too," she said. She also went hopping to her, and she got hold of her, and also put her in the boiling water where she put the first one. Then the bird said to the coyote, "You just wait for a while until they cook. When they are cooked, then we will have something to eat," the brown bird said to the coyote. The coyote was watching and she thought it was interesting the way she did this. And after when they were cooked, she went into the other room and got out a food bowl, and she dumped the two little birds and the boiling water in that food bowl. Then she went in that room and brought out a yucca sifter—made of yucca plants. She brought that out and set it by the side of the food bowl where the little birds were ready to be eaten. Then she said to Mrs. Coyote, "All right, let's eat. Move over here and let's have our dinner; you must be tired." "Yes, I'm very tired," she said. So they sat down there and began eating. Then the brown bird said to Mrs. Coyote, "Do not eat the bones, but put them on that sifter that I brought out. Just eat the flesh, but don't eat the bones," she said to Mrs. Coyote.

And so they were eating there, and the brown bird just pretended to eat, but she was not. But Mrs. Coyote all that time was eating the flesh of those little birds. She did what Mrs. Brown Bird told her to do, and she didn't eat the bones.

After they were through, the bird said to Mrs. Coyote, "Let's go out on top of that rock where I was standing, where you saw me," she said. "All right," the coyote said, and so they went out. Then the bird came to the place on the edge of that rock where she had been standing before, carrying those bones in the sifter. She went on singing, singing in a low tone.

In a low tone she was singing. Then she threw the bones down off the high rock. Instead of falling, they flew. The little birds came to life again and flew, and then came back to their mother and sat by her. The coyote said it was interesting, and she said that she will be friends with the brown bird and asked her to be her friend. Then the coyote said, "I also have two little ones and they will be friends with your little young ones." So the brown bird agreed that they would be friends. And so Mrs. Coyote said to the bird, "Come to us, to visit." Then the brown bird said to her, "Where do you live?" "Just right across at the foot of that mesa." She could see that point where her little pups were. That was their home, the coyote's home.

And so, after they had their meal and saw all this, Mrs. Coyote went on to look for food for her little pups. She went toward Walpi and she found some food. The sheep had some lambs there and she found the afterbirth and took it home. When she got there, the little pups were on top of that rock, watching for their mother to return. She came there and brought it for them and they all had supper. Then she told them that she made friends with a bird, who also had two little ones. "I made friends with their mother," she said, "and I asked them to come to visit us tomorrow. When they come, you make friends with the little ones, and you must be quiet so they won't be afraid of us." This is what she said to her pups.

So then it was evening, and they went under their rock where they were living and slept the night. The next morning they got up early and they were watching the birds. As they were watching, they could see them coming. Then Mrs. Coyote said to the little pups, "There they are! When they come you must be very quiet." As those little birds weren't strong enough to fly very far, they flew a little, then hopped along by the side of their mother, when they were coming to Mrs. Coyote's home. Finally, they got there and they were all sitting on top of the rock, the flat rock. Then Mrs. Coyote told them to come in, and they went under the rock.

The mother bird whispered to the little ones to watch the little pups and the mother coyote, for they might eat them. And so they went in. Then Mrs. Coyote said, "You must be tired." The brown bird said, "Yes, we are very tired." "Well, you just rest here and wait a while and we'll have something to eat." And as they were sitting there, she went in the other room—it was a cave. She also brought a bowl, an old bowl, and then she went out and gathered some chips and made a fire. Then she poured some water in that bowl. It was all mended with pitch that they get off the pine trees. It was an old broken bowl which she had. So she put the water in there and put it on the fire. They waited a while and the water was boiling. Then she said to one of her little pups—it was a little boy-pup—"Come here, my little one," she said. But the little pup got scared and was running within the house, jumping here and there, trying to get out. And so the mother chased him around and finally she got hold of him. She dragged him to the boiling water and put the little pup in the boiling water. Then she asked the other one to come but she too didn't want to. She ran around the room there and got hold of her and put her in the bowl also. Then Mrs. Coyote said, "We'll wait for a while until they are cooked and then we'll have our dinner."

They were waiting a while and then she said, "I guess they are ready to be served." So she went in the other room and she brought out an old food bowl and dumped that boiling water and the little pups in the bowl. Then she said, "Now we are ready to sit down to eat." And so the little birds moved to the place where the bowl was, where the little pups were in the bowl. She went in the room again and got an old yucca sifter and brought it out, and said to the birds, "Do not eat the bones; put them on this sifter that I brought out." Now the birds were just acting like they were eating, but they were not, but Mrs. Coyote herself was eating the boiled meat of her little ones and putting the bones on that sifter. After she ate all of the little pups' meat and put the bones on that sifter, then she said, "Let's go out on top of our house." So they all went out, and the little birds were just a little distance away from Mrs. Coyote. She was standing there and humming a song, but I don't know what kind of a song she was singing. Then she threw the bones down from above that rock, down to the ground, and all the bones fell on the ground. The little pups never came alive.

So she got mad and was chasing those birds; she wanted to get their mother before she got the other ones, she thought, and so she was chasing the mother bird rather than the little ones. And so the little birds were hopping along, flying a little ways then hopping again toward their home. Mrs. Coyote got tired of chasing the mother bird and so she gave up, and the birds went back to their home. She was sure mad and so she left that place. "I won't live here anymore," she said. Then she went up north toward Wepo to find a new home. She must still be around there somewhere.

The coyote is always being fooled because she doesn't wait until she gets the truth of what anyone says to her. Both the female and the male coyote, they always get fooled. So we ask you to be patient when someone is talking to you or wants to do anything with you. Because the coyote was like that, she boiled her own pups. But the brown bird had the power to do so, that's why the brown birds came back alive. This is the end of the story.

The Coyote and the Bluebirds

(TEWA)

Once upon a time there were bluebirds living on top of the mesa at Tewa, on top of a big draw. The nest was on top of a cedar tree and there were two little birds, bluebirds, and the mother bird and the father bird, so all together there were four of them living there. While they were living there, the mother bird was keeping track of them while they were growing, the little birds. Every morning they both went looking for food for those two little birds. They were bringing them food, as they were not able to fly yet. They kept on doing that until they had their wings coming out, and every morning the mother bird asked them if they were strong enough to fly and they said, "Not yet." They were not able to fly, they said, and so she waited a few more days.

So one morning she said to them again, "Now, my little birdies, you have to exercise, try to fly." And so they said, "All right." So one morning after they had their food which the mother bird and the father bird brought for them, she asked them if they will practice trying to fly, and they said, "All right." She said she had a song to sing. When she stops singing, then they will fly up in the air, not down below on the ground. "Try to fly up in the air," she said to the little birds. And the father bird was also with them. So they sang a song, the father bird and the mother bird sang a song. When they stopped singing, they flew up above. This is the song they sang:

> 'áh 'áh níkosa· sá·
> má' iy kó·nìy
> kó·nìy 'ìsta
> 'áh 'áh
> 'áh 'áh

This is what the song was. When they stopped singing, then they flew. They didn't fly very high up when one of them said, "I'm tired," so they came back down and sat on that tree again. That was the first day they tried to fly. Then the mother bird said they would try the next morning, and that's all they did that day. They flew all right, but they were not strong enough to fly any higher.

They waited that day and were all together on top of that little tree where the little birds were in the nest. So the next morning, early in the morning, they went for food again, both of them—the father bird and the mother bird—and brought them food again—worms, insects, and whatever they can find that the birds eat. After they had their meal, the mother bird said again that they will try again and the little birdies said, "All right." So they were singing again:

> 'áh 'áh níkosa· sá·
> má' ìy kó·nìy
> kó·nìy 'ìsta
> 'áh 'áh
> 'áh 'áh

Then away they flew up in the air. This time they flew a little higher and then one of them said, "I'm tired," and so they came down again. While they were singing, an old coyote heard that song and was coming towards them. He heard the song and so he came direct to where they were. When he came there he said, in Tewa, "yági yági, sáha péy 'éy. What are you doing?" he said. He said, "yági yági"; of course, I can't describe what that word is, but sáha péy 'éy is "my grandchildren." That is what the old coyote said to them.

"When I was coming," he said, "I heard your song and it is a very nice song, and will you sing to me?" He was standing down below looking up at those birds sitting on that cedar tree. And then he asked them to sing the song again and so they sang again:

> 'áh 'áh níkosa· sá·
> má' ìy kó·nìy
> kó·nìy 'ìsta
> 'áh 'áh
> 'áh 'áh

They sang that to the coyote. He was still listening to them. He said to them, "sáha péy 'éy" again. "You've got a nice song and I know when you sang that song yesterday, you flew up in the air." And the father bird said, "Yes, we did." The coyote asked them if he would fly with them after they sang that song. The father bird and the mother bird said to him that he had no wings, that he can't fly.

Then the coyote asked them to give him their wings and their tails, all of them to give him their tails and wings to put on him. So the coyote asked them again to give him their wings, at least two apiece, for there were four of them, the father bird, the mother bird, and the little birdies. And they agreed that they would put wings on him. And so they took off two of their wings from both sides and their tail. They fixed the wings on the leg of Mr. Coyote, and they fixed the tails that they had taken off themselves and put on the coyote. Now he was ready to fly, and the father bird said to the old coyote, "Let me hear you sing the song that we sang; you have heard us and we want to hear you sing to us before we all sing." So the old coyote began to sing.

> 'óh 'óh níkosa·
> 'óh 'óh níkosa·
> 'óh 'óh níkosa·
> má' ìy kó·nìy
> 'óh 'óh
> 'óh 'óh

Then the bird said to him, "You've got a fierce voice. You haven't got a voice like us." The coyote said, "My *sáha péy 'éy*," he said again, "my grandchildren. That is my voice, I can't help it," he said, "and I'll sing in the tone that I have, and you sing, for you have nice voices." And so they all sang then. The birds sang and so did the coyote.

> 'áh 'áh níkosa· sá·
> 'áh 'áh níkosa· sá·
> má' ìy kó·nìy
> kó·nìy 'ìsta
> 'áh 'áh
> 'áh 'áh

"Now fly," they said to the old coyote, and he got up and he flew up with them in the air. And then when they got way up, then the father bird and the mother bird told the little ones to take their wings away from the coyote. They said, "He had a fierce voice and might eat us after all." And so they took their wing and their tails off of the coyote.

From there the old coyote was coming down, whirling down, and with all the heavy body he had, fell down on the ground on top of the rocks. And he was dead. The birdies came to him and he was dead. And so they said, "You are a mean old man and we know you are trying to get us." This is what they said to him. Now they said, "Now what shall we do with him?" and he was on top of that high rock, on top of where their home was. So they all got together and with their claws they dragged the old coyote down and threw him down the cliff. And that was the last of the coyote. That's how those birds killed that coyote.

The old coyote always gets fooled, and so we advise you children to never get fooled by anyone. Always try to be patient when they are talk-ing to you because the coyote was a fool is why he got fooled, to have the wings put on him to fly. And this was the end of the old coyote. So the birds went away from that place after they threw the coyote down the cliff. They say the bones used to be there, below that high standing rock, where that cedar tree stood where the birds were living. This is the end of this story.

PART THREE

EDITOR'S NOTES

The Aftermath of
the Migration

The numerous accounts of the Tewa migration to First Mesa (see Appendix 1) all provide justification for the Tewas' indignation at their mistreatment by the Hopis. In the dialogue between the Tewas and the Hopis, feelings of resentment serve to support the Tewas' moral integrity and rectitude regarding their grievances. The Tewas complained about the delay in being given adequate land and food and the poor quality of the land they eventually received (Dozier 1954:353, 1956:176). Furthermore, they believed the Hopis had "bad hearts," were responsible for their poor crops, had encroached on the land that had been given the Tewas, and had stolen Tewa property.

The antagonism between the Hopis and the Arizona Tewas can be attributed to a clash of basic values. According to both Edward P. Dozier and Victor Mindeleff, the Tewas perceived the peacefulness and passivity of the Hopis as a sign of weakness. Conversely, the Hopis viewed Tewa aggressiveness and warrior behavior as undesirable, even if it was useful when protection was needed (Dozier 1956:176; Mindeleff 1891:37). Hopi mistreatment of the Tewas can perhaps be better understood as a defensive response to Tewa aggressiveness, which posed a threat to the Hopis' worldview and values. The Tewas were seen as militant intruders encroaching on Hopi land, a characterization that made the Tewas all the more determined to resist Hopi domination by asserting their differences.

The "curse"—that the Tewas will be able to speak the Hopi language but Hopis will never learn the Tewa language—has consistently been used by the Arizona Tewas to perpetuate the shaming of the Hopis for their past selfishness and ingratitude. It has also served to enhance Tewa self-esteem and feelings of superiority. The curse became both a defense mechanism and a weapon, as seen in the following rebuke of the Hopis by Tewa elders: "Because you have behaved in a manner unbecoming to human beings, we have sealed knowledge of our language and our way of life from you. You and your descendants will never learn our language and our ceremonies, but we will learn yours. We will ridicule you in both your language and our own" (Dozier 1954:292).

Tewa ceremonial practices have also been used to remind the people of the sacrifices made by their ancestors who came to First Mesa. During the second night of the Winter Solstice Ceremony in Tewa Village, the narrative of the coming of the Tewas is repeated to the men and boys. The town chief tells how the Bear clan people came to this place from their place of origin and describes their reasons for coming. He says, "We must remember the story of how those Walpi chiefs sent for us. Whenever any Walpi person says anything bad to us, remembering the story, we must not mind what is said to us" (Parsons 1925:122).

Dozier recorded another indictment of Hopi behavior by the Tewa elders: "How pitifully ignorant must have been our ancestors to believe the Hopi. Little did they know that they would be so miserably deceived. When our ancestors had defeated the Utes and made life safe for the Hopi, they asked for the land, women and food which was promised to them. But the Hopi refused to give them these things. Then it was that our poor ancestors had to live like beasts, foraging on the wild plants and barely subsisting on the meager supply of food. Our ancestors lived miserably, beset by disease and starvation. The Hopi, well fed and healthy, laughed and made fun of our ancestors" (1956:177).

The Tewa elders advised their people to accommodate to their erstwhile antagonists: "You have to go, just like walking on a sharp knife. That's the way the road is. You have to keep straight. You cannot be jealous, you cannot be mad at anybody. You cannot go against anybody or anything that they're doing to you. You have to take everything the way it hits you. You have to take everything they criticize you on. That's the way you're going to see another life. Don't try to live up with them. Of course, associate with them; be good to them, but remember, our authority has ended" (Dewey Healing, in Black 1984).

The Tewa elders further admonished their people how to maintain their resistance to the Hopis and, at the same time, how to be of help to them: "Whatever you're going to see in the life of the Hopis, you're going to be persuaded about lots of things. But if you see something that you think will hurt the Hopis, tell them about it; don't be afraid. Even if you have to go up to their chief and get a hold of his ear and shake him. Tell him, 'You're off the line; you're mistreating my people.' Don't be afraid of him. That's your duty. Then whenever they call for you to help on certain things, do it" (statement by Pot'óko, a member of the

Corn clan, heard by Tom Polacca, Dewey Healing's uncle, and re-counted by Dewey Healing, in Black 1984).

The Tewa migrants showed ingenuity in accommodating themselves to the Hopis by adopting many of their customs and instituting changes in their own kinship, social, and religious systems. By moving toward greater cultural integration with the Hopis, they reduced friction and helped unite the villages of First Mesa. Of primary importance in achiev-ing this integration was the adoption of the Hopi matrilineal kinship sys-tem in place of their Rio Grande patrilineal organization.

By observing the rules of matrilocal residence, the Arizona Tewas were able to maintain their social identity and preserve their functioning language community. Tewa women, whether married to Tewa or Hopi men, generally lived in Tewa Village, ensuring that all their children were brought up in a Tewa-speaking community. Hopi husbands and fathers were addressed in the Hopi language; if they tried to respond in Tewa, their awkward attempts were taken as evidence of the viability of the curse. A Tewa man married to a Hopi woman lived in the Hopi vil-lage in accordance with Hopi residence rules, and their children were brought up in a Hopi-speaking community. An increasing number of families of mixed marriages took up residence in Sitsomovi, the middle village established between Walpi and Tewa Village. Thus, by adopting certain aspects of Hopi culture, the Arizona Tewas paradoxically ensured their own persistence as a discrete and bounded ethnic group (Eggan 1966:124). On their arrival the Arizona Tewas also borrowed and incorporated the Hopi clan system. It is therefore highly unlikely that Rio Grande Tanoan people had fully functioning clans before they migrated to the Hopis (Parsons 1936b; Eggan 1950; Ellis 1951b; Dozier 1954).

Pabanale's detailed version of the Tewa migration legend contains a list of clans that undertook the journey: Stick, Cloud, Tobacco, Sand, Sun, Cottonwood, Katsina, and Butterfly. Although none of the extant narrative accounts mention migration by clans, some contemporary Tewas maintain that the Tewas indeed journeyed by clans, but they take exception to Pabanale's list. Dewey Healing asserted that the Tewas did not have a Katsina or Butterfly clan on the first migration. He also said that Pabanale omitted mention of the participating Corn and Bear clans. Alternatively, Healing listed the following clans in the order of their arrival at Hopi: Tobacco, Stick-Spruce, Corn, Cloud, and Bear. Healing was uncertain about the Sand clan but noted that the five clans in his list were the only ones that had possession of the *tipony* (sacred medicine bundles) that symbolized authority (Black 1984). Pabanale's niece, Effie Tengyo'tse, believed that only four clans originally came to First Mesa: Tobacco, Bear, Corn, and Sun, followed later by the Parrot, Stick, Sand, and Katsina-Crow clans, the last one coming from Zuni (Black 1984). Such differences of opinion reflect diverse clan traditions and have political and ritual implications. The importance of clans in the life of the Arizona Tewas cannot be underestimated. They play a vital role in perpetuating historical and ceremonial knowledge and fulfilling social obligations.

The most likely reason for the borrowing of the clan structure was the need of the Tewas to accommodate themselves to the existing Hopi clan traditions to facilitate interaction. Dozier points out that borrowing fostered rather than threatened the preservation of the Tewas' way of life: "When elements [of culture] could be incorporated within the Tewa pattern without endangering cultural aloofness, borrowing was in order" (1951:61). Thus, by adopting the clan system and observing the rules of clan exogamy, the Arizona Tewas were able to intermarry more easily with the Hopis. It also gave legitimate form to Arizona Tewa landholdings, since all land was owned and distributed by the clans (Kroskrity 1993:25).

In the process of the Tewa integration on First Mesa, the newly adopted clans were divided into two groups, each with its own kiva, ceremonies, and kiva chief. Every Tewa belongs to one of the two kivas. The main, or central plaza, kiva (*munéteh*) is also called the summer kiva and is owned by the Corn clan, to which the Bear, Stick, and Tobacco clans also belong. The outside, or winter, kiva (*p'endite'h*) is owned by the Sand clan and includes members of the Cloud and Cottonwood clans (Parsons in Stephen 1936:xliv–xlv).

Although the Arizona Tewas integrated their kinship and clan organization with that of the Hopis, the Tewas' ceremonial practices have preserved their distinctive Rio Grande–based culture. These practices are carefully guarded, and most Hopis are prohibited from attending. Dozier (1951:53 n. 27) notes that "the Tewa are farthest removed from the Hopi in their ceremonial system": unlike Hopi practices, which are concerned with weather control and crop fertility, Tewa ceremonies focus on curing the sick. There is also a strong emphasis on warfare in Tewa society. The theme of warfare and its associated imagery provided the Tewas a symbolic means of defining and preserving their cultural heritage (Ellis 1951). This military element in Tewa culture has its historical roots in the Tewas' occupation of the eastern frontier of the Rio

124

Grande valley, where they were in contact—and conflict—with Southern Plains Indians.

In their later encounters with the outside world, the Arizona Tewas proved to be more aggressive and outgoing than the Hopis. They were more willing to accept white ways and cooperate with local Indian agents. Individual Arizona Tewas were friendly to whites and had little of the reticence characteristic of both the Hopis and the Rio Grande Tewas (Dozier 1954:367). Dozier comments on the Arizona Tewas' ability to adapt to radical changes: "Hopi-Tewa social and ceremonial organization thus appear to be the result of (1) a core of elements indigenous to the group and bearing resemblances to the Rio Grande Tewa, (2) elements borrowed from the Hopi over a period of two and a half centuries during which the two groups lived as neighbors, and (3) a unique integration of the two that appears to be becoming progressively a new whole" (1954:368).

In 1949, in a letter to Elizabeth Shepley Sergeant, a member of Friends of the Indians and a friend of John Collier, former commissioner of Indian affairs, Dozier further observes: "I have been impressed how much like an ethnic minority group (within the Hopi majority) the Tewa here [at First Mesa] are—they hold steadfast to their language and culture and in addition have adopted 'aggressive' overbearing attitudes so much like other minority groups" (Collier Papers, Reel 17, No. 349, Newberry Library, Chicago). Kroskrity, however, believes that the Arizona Tewas cannot easily be set apart from their Hopi neighbors: there is "little if anything that distinguishes the Tewa from the Hopi. The clothes they wear, the food they eat, the houses they live in, and the fields they tend are not significantly different" (1993:7).

Perhaps the most astute observations on this matter were made by Albert Yava, Arizona Tewa elder and interpreter: "We are interrelated with Hopi families in all villages. Many of us have become members of the various Hopi Kiva Societies. We share dances and festival days with the Hopis. We belong to the same clans. We are usually represented on the Hopi Tribal Council. In many ways we are indistinguishable from them, and often you hear us say in conversation, 'We Hopis,' not because we have forgotten that we are Tewas but because we identify with the Hopi in facing the outside world" (1978:129–30).

The Early Years

BOARDING SCHOOL AND THE
PROBLEMS OF CULTURE CHANGE

By the 1880s the government had established a comprehensive public school system for the rapid assimilation of Indian children. The system consisted of day schools on the reservation and boarding schools both on and off the reservation. The boarding schools imposed severe restrictions on the Hopi children, who were forcibly taken there by Indian agents and government troops. They were prohibited from speaking Hopi, their hair was cut, and they were given strange clothing to wear. English names replaced their Indian names, and they were compelled to undergo religious indoctrination conducted by Christian missionaries who operated freely on the reservation with the approval of the government and who most often were the teachers at the schools.

Commissioner of Indian Affairs William A. Jones stated the choice for Indians succinctly in 1903: "To educate the Indian in the ways of civilized life . . . is to preserve him from extinction, not as an Indian, but as a human being. As a separate entity he cannot exist encysted, as it were, in the body of this great nation" (U.S. Department of the Interior 1904:2–3). Ultimately, the mandate of the government was to do away with the reservation schools and all things distinctly Indian.

A few years earlier Commissioner of Indian Affairs T. J. Morgan, noted for his ultimatum to the Indians, "assimilate or die," had articulated the goals of the government schools: "It is the duty and design of the government to remove, by the shortest method, the ignorance, inability, and fears of the Indians, and to place them on an equity with other races in the United States. In organizing this system of schools, the fact is not overlooked that Indian schools . . . should be preparatory and temporary; that eventually they will become unnecessary and a full and free entrance for Indians in the public school system of the country will be possible" (U.S. Department of the Interior 1890:cxlvi). A former Civil War general and Baptist minister, Morgan moved with conviction and fervor to institutionalize compulsory Indian education and apply

Christian principles to the recently formalized structure of the Indian school system. Morgan was influenced by a group of self-styled "Friends of the Indian," Christian humanitarians who assembled annually at Lake Mohonk, New York, to plan Indian reform. These reformers intended to "solve the Indian problem" by abolishing the reservation system through the allotment process and undermining traditional kinship systems and modes of inheritance. The goal of assimilation was also to be accomplished by emphasizing such values of the American ethos as hard work, private property, and the acquisition of material goods.[1]

Not to be overlooked in this process was the relentless pressure brought by various missionary groups on Indians to abandon their tribal religions and adopt Christianity, thereby hastening their absorption into the broader American society. A key element in Morgan's program was a new Indian educational system. For him there were no alternatives: "The Indians must conform to the white man's ways; peaceably if they will, forcibly if they must. They must adjust themselves to their environment and conform their mode of living substantially to our civilization . . . they cannot escape it, and must either conform to it or be crushed by it" (U.S. Department of the Interior 1889:3).

Such a program of education was intended to inculcate those values that would "prepare the rising generation of Indians for the new order of things thus forced upon them" (U.S. Department of the Interior 1889:3), including the love of flag, the rights and privileges of citizenship, and an awakening of a sense of independence, self-reliance, and self-respect. Systematizing the Indian schools was one of Morgan's primary concerns, for schools were "to be the medium through which the rising generation of Indians are to be brought into fraternal and harmonious relationship with their white fellow-citizens" (U.S. Department of the Interior 1889:3). Every Indian community was to have a day school that would funnel children into boarding schools located close to the population centers of the tribe. Last in the series of Indian "training centers" were the off-reservation industrial training schools, located near large cities and far removed from the "destructive" influences of the reservation. Here the transformation could be made from the "native condition of indolence and uselessness into civilized and useful members of society" (*Arizona Graphic*, Sept. 1899).

As a result of these governmental efforts, the Indian world into which Irving Pabanale was born around 1890 was witness to the rapid disappearance of many of the old tribal practices and customs and the inexorable drive to acculturate the population, especially the children. For

127

the Hopis, with their theocratically structured communal lifestyle, this process was somewhat slower than for other tribes, though the inevitable consequences of Euro-American directed culture change were readily perceivable. Thus, at the age of five, Pabanale found himself among the first group of children to attend the Polacca Day School, a small makeshift structure that was to serve until a new school was finished at Keams Canyon.

The catalyst in establishing the school system at First Mesa was the energetic and charismatic Tom Polacca, a Tewa who was interested in having the children attend the government school to get a modern education. Oblivious to criticism, Polacca exerted a great deal of influence in supporting government education. The more conservative Hopis, who opposed sending their children to the government school, called Polacca and his followers progressive, or friendly, because of their inclination to accept white influences and cooperate with government policies. But according to Dozier, Polacca was "a traditional Hopi-Tewa, . . . little different from other Hopi-Tewa" (1954:295–96).

The Arizona Tewas historically have held the position of interpreters for the Hopis in their contacts with the government. Polacca served in this capacity and was highly respected for his work. In 1890 he accompanied four village chiefs to Washington for a conference with Morgan and Agent C. E. Vandever in the hope of obtaining relief from the continuous intrusion of the Navajos on Hopi land. Permission for the meeting was given on the condition that the Hopis provide sufficient children to fill the Indian school at Keams Canyon. The group consisted of the five Hopi village chiefs: Simo, Anawita, Loloma, Honani, and Polacca. Polacca, who represented Tewa Village and served as interpreter, expressed to Morgan and Vandever his eagerness to adopt change and to accept the ways of the whites: "I am not a Moqui [Hopi], but a Tewa. Although my father has the old religion and all the old ideas, yet I have listened to the whites and have moved down from the mesa and have a good house and horses and cattle. We want horses and cattle, stoves and wagons. When I go back I think we will be willing to do as you ask. I am younger and stronger than most of these, and have taken the white man's way and I think after coming here and seeing things the others will do as I have done" (U.S. Department of the Interior 1890).[2]

By the time Irving Pabanale was settled in at the Keams Canyon Boarding School, almost a decade of uninterrupted government effort to educate Hopi children had passed.[3] The school opened in 1887, the same year the Indian Allotment Act was passed. The allotment system was to have limited success altering traditional Hopi landholdings, but the boarding school at Keams Canyon effectively polarized the Hopis over the issue of compulsory school attendance, whether at day schools or boarding schools.

The Tewas accepted the boarding school, but other Hopi villages vigorously resisted the compulsory removal of their children to Keams Canyon. This location was far enough from the villages to allow the government teachers a free hand with minimal parental interference in the educational process. Hopi parents felt that boarding schools severed the child's ties to family, religion, and language and that the government was determined to strip Hopi children of their culture. John H. Bowman, the Indian agent attached to the Navajo Agency (which also served the Hopis),[4] noted the purpose in establishing the boarding school at Keams Canyon: "Keams Canyon is twelve miles east from the Moqui [Hopi] villages. The children being removed to school at this place would preserve them from the annoyance and interruption of daily visits from parents and relatives" (U.S. Department of the Interior 1884:137).

The school occupied several buildings rented from Thomas Keam and employed a matron, a seamstress, and a cook. The boys cut wood, hauled water, worked the garden, and maintained the buildings. The girls were taught how to sew, cook, and launder and worked in the dining room. In addition, the basic skills of arithmetic, reading, and writing were taught. Superintendent John Gallaher sought enrollees for the school, obtaining a total of fifty-seven, most of whom came from First Mesa, when the school opened. The school experienced difficulties with runaways and parental hostility for several years until the government instituted a policy of compulsory attendance in 1890. Tom Polacca and Thomas Keam both assisted in this effort. The children faced a bewildering array of strangers and frightening experiences at Keams Canyon school. Life was regimented, and strict discipline was enforced. Punishment for violation of the rules was freely administered. The children learned to cope with their new environment, however. Most adapted as best they could, showing acceptance externally while quietly retaining their Hopi values. "Others accepted Anglo-American values and customs and broke with traditional patterns although maintaining a strong identity as Hopis" (Eggan in Spindler 1963:327).

129

The Phoenix Indian School

Pabanale arrived at the Phoenix Indian School in 1901, nine years after it began operating as the newest of the off-reservation industrial schools.[5] It had already made a considerable impact on Indian education; its steadily increasing enrollment reached seven hundred that year and included Indian students from numerous tribes in the Southwest. In the eyes of its administrators, the Phoenix school was a model of aesthetics and efficiency, well suited to the tasks of "civilizing" and assimilating its wards. Its prototype was the boarding school at Carlisle, Pennsylvania, founded in 1879 by Richard Henry Pratt, a Civil War veteran and frontier officer. All boarding schools followed Carlisle's practice of rigid military discipline and corporal punishment to enforce adherence to assimilationist policies.

The stated goal of the Phoenix school was to provide a controlled teaching atmosphere in which only the English language would be tolerated. Separated from their cultural background, children would be trained in industrial, mechanical, and domestic skills.[6] The school operated on the self-proclaimed virtues of punctuality, obedience, and regimentation. All aspects of work, study, and recreation were organized with military discipline. Helen Sekaquaptewa recalls the school environment when she was a student at Phoenix: "It was a military school; we marched to the dining room three times a day to band music. Everything was done on schedule and there was no time for idleness." She continues: "School life was obnoxious to many students and discipline was military style. Corporal punishment was given as a matter of course; whipping with a harness strap was administered . . . to the most unruly" (1972:134, 136). For the Indian students, these new ways of living were confusing: the wearing of a different style of clothes, practicing white habits of cleanliness, bathing, using toilets, eating white foods, and living by fixed schedules and a strict adherence to obedience. The pressure to conform to an alien culture produced anxiety and tensions.

The "outing system" provided yet another opportunity for teaching the Indian students "good work habits" and proper behavior in the white world. It was the school's most valuable contribution to the local economy—cheap labor. Some two hundred students were placed with private employers and rural farm families to work as laborers, field hands, and domestics. Though students received wages of a dollar a day for their work, the greatest advantage accrued to members of the local business community, who could draw on an ample supply of inexpensive labor for extended periods of time.

Almost from its inception, the Phoenix Indian School was beset by the problem of runaways, averaging ten to twenty a month in 1890 (Trennert 1979:317). It was inevitable that student disaffection would develop in the face of the harsh, insensitive, and inflexible policies requiring conformity to an alien culture. School officials spared no effort in apprehending the deserters, employing reservation police, disciplinarians, trusted students, and civil law enforcement officers to locate and return runaways. Agency police were empowered to arrest and return children who were being detained by their parents or relatives. Parents themselves were subject to arrest and punishment for hindering the performance of the agent's duties (U.S. Department of the Interior 1898). Punishment for runaways was usually severe. As we have seen, Pabanale avoided punishment by returning to the school voluntarily after running away.

Helen Sekaquaptewa recalls some of the experiences of Hopi students who tried to escape: "Sometimes boys and even girls would run away; even though they were locked in at night, they managed to get out somehow. Often a boy and a girl would have it planned to go at the same time. Older boys, with records of dependability, would be sent to find and bring them back. Punishment for the girls might be cleaning the yards, even cutting grass with scissors, while wearing a card that said, 'I ran away.' Boys were put in the school jail . . . repeaters had their heads shaved and had to wear a dress to school. Some of them forgot how to wear pants" (1969:137).

While at the school, Pabanale developed an interest in music and learned to play the cornet. He joined the school band in 1904 and shared in its prestige. The band was a highly acclaimed asset for the school. Its forty members—students with good grades—traveled throughout the Southwest and California performing at school functions, fairs, and town events. The band had elite status, and members took great pride in their accomplishments (Trennert 1988:127). The band also had an impact on outside opinion, reassuring the public that the efforts to educate the Indians were achieving success and that the "Indian problem" was being eliminated..

After hearing the band's performance at the Great American Exposition of 1899, the commissioner of Indian affairs commented to the band director:

131

You have a fine band. I'm astonished. The boys play delightfully in tune. That band is a constant wonder to me. If my own eyes had not seen them, and my own ears heard their playing, I would not have believed such improvement could have been made by an Indian. Their playing is only equaled by their marching, which is perfect.

The contrast between your band and those old Indians yonder is certainly inspiring and hopeful. It is time to embalm that odious expression "The only good Indian is the dead one," and substitute "The only good Indian is the educated one" (U.S. Department of the Interior 1899:384–85).

Problems of the Returned Students

How successful were the boarding schools in changing the lives of their students? How well did they enable the Indians to adopt the values of American society? The results were certainly mixed and proved to be disappointing to school officials, who anticipated a quick conversion of Indians to the ways of "civilization."

In 1917 Hopi agent Leo Crane voiced strong criticism of the boarding schools as an ill-conceived "white-washing process" that attempted to turn the Indian into an "imitation white man." Nevertheless, Crane recognized that the Hopi student "essentially retained his Indian identity and manner of life, while simultaneously he felt a strong sense of political loyalty to the national government and possessed a general understanding of white ways" (Adams 1979:353).

The Bureau of Indian Affairs found it advantageous to cultivate the abilities of a number of astute Indian men with boarding school experience. These individuals were encouraged to move into positions of leadership, either as go-betweens with the whites or as recognized representatives and advisers in their home communities. It was through such men that the BIA was able to deal with the southwestern Indians. Some became judges and leaders in their communities (Spicer 1962:441).

Many who returned to the reservation found that in their absence tribe and family members had changed, as had circumstances in their villages. They felt strange and out of place, alienated from traditional social, political, and religious life. Furthermore, they were objects of suspicion and hostility on the part of older people and were subject to ridicule. Parents and elders frequently put great pressure on them to resume the old ways, a process that many resented. Some returnees found reservation life too restricting and resisted assuming their village and ceremonial obligations. Their new values and ideas were in conflict with the old traditions, and they felt that their school training had little application to reservation life. Consequently, alienation was a major problem, and many former students resorted to periods of wandering and working at odd jobs. A number found employment in distant cities and rural areas, working in factories and on farms. Freed from the restraints of cooperative labor and economic dependence on the extended family, some of these individuals adapted to life as independent wage workers (Spicer 1962:490). Some of those who remained on the reservation found it satisfying to live on the margins of white and native society, becoming the vehicle for the introduction of new ideas from the Euro-American world.

Pabanale's account of his experiences at the Phoenix Indian School is sparse. Missing are observations, descriptions, and personal feelings about the structure, routine, discipline, military drill, and regimentation of school life and how he coped with it all. Was he made to participate in the outing system or other aspects of school life? Was he totally accepting of white values and customs or were there some that he objected to? These questions remain unanswered. Pabanale generally liked his school experiences, he told me. He gained some knowledge and experience of the larger world and learned the English language and how to handle money. He also seems to have accepted the precepts of obedience to and respect for authority and the organization of the government's power structure within the school.

Yet Pabanale reveals nothing about his expectations, such as the roles or occupations he hoped to achieve as an educated Arizona Tewa or, more to the point, how his school experiences directed his sense of self-fulfillment. Did he see himself as a marginal man, striving to find a place in the interface between white and native societies? His experiences do not reflect any bitterness; his self-definition as a Tewa and a Hopi remained intact, perhaps with an implied understanding that his future success would depend on his ability to work with the sources of power on the reservation.

Hopi Allotment

133

Under the Indian Allotment Act of 1887, allotment was attempted on the Hopi reservation from 1892 to 1894 and again from 1907 to 1910. Surveying began in 1891, causing great concern among the Hopis, as noted by the anthropologist Jesse Walter Fewkes, who was present at

First Mesa at the time: "The Chiefs were very much disturbed and resented the white people looking over the land through tubes and—in their eyes a more grievous sin—mysteriously putting wooden sticks in the ground. They were desiring to know the meaning of this; it was explained to them that the white man was preparing to grant each family a plot of land which would be registered in Washington and be protected as the property of their children forever" (1923:273–74).

One of the government's objectives was to force the Hopi to abandon their mesa-top homes and accept new houses below the mesas. This measure, it was believed, would break up the solidarity of the traditional Hopi villages and speed the process of assimilation. Most Hopis vigorously opposed allotment, and many went out at night to pull up the surveyor's stakes and destroy survey monuments, especially at Third Mesa (Donaldson 1893:37).

Recommendations for the termination of the allotment program were made in 1910, and it was finally abandoned in 1911. Laura Thompson and Alice Joseph observe: "It is noteworthy that the unbreakable resistance of the Third Mesa group to allotment finally in 1911 persuaded the authorities to desist. In the years 1907–1911, it was the announced purpose of the Government to allot all the reservations in the Southwest. The Hopi's resistance appears to have had the historic effect of saving the other Pueblos and the Navaho, the Mescalero, White River and San Carlos Apache, and the Papago from allotment and its disastrous consequences" (1944:136 n. 33).

Dewey Healing commented:

We got into controversy ourselves over Tom Polacca. This was over land. At one time the government was trying to assign us a plot of land, each to ourselves. At that time, being a policeman, Polacca had to relay messages. He had to go around to the people telling them what the government was planning. He went around telling the people to get themselves grouped according to clans, so that each one would have a plot of land surveyed out and given to them. They got mad over this because Tom Polacca was telling this among the people and this other group was against it. They didn't want to have nothing to do with whatever Polacca told them. He was a very courageous man. He went around, and when this [special allotment agent Matthew] Murphy started surveying around here, they found out that he couldn't cover the area that he was supposed to cover, way up north. In order to cover the area, he got some Hopis from Walpi, who in a way were supposed to be related to the Corn clan.

He got those people and asked for some other people to voluntarily help if they wished to get that plot up north surveyed. A lot of them responded to his wishes, so they tried to get that area covered, to give those people a plot of land. This brought about turmoil, with people going against each other. But then, somehow, at one time, they were telling each other what was going on. Some of these Tewas took sides with this group over here—those that were opposing Tom Polacca. They got together and planned to kill him, over at Wepo Spring. That day, they invited Tom to be there. Tom wasn't afraid, so he goes there, without any other policemen. So when they meet over there, Tom's boys, who were all grown, got their bows and arrows and they were going to fight it out if these other men were going to do something to their father.

They had a talk there, a lot of them who were against him. Even those that were not related to our clan.

So some of those men started to go for him, trying to get a hold of him on horseback. He got mad and started running in the midst of them and got a hold of one of the men, tied his hair on his saddle horn and dragged for a long time and dropped him off.

The others got scared; they all ran away; that's what happened. But this group here [Corn clan], they don't like to talk about it. When that controversy was over, those people didn't feel too good about Polacca, so that's why they isolated us over that way. But this group [Corn clan] went along with the Hopis because the Hopis were always going against us on any issue, whatever our uncle [Polacca] is doing (Black 1984).

Marriage

Pabanale's marriage by the Mennonite missionary J. B. Epp was a radical departure from traditional Hopi and Tewa customs. He was proud to hold the first marriage license issued by Superintendent Horton Miller of the Hopi Agency at Keams Canyon.

Indian agents, working with the reservation missionaries, made every effort to eliminate traditional marriage practices among the Hopis and Tewas in order to accelerate the process of assimilation.[7] Hopi marriage customs were particularly onerous in their eyes because they

135

perpetuated tribalism and resistance to change. The Hopi marriage ceremony established close ties between households and among clans, since clans served to regulate marriage by excluding marital ties with members of one's clan. Marriage within a group of linked clans, or phratry, was also prohibited. Thus, through the practice of clan and phratry exogamy, the Hopis were able to ensure the perpetuation of social and economic ties beyond the confines of the clan. The marriage ceremony brought the families of the bride and groom together through formal reciprocal exchanges of food and services; it further strengthened the bonds among a wide range of extended kin. The ceremony also made possible an eventual safe journey to the afterworld, secured by the weaving of the bride's wedding robe and the making of the groom's wedding plaque (Eggan 1950:53). Before the marriage of two people could be considered, the boy had to be initiated into the Winter Solstice Society, signifying the achievement of manhood, and the girl had to go through the puberty ceremony.

When both sets of parents gave their approval, the respective families became involved in a protracted series of reciprocal ceremonial exchanges—primarily of food—during the inception and culmination of the marriage ceremony. The bride was responsible for the grinding of large quantities of corn and the presentation of piki bread to her future in-laws. For several weeks, her relatives helped her grind corn. The groom's relatives were responsible for making the bride's wedding garments—weaving a belt, robe, and dress and making moccasins. When these tasks were completed, the bride ground corn in her in-laws' house for three days, after which her hair was washed in yucca suds. She dressed in her wedding outfit, and she and her husband were taken by his mother to the bride's mother's house, which would be their new residence. Early the next morning the boy's head was washed by the girl's clanswomen. At a later time a large quantity of food was given to the groom's family for the loss of a productive family worker (Dozier 1966:63).

Residence patterns were matrilocal, but a couple could build a new home in another part of the village or below the mesa at Polacca. Dozier notes that the term *matrilocal residence* is justified because the new residence is built primarily with the help of the girl's extended family and on her clan land (1954:330).

Pabanale was separated from the old village life by the time he left First Mesa to work in Winslow. The coercive indoctrination of the

136

Phoenix Indian School no doubt contributed to his estrangement from tradition. The prospects of independence from village obligations and the attraction of personal achievement also drew him toward the Euro-American world. Unfortunately, we have no information regarding why his wife's family did not pursue a traditional marriage ceremony.

Trading

The Hopis and Arizona Tewas were recognized for their trading abilities and were often called "born traders." White traders on the reservation regarded the Hopi traders with awe and some trepidation: "They say that they would rather deal with six Navajos than one Hopi, because the Navajo does not haggle, while the Hopi, with a thrift that is bringing him to the front, is determined to get the benefit of a bargain" (Hough 1915:38). A white trader described the differences between the Hopis and the Navajos: "A Navajo . . . starts off for the trading post with some money. He intends to buy flour and other supplies. On the way he meets a Hopi and they have a visit. When the visit is over, the Navajo has a bracelet and the Hopi has the money" (O'Kane 1950:151).[1]

Irving Pabanale spoke with animation about his early life as a trader. His energy and perseverance took him to many places to trade and sell. He was interested in the outside world and sought to explore the new and the unknown; he especially enjoyed going among white people as a Hopi and a Tewa. The friendly working relations he established with many Navajos contributed to his trading success.

Dewey Healing commented:

When Irving came back from school, he was trying to work himself up to something to live on—to earn a living, but he didn't quite succeed. He tried here and there. I remember the time he went to California and went around with some group that went to an exposition [San Diego Exposition of 1915]. Then after coming back from there he had a job at Grand Canyon, but not for very long. Then he went to Santa Clara, where he spent quite a few months. He did a lot of trading. He traded anything he could get a hold of. In those times, those men who traveled around, had in their mind that they wanted to get stock to start a herd, maybe cattle or sheep, horses. That's why they got *mantas* [women's woven dresses], silver, beads—whatever of value. When they got to those other villages they traded that for animals. From here [Tewa Village] they would go to a distant village to buy even one sheep or one cow, or one horse. It would take them time to drive them back over this way. That's what they did. No matter how long it took them to drive those animals, they'll do it. And they're always trading, especially these deer hides and buckskins. Everyone traded; Hopis, Tewas. There's a lot of them that did that, but they never talk about themselves.

I went with him several times to Zuni when I was a boy. He used to have a little Ford; he always had something to trade—*mantas*, women's belts, or anything he could get a hold of (Black 1984).

Emory Sekaquaptewa observed:

The Tewa were always active traders. They were close to the Rio Grande Pueblos from which they were able to obtain things they needed—buckskins, seashells, horses, turquoise beads. Awatovi excavations indicate prehistoric trade with the Rio Grande Pueblos and others. In the Mogollon ruins of southern Arizona, many Hopi pots are found. Trading is rooted in the prehistoric tribes. It built up a sense of enterprise and trade in Hopi men. Hopis always traveled and traded, even in Spanish times, carrying news and information.

These traders were diplomats . . . they carried rumors which would get them by. Hopis traveled to Zuni, Acoma, Laguna and traded their woolen leggings. Hopis wove these leggings; women wore them until recent times—for everyday use, not solely for ceremonial purposes. Hopis had a predilection for travel and trade. [The Hopi term that best describes this is] *tsitsipölhoya*—"one who hitches rides with his wares and is ready to go off on his selling trip." Travel was not only an economic event; it was an opportunity to meet people, meet women, and share new ceremonial songs with his eager hosts in the New Mexico Pueblos.

Hopis in the past were good traders. Today the Santo Domingos have the distinction. Surplus commodities were traded in the villages—beans for corn. Pabanale was not unusual (Black 1984).

Rabbit Hunting

The Hopi hunted extensively in earlier times, before the depletion of grasses and erosion cycles reduced the range of the animals. Rabbit, antelope, deer, fox, coyote, and other animals were hunted. As Misha Titiev noted in 1944, "It appears likely that at one stage of their cultural development, the Hopi were far more dependent on game as a food supply than they are at present" (1944:188). After the Second World War there was a considerable decrease in hunting, although the pursuit of rabbits and other small game still enjoyed wide popularity. Rabbit hunting, especially, found great favor among men and boys as it combined elements of skill, sportsmanship, communal effort, and the ritual of the chase.

A good deal of hunting activity was accompanied by ceremonial rites, both before and after the hunt. They usually involved the preparation of offerings in the form of prayer sticks (*pahos*) or prayer feathers (*nakwákwusi*) to the various spiritual and life forces, intended to help bring about the desired results. For rabbit hunting, prayer sticks or prayer feathers were offered to Masawu, the Earth Father deity, as well as to the female deity Tuwapongtumasi, the Mother of All Animals. The prayers asked forgiveness of the "rabbit people" for having to "take" them, explaining the hunters' need for food, thanking the deities for their sacrifice, and asking for their continued assistance.

Rabbit hunting usually took place in early summer and autumn, although special hunts were held in conjunction with the Wuwtsim Ceremony in November and to initiate young boys into hunting (Beaglehole 1936:14). Any man could organize and lead a hunt, assuming the responsibility for making the prayer sticks and determining the route. On First Mesa the organizer of the hunt took the prayer sticks to the Rabbit clan chief and told him of his plan for the hunt.[1] The chief proceeded to announce the event that evening from the rooftop of his house. The announcement served to broadcast the news about the hunt to the village and to induce men and boys to participate on the following day (Voegelin and Euler 1957).

At dusk the call of the crier could be heard throughout the village. People would stand outside their doors, listening attentively to the rhythmic incantations of the announcement and the message it contained. The announcement format is of great antiquity and was functionally adaptive to a small village. The structure of secular announcements was intended for the ears of the people. The words of the village crier, or announcement maker, drifted across the serenity of dusk. The message, relayed in chanted paragraphs, audibly rising and falling in even pulses, brought village activity to a momentary halt.

Rooftop announcements were common to all villages, with only minor variations in content and internal organization. The format of the announcement usually consisted of three independent units: the introductory call to attention ("listen to me!"); the substantive portion, containing the essential information; and the closing segment, signifying the end of the announcement. The final "paragraph" usually consisted of a brief and stylized statement such as "It is already like that" (there is no more). In the case of rabbit hunt announcements, the crier (Tsa'akmongwi, the crier chief) would often conclude with the phrase "Go to sleep and have dreams of fulfillment," an allusion to the pleasurable anticipation of a good hunt (Black 1965:107).

Two variants of the rabbit chant from First Mesa are presented in Table 1. I obtained the first one in 1957 from Sylvan Nash, son-in-law of Irving Pabanale, in the village of Sitsomovi. The second was made by Jesse W. Fewkes from Kutka, chief of Walpi and Sitsomovi, in 1925 in Walpi and was issued in 1926 as a ten-inch commercial recording on the Gennet label. Comparing these texts, we can note the conservative nature of announcement structure as well as stylistic differences and variations in content and paragraph organization.

Such announcements were made four times, to each of the cardinal directions, following the prescribed anti-sunwise ritual pattern: east, north, west, and south. The meeting place for the hunt and its itinerary were given in some detail. Allusions to pleasurable associations with the game animals were frequently found in context with the route of travel. Some of these sentiments were "going happily among them," "being joyful over good luck among them," and "so many meat-tasting animals" (Black 1965:92). On the morning of the hunt a ceremonial fire was built at the gathering place and prayer sticks and other offerings were made. The specialized throwing stick (*putskoho*), used in small

Table 1. Two First Mesa Rabbit Chants.

I. Sitsom'ovi 1957 (Nash)	II. Walpi 1925 (Kutka)
INTRODUCTION	
(1) Ya-ha ha, boys and men listen, all of you.	(1) Ya-ha ha, boys and men listen.
BODY OF ANNOUNCEMENT	
(3) Tomorrow, we will walk somewhere for those jackrabbits and cottontails.	(3) Tomorrow, we will walk about somewhere, after those jackrabbits and cottontails.
(4) When those women make fires after getting up early, we will eat, early, and go out along the north side.	(4) Tomorrow, when it gets light, these women will make fires, early, and after they cook, we will eat, early, and then go out to that location, along to the north.
(5) It is said that we will gather there at Teves Place to the north. From there, moving out to the north, going happily among them [rabbits], arriving at Blue Reed Bush. From there, going to the west, arriving at Skeleton Hill, we will go back from there, going to the south, again going happily among them. After arriving at Paqoy Hill, we will go back to the east, again going happily among them. There, at our destination, at the White Clay Place, we plan to stop.	(5) From there we will come up from below where we will gather at that location Totokchomiq.

game hunting, was passed through the fire to harden it and ensure its accuracy.

Stephen describes this ritual, which he observed on First Mesa in 1893:

On the night previous to the hunt or early the same morning, [the hunt leader] prepares four prayer feathers and on the hunt day when all the hunters have assembled he scratches in any sand mound a shallow cavity. . . . Within this cavity . . . he sprinkles a circular line of

Table 1 continued.

I. Sitsom'ovi 1957 (Nash)	II. Walpi 1925 (Kutka)
(6) From there, heavily loaded with game on our backs, we will come back up to the village on the mesa.	(6) After gathering there, somewhere, and after arriving from all directions, we will find them [the rabbits] there in their dens among the cedar trees. We will then be joyful over our good luck.
(7) Perhaps when the girls make food, they will go with the men.	(7) After arriving from there, we will move out to the north, arriving at Pokvastu-oahaq. From there we will again move to the west; after arriving at Skeleton Hill, we will go back from there, encircling them [the rabbits] as we move out to the east. Over at the White Clay Place we plan to stop and pursue them.
	(8) At that place, there, they will become too heavy to carry. Going from there, we will go along happily with heavy loads, climbing back up to our homes.

prayer meal. . . . Then with a slight motion toward the cardinal points he casts four lines toward the centre of the cavity. On these lines at their intersection he lays four pellets of hare dung, and on each of these lines, a prayer feather.

He had gathered a handful of dry grass and a few dry twigs and these he cast in the cavity and . . . set fire to them. He sat squatted beside the fire and passed his boomerang and oak club throwing stick lightly through the blaze, and all the others who take part in the hunt do the same, each one first plucking a small tuft of grass, herbage or twig, and casting it on the small fire just before he passes his weapons through the blaze. The ceremony is called . . . hunt fire. (1936:1024)   143

Rabbit hunts were also the occasion for conviviality and courtship, especially when unmarried girls accompanied the hunters: "The girls used to accompany the youths and some girls would carry a rabbit club and a few could throw it and strike. The line was deployed so that youths and maidens alternated,[2] and when the youth knocked over a hare or rabbit, the maiden accompanying him would race to him and strive to get to the game first; if she did it was hers" (Stephen 1936:1023).

On returning to the village, the hunter presented the game to his mother, who sprinkled it with cornmeal and offered a prayer of thanks to the rabbits (Stephen 1936).

The Indian Police

The Tewas played a significant role in implementing the government's program of change on the Hopi reservation. Along with the Navajos, they became members of the fledgling police force in the 1890s. By act of Congress in 1878, provisions were made for organizing Indian police forces on most reservations, under the supervision of the various agents (U.S. Department of the Interior 1878). The duties of the police were to preserve law and order, prohibit illegal traffic in liquor and arrest offenders, protect government property, restore lost or stolen property to its rightful owner, drive out trespassers, enforce school attendance and return truant pupils to school, and make arrests for disorderly conduct and other offenses (Regulations of the Indian Department, Sections 577, 578; Act of Mar. 3, 1885).

Indian policemen were carefully selected from among those who were considered progressive and supportive of American policies. Indians who had taken their land in allotment were shown preference in hiring for they were deemed to be the most energetic, courageous, dependable, and loyal. In their annual reports to Washington, Indian agents lauded the service of the Indian police: "They are not only of practical assistance in making arrests, . . . but they also act as a deterrent upon the lawless elements of a tribe" (U.S. Department of the Interior 1890).

One of the staunchest advocates of a strong "law and order" police force was Leo Crane, who served as superintendent of the Hopi agency at Keams Canyon from 1911 to 1919. He had an intense dislike of the Hopis (as well as the Navajos)—their culture, their religion, and especially their "pagan" dances. He could not accept or understand their "unwillingness to advance" and their continued "immoral" practices of marriage and divorce. He railed against the "hostiles" (conservatives) who refused to accept government regulations, which he felt were made for their betterment, such as the dipping of sheep and the institution of sanitation measures to combat disease. He was also a strong advocate of compulsory education for children and summarily jailed many dissenters.

Although he disliked the nomadic Navajos, Crane felt that the Hopis held an unfair advantage over them, a prejudice he voiced repeatedly in his annual reports: "As the reservation is closed as a Hopi or Moqui reserve, the impression may be conceived that the Navajoes residing thereon have had the same advantages. This is not so. Had the Navajo received the same attention, their progress would undoubtedly have been much greater. It is the judgment of those who have lived in close touch with both tribes that the Navajo is in every respect superior" (Crane 1915).

His disdain for the Hopis in general extended to their performance as policemen: "The Hopi do not make good policemen. . . . Their towns are ruled largely by pueblo opinion. If a resident acquires the reputation of being unreasonable and unfeeling, as a policeman often must, his standing in the outraged community may affect all other phases of his life. Therefore the Hopi is not likely to become a very zealous officer when operating alone. And too, the Hopi fear the Navajo, as it is said the Navajo fear the Ute, and are useless when removed from the neighborhood of their homes" (Crane 1925:136). Crane was uncomplimentary of the Navajo police as well: "The Navajo population is nomadic and secretive. It is reached only through five ignorant and superstitious Indians employed as policemen, who are no better or brighter or more progressive than the Indians they carry orders to, and under such circumstances the Navajo population is very hard to reach" (1916:12). Toward the end of his 1916 report Crane dismisses Indian police in general: "The Indian police have no conception of their authority, and little tendency to make use of their authority against their friends, or influential opponents, when they are thoroughly informed. All this means that it is easy to go on the range, distant from the personal influence of the Superintendent and Agency, and do anything that it pleases the Indians to accept; but that it is infinitely difficult to get anything done that the Indians of either tribe do not especially wish done" (1916:28).

Crane was not entirely disdainful of the Indian population. One small segment of the Indian community did meet with his approval: he liked the Tewas and admired his Tewa police, particularly Nelson Oyaping, Pabanale's older brother. The reputation of the Tewas as effective police officers started with Tom Polacca, who became the first policeman on the reservation around 1890. Polacca was a staunch advocate of adopting the white man's ways and was noted for his zeal in enforcing the

146

compulsory school-attendance ruling of the Indian Service. Polacca spoke Hopi, Tewa, Navajo, Spanish, and English. By 1903 he and Charlie Avayung were the two Tewa law officers who enforced school attendance and sought out truant children.

Some years later Polacca recommended Nelson Oyaping for the police force, a man Crane found to be dependable, courageous, and even belligerent. Crane noted in his memoirs of his service as Indian agent that Tewa policemen "will fight when it is necessary, and, strange thing among desert Indians, with their fists, taking a delight in blacking the opponent's eye" (1925:137). Dewey Healing commented: "Brother Nelson wasn't afraid to go after anyone—he went after those Navajos. All the people here [in Tewa Village] wanted a policeman and they made him one" (Black 1984).[1]

It was through Nelson's efforts that Irving Pabanale was appointed to the police force in 1916. Pabanale revered his older brother and sought to emulate his accomplishments and status. According to Tewa custom, a younger brother is expected to show deference to an older brother, who can command obedience and acquiescence (Dozier 1954:319–20). In the case of Nelson and Irving, Nelson was recognized as his younger brother's guardian and protector and was concerned with his welfare. As a policeman, Nelson was Irving's mentor, and Irving sought to prove himself a capable student.

The performance record of the Tewa police is indicative of the relative ease with which they adapted to American cultural patterns. They readily accepted schooling for their children and the material and ideological aspects of the new life. A large number of Tewas built new homes below the mesa, which not only facilitated their farming and sheep-raising efforts but also enabled them to integrate more effectively in the reservation's governmental and administrative functions. They sought jobs with the agency at Keams Canyon, and because of their cooperative attitude toward the government they acted as a liaison between the Hopis and the agency (Dozier 1951:56-66). By doing so, the Tewas raised their own self-esteem, taking special pleasure in stressing their unique roles as "protectors" of the unappreciative Hopis (Dozier 1954:291; Kroskrity 1993:177–79).

Irving and Nelson, along with another Tewa, Conner Kylily, worked together as policemen and were fluent in Navajo. Assessments of Pabanale's performance as a policeman were positive, as noted in the following comment by Dewey Healing: "He did pretty good work for the government. They respect him because he knew what to do. When they

147

asked him to do things, he went right ahead and did it" (Black 1984).

In those early years the Hopis did not perceive themselves as enforcers of government laws and regulation and left it for the Arizona Tewas to assume such disagreeable tasks as being policemen. The Tewas accepted the charge with a moral and almost sacred dedication. Elsie Clews Parsons heard a Tewa man invoke the commitment his people made to the Hopis when they first arrived at First Mesa: "If danger comes, we Tewa people leave to go first. We are Watchers for the Snake clan, and if ever the Snake clan people go wrong, we make them behave" (Parsons 1925:116).

By willingly cooperating with the government and acquiring new status as intermediaries, interpreters, and policemen, the Tewas strengthened their historic role as protectors of the Hopis. Dewey Healing observed:

When the early police force was established, the Tewa joined up. This was what was in their mind: "This is my duty; this is what I'm here for." Those things the Hopi didn't want to do, they put the Tewa in there.

When the government couldn't get something done with the Hopi, they would come to the Tewa and the Tewa accepted it and it went over. That's the way it's been working. Then the Hopi went along with what was happening. Now the Hopis want the credit. Tom Polacca was the first to do that. Then the police force came on and there were a lot of them that went on that police force, Nelson, Irving, Travers Mali.

Those police inform the people what the agency wanted them to know—how to follow them. Agency couldn't trust Hopi to follow the regulations, so they went to the Tewa—to the police, for implementation.

Sanitation, personal cleanliness, plague treatment, setting up privies. There was no money, but they [the Tewas] did the best they could do.

Those Tewa took all of the recommendations of the government and convinced the Hopi that this was good for the people. If the Hopi wouldn't accept something, the Tewa would tell them, "Why don't you take it; it's the best thing you'll ever have. If you don't take it, someone else is going to get it."

The Tewas went to talk to all the other villages. The Hopis wouldn't tell each other, but the Tewa had nothing to bind them.

They would go out and tell them, "This is what we going to do; this is good for you."

The Hopis didn't want to take action because they didn't want to go against their people; they wanted to remain in the middle (Black 1984).

Albert Yava also invoked the traditional role of the Tewas:

There may be some Hopis who think we Tewas are too aggressive, that we try too hard to be out in front. I don't think that is really the case, though it may be true that we are a little more outgoing by nature and temperament than Hopis are. Hopis tend to draw back. Traditionally they have taken their blows and waited for prophecies to be fulfilled. That is one reason they had such a hard time in their dealings with the white man. Things that had to be done to cope with the sudden changes around us could not wait for the fulfillment of prophecies.

On the Tewa side, our old-timers had a sense of commitment to the compact that was made when we came here to defend Walpi from the Utes, Paiutes and Apaches. The Tewas pledged themselves to be protectors and watchdogs against any kind of threats to the Hopis. They believed they were expected to stand up front in critical times, and they have done this. You can call this "pushing" or "leading" if you want to. I know that some Hopis resent it. But the Tewas, particularly the older generation, see it as an obligation undertaken when our people came here from Tsewageh (1978:131).

An important function of the police was to enforce emergency procedures during epidemics. The Hopi reservation has periodically been plagued by influenza, measles, and smallpox. The government attempted to contain these outbreaks with vaccination programs and the wholesale immersion of villagers in vats of sheep dip. Most villages accepted "dipping," but Hotvela, hostile to any form of government interference, staunchly resisted. Crane noted the influenza epidemic of 1918, which continued into early 1919, citing the deaths of 135 Hopis during the months of October–December 1918. (At the time, the total Hopi population was estimated at 2,158.) He also reported the occurrence of a smallpox "visitation" during January, February, and March 1918 (Crane 1918:20). Although he makes no mention of the forced dipping incident at Hotvela in 1918, which Pabanale so vividly describes, it is possible Pabanale confused the dates.

Two years after Crane's departure from the Hopi agency, his successor, Robert E. L. Daniel, reported in some detail in his annual report for 1921 the campaign to prevent the spread of typhus fever by delousing the people of Hotvela. Pabanale most likely took part in this confrontation, since he was on the police force until 1927. The incidents bear resemblance to those described in Crane's Narrative Report for 1918:

> When every other Indian on the reservation, both Navajo and Hopi, gladly dropped into co-operation with us in the campaign against lice, to prevent spread of typhus fever, the Hotvelas sent me word they would not delouse, and if I tried to force them, they would kill the Principals of Hotvela-Bacabi and Orayvi Day Schools and the Hotvela policeman; they were willing to sacrifice two of their number to accomplish this.
>
> On June 10, 1921, we went to Hotvela village with eight employees and seven policemen, all well armed with revolvers, and requested the Indians to meet me in the Plaza for conference. They refused to come out, as I expected from previous experience, but following my invariable rule to first explain my object before taking drastic action, I ordered our people to go and each bring a man into the plaza. After assembling about twenty-five by force, I explained clearly, the purpose and methods of delousing and told them I preferred that they come voluntarily and take the treatment, but if they did not, they would be taken by force. I also told them I had heard their threat against certain employees and I warned them if they attempted violence, I'd wipe up the face of the earth with them.
>
> The next morning by seven o'clock, about seven or eight well meaning men and women presented themselves and were bathed and their clothing deloused. At eight o'clock, not another Indian had appeared. I then issued hickory buggy spokes to my delousing party and police. Directing them not to use their revolvers, except as a last resort in self defense, we then went to the village, where all able-bodied men were stationed in and on top of certain houses (two or three) the women and children on other house tops. I again called upon them to come down peaceably, and gave them three minutes to comply. (May as well have given them a month.) Upon their failing to do so, I directed my force to bring them down. After about forty men had been forced to the street, they refused to budge, and suddenly turned in a threatening manner and show of resistance, when a policeman undertook to hand cuff a man. At this point the spokes

came into play, and several heads were cracked. The ring leader was knocked down and received a scalp wound which bled freely; this lasted perhaps a minute or two, when I cautioned all my men to ease up on the use of the spokes. I then personally examined the man, lying on the ground, and found he was not seriously hurt, but "playing possum" to excite others. I called the blacksmith to my side and directed him to get my car and bring the doctor to dress the fellow's head. The man was removed to a house a few feet away. We then commenced the task of dragging and shoving till we finally got them strung out toward the School, where the bathing equipment was, and where, in a short time they were deloused and their clothing boiled. We returned to the village for the next lot. At this time, the doctor arrived from Orayvi and was refused permission to see the man who was knocked down, until the house was cleared. The doctor pronounced the hurt superficial and of no consequence. I believe he applied some simple remedy and left.

The second lot was not quite so hard to handle, and by noon, practically all able bodied men were deloused. In the afternoon, the balance of the women were brought up on foot. Old men and women and cripples were brought by team, and handled with utmost care.

Only men were handled in one building; the women in another building two hundred yards away, by female employees and assistants, until they developed such offensive opposition that I detailed a squad of men to assist; then they were put into the bathing vats, without removing their clothing. I desire to state here that those women wear only a one piece garment, and putting them into the solution without disrobing was as effective as stripping them and boiling their clothing. Black leaf 40 (sheep dip) was used and it was as effective, and in many respects better than kerosene. It does not blister and is easier and quicker to handle.

There was no attempt by any employee to make an indecent exposure of any woman or child, and the only objectionable feature of the work was the obscene and revolting vituperation the Indian women hurled at the employees.

The language of the English speaking Indian men as applied to every one, Indians and Whites, assisting in the work, was too filthy to be recorded verbatim here.

A check of the Census, when the day's work was done, showed fifteen had escaped. The following Monday these were routed out of the rocks and other hiding places, by the police, brought in and deloused.

151

Editor's Notes

We prepared their baths at the proper temperature, bathed them, and boiled and dried their clothes for them while they were being bathed. Yet they had to be driven or dragged to the tub, and forced into it like some wild beast, unblessed with human intelligence. Pure unadulterated fanatical perversity is the only explanation, and I am assured by those who know the Hotvela Hopi best that if it had been necessary to repeat the work next day, that whole deplorable incident would have had to be reenacted, with perhaps, more serious resistance.

Not one of those lousy Indians, whom we cleaned up, had enjoyed his first night's peaceful sleep since he or she became infected, and that was so long ago that they had learned to believe lice a necessary part of their existence.

This is, briefly, a history of our last attempt at enforcing law and order at Hotvela.

These four hundred Hopis are fanatical and willful degenerates, because most of them have had every opportunity, for years, to learn and know better; and I state now and here as my candid opinion that they do know better.

They were driven out of Orayvi, by their own people, for this same willfulness, and, I am told, are seeking other more inaccessible dwelling sites, in an attempt to defeat Governmental supervision. Each time they offer resistance, it is stronger and more offensive, and I believe sooner or later it will result in bloodshed. The employees of this Reservation are red blooded men and women, and will go where I lead the way, or send them, but I shall not in future lead them into or expose them to such serious possibilities. I say this without having heard one word of resentment or complaint from a single one of those loyal men and women, who are struggling with a cross because no one seems to possess the backbone to point the accusing finger at those responsible for this condition.

Those people were not employed to do police duty, and in the name of red blooded Americans, I protest that they must not be forced to do it in order to hold their position, in the absence of adequate police force to maintain a respectable amount of law and order (Daniel 1921:11–16).

The Tewa police and the First Mesa villagers assisted the agency in these procedures, preparing galvanized watering troughs, normally used for animals, for human dipping. The resistance of Hotvela was looked on by some Tewas with indignation, as Dewey Healing noted: "Hotvelas always object to whatever the government is doing, see. Even though it's going to benefit them, they're still opposed and they're still that way. But one thing you have to learn. Even though they object to a lot of things, when there is a good thing, they're the first ones to go for it. They're just like anybody; that's the way they are. Right now [1984], they're like that—they object to everything" (Black 1984).

The people of Hotvela saw those events in a different light, as expressed by a Hopi woman in 1955:

We have been living in this village for a long time now and at that time most of us live like the Hopi have been living in those days, and we all know that many things have taken place. At one time the soldiers came and do many things to us and one time we seem to have another trouble coming up so that most of the women folks were gathered on the Fire clan house and on top of the house there were many men folks gathered. Soldiers came to the house where men folks were gathered and we saw they all had a stick in their hand and they went up on top of the house and forced people down. (A Hopi man interrupts and says the sticks were wagon spokes.) They pushed many of the men down and began to strike them. There were three men knocked unconscious. I saw one lady standing on top of the Kiva and said to us, "I knew this was going to take place. You people should have cooperated. This will happen to you." Her name was Kootsnimka who lives in Bacabi. Then we saw many people come to us. One of the men is Mawa, along with other white people. They came up to us with clubs and drove these men away from that house and they were taking them to a place where they said they were going to give us a bath. Later on they came back after the women folks and drove us over to them. Many of us had no shoes and the sand was hot. We were driven over to a place where this was to take place.

They drove us to a place where there is a clinic and there they forced us into a door and inside were many men who would grab us and throw us in a tub full of water. There were many Hopi people and some from Walpi. I do not know who they were but they were there and we women folks had these Hopi belts and they would grab our belts and pull our clothes off and throw us in the tub. When one falls in it and swallows it, it burns your throat. It must be the same thing that they dip the sheep in. And when we were thrown in these vats the men folks would reach to a woman and grab every place and rub us

153

all over. Men they were, yet they acted in this manner. We suffered and when they were through with it they took our shawls and dipped them in this vat again and then threw it at us and we carried them off to our homes and had to dry ourselves in the sand. When you came out of this house they would hold you and pour coal oil all over your head in a rough manner so this oil was all over a person. We tried every way to get rid of this greasy stuff by rubbing it in the sand. This is how they treated us in that place, and when we came home to our houses again two men came through the houses and went through every house spraying this smelly stuff on our bed rolls and on our corn and in every room. It made us sick for many days after that. We suffered that (Hopi Hearings 1955:1:72–73).

Medicine Men

Irving Pabanale was one of a number of Arizona Tewas who became medicine men, or curers. Some of them went to the Tewa Pueblos on the Rio Grande to acquire training and to be initiated into the curing societies. Pabanale's brother, Nelson, was persuaded to travel to Santa Clara Pueblo in the early 1920s for this purpose and spent two years training for initiation into one of the curing societies. It is not clear whether Pabanale was invited to join him, but he never went to Santa Clara for this training. Instead, he relied on Nelson to teach him the various techniques of curing, and he joined other uninitiated men in the practice of native medicine.

The Tewa-speaking Pueblos of the Rio Grande are noted for their curing societies and the skills of their medicine men. Among both the western and eastern Pueblos, it is believed that failure to abide by culturally prescribed rules of conduct and the neglect of ceremonial obligations and responsibilities were the causes of supernatural sanctions resulting in illness. At Santa Clara Pueblo individual curers—both men and women—who were not members of the curing societies could provide treatment for such illnesses (Hill 1982:309). Individual members of the two curing societies at Santa Clara "were called upon to treat a patient. Sometimes all the members of one society are involved in treating a patient or performing a ceremony for the well-being of a family. . . . At certain specific times the two societies cooperate in an elaborate ceremony to rid the village of 'witches'" (Dozier 1954:267 n. 12).

The Arizona Tewas established their own curing society on First Mesa based on their Rio Grande traditions. The Shumakolil Society, controlled by the Cloud clan, was formerly owned by the now extinct Sun clan.[1] Its specific responsibility was to cure sore eyes. Requests for a curing ceremony could be made by any Arizona Tewa or even a Hopi from First Mesa.

The Hopis also have institutional mechanisms for treating a wide variety of illnesses, but they have no specific curing societies. Curing functions are associated with the non-kinship secret societies or fraternities, many of which have a reputation for treating specific ailments. For example, Snake Society members are skilled in curing snakebite or swelling in the stomach. On recovery, men are expected to join the society. The Masawu Society in Musangnuvi and Walpi, which became extinct around the turn of the century, cured head swellings and headaches. Cured patients likewise joined the society after recovering (Parsons 1939:866). In Walpi the Wuwtsim Society treated a form of paralysis.[2] People who had rheumatism sought treatment from the Powamu Society, and lightning shock was treated by the Flute and Marau Societies. It was also reported that the Mamzraú Society at Walpi cured syphilis and a "twisting or distorting" ailment (Fewkes and Stephen 1892:226 n. 3, 242 n. 10).

Parsons (1933:9–16) notes that on First and Second Mesas there once existed a society called Povoswimkya devoted exclusively to curing. The Hopi curer—*tuúhikya*, or one who revitalizes—used a variety of techniques: herbs, massage, the laying on of hands, sucking out foreign objects, and a good deal of psychology. Juniper tea was used as a laxative; mixed with sand sagebrush, it cured indigestion. Snakeweed tea was used to treat stomachache (O'Kane 1953), and geranium roots were used for cataracts, stomach ulcers, and general sores.

Hopi curing practices distinguished between naturally and supernaturally caused illnesses. Naturally caused diseases were treated by herbalists, bone setters, massage specialists, and others skilled in treating various internal disorders. Such ailments resulted from bad thoughts and anxieties. Supernaturally caused diseases usually involved the violation of a taboo, lack of attention to ritual instruction, or ignoring food or sexual restrictions related to ceremonial activity. Such maladies were treated with prayer and ritual by the priests of the society concerned (Titiev 1944:106). Cases of witchcraft were treated by a shaman who went into trance to determine the causes and nature of foreign objects that had intruded into the victim. The objects would be removed by sucking (Levy 1982:1).

Pabanale states in his narrative that when his brother Nelson returned to Tewa Village after an absence of two years, "no one but us Tewa knew that he had been initiated as a medicine man." This secrecy perhaps reflects the social distance that existed between Tewa Village and the Hopis.

Troubles with the Navajos and the Establishment of the 1882 Area

The troubles with the Navajos experienced by Pabanale and the Hopi people reflect centuries of intergroup conflicts between two culturally distinct societies. The Hopis lived in a group of independent sedentary farming villages with clan-allotted lands and outlying hunting and gathering regions. Outlying non-clan lands were farmed, and sheep, cattle, and horses were grazed long before the Navajos arrived. The Navajos were a recently arrived, rapidly expanding society of former hunters and raiders who became semisedentary as they adopted goat and sheep herding from the Spaniards and maize agriculture from the Pueblos. The Navajos were divided politically into independent bands, each of which sought to replace its depleted grazing lands by encroaching on Hopi territory. First Mesa people who attempted to build new homes below the mesa were harassed and thwarted by Navajos who moved ever closer, and relations between the two groups continued to deteriorate.

Since the seventeenth century the Navajos had raided Pueblo villages, stealing food and taking women and children captive. In the 1860s, as part of the government's program to contain Navajo marauding, Kit Carson was authorized to round up the Navajos and remove them to Fort Sumner (Bosque Redondo) on the Pecos River in east-central New Mexico. Many bands of Navajos, however, eluded capture and continued their depredations against the Hopis. In 1865 Agent John Ward reported: "A short time previous to my visit . . . [the Hopis] had been attacked and robbed by the hostile Navajos. Their location and circumstances make them an easy prey for their more formidable and warlike foes . . . by which they are surrounded" (Ward to M. Stecke, Apr. 1865, New Mexico, 5-658/1865, Museum of Northern Arizona Library).

In 1868 the Navajos were permitted to return home after signing a peace treaty with the United States. The treaty established a defined area as the new Navajo reservation; the boundary was dozens of miles from the perimeter of the later 1882 Hopi reservation. In between lay vast areas of public lands belonging to the United States. After their return from Bosque Redondo the Navajos were encouraged by the government to establish a pastoral economy. Sheep and goats were distributed to them as an incentive to prevent further raiding. The Navajos soon found themselves overcrowded on their treaty reservation and began expanding westward, pushing into Hopi territory.

Emory Sekaquaptewa made the following observations:

> The Hopis had to rely on the superintendent to force the Navajo to move away. The Hopis could no longer do this on their own. From 1865 to 1882 the Navajo were still a big threat.
>
> The Hopis thought the federal government intervened with Kit Carson because they were recognizing their duty to the Hopis. But actually it was probably not the case. Kit Carson moved in there because he needed to do something to keep his military powers. By that time American settlers were coming through there and it was really for their protection rather than for the protection of the Hopis that Carson undertook his military campaign.
>
> An interesting thing follows the Kit Carson incident. A few Navajo were not able to be rounded up; they successfully hid out. But the Hopis knew where they were. Those Hopis who still had a hard feeling against the Navajo because of Navajo depredations against their families, who were killed by the Navajos in the last big attack, secretly, without the consent of the Hopi chiefs, organized small war parties and went out into the wilderness and attacked the Navajo camps. Some Navajo children were taken captive and were brought back to Hopi and raised there. As a result of these short raiding forays by the Hopis, the Navajo who were left behind probably wished that they had been rounded up by Kit Carson (Black 1984).

The government, favorably impressed by the Navajos' industrious achievements and aware of their rapidly expanding population, sought to address their needs by making numerous additions of land to their reservation through executive orders and rulings of the secretary of the interior. These additions came from the public lands of the United States and were designated not annexations to the Navajo reservation but public lands set aside for Indian purposes and needs. An act of 1934 declared all the additions to be reservation land for Navajos and "other Indians already settled thereon"; the "other Indians" were the Hopis at

158

Munkapi (Tuba City). This expansion westward was permitted without any long-range planning or consideration of its effect on the Hopis.

The Hopis had no reservation authorized by the government until 1882, when Hopi agent Jesse H. Fleming raised the issue. Fleming had been unable to evict some undesirable people from the Hopi villages since there was no reservation status. He threatened to resign if the commissioner of Indian affairs failed to take action (Fleming to Commissioner H. Price, Nov. 11, 1882, Bureau of Indian Affairs, Letter Received, 21371/1882). The commissioner's reply was brief: "Describe boundaries for reservation that will include Moqui villages and agency large enough to meet all needful purposes and no larger" (Price to Fleming, Nov. 27, 1882, Pressbook Copies of Letters Sent, Land Division, Vol. 52, Letterbook 104, p. 132).

Fleming's recommendations, including proposed boundaries for the reservation, were approved by Commissioner Price and presented to President Chester Arthur by the secretary of the interior for his signature. President Arthur withdrew 2.6 million acres from the public domain to establish the reservation, indicating in the executive order that it was for the Hopis and, in a controversial phrase, "such other Indians as the Secretary of the Interior may see fit to settle thereon." Although they were not named specifically, the reference was to the Navajos. The boundaries formed a rectangle arbitrarily drawn on a map without regard to topography, geography, or historical occupation.

It is estimated that in 1882 there were some two thousand Hopis within the executive order reservation and only a few hundred Navajos. Efforts to deal effectively with Hopi complaints about Navajo encroachment were thwarted by the bureaucratic bungling of the agency system. In 1884 the Navajo and Hopi agencies were combined, an act of Congress that served to favor the Navajos (U.S. Department of the Interior 1884:136). Bureaucratic procedures did little to diminish the problem, as noted in the report of Superintendent Charles E. Burton, the first bonded agent for the Hopi reservation. It is reminiscent of the observations of many of his predecessors who reported on Navajo trespass and lawlessness: "Many Navajo . . . have settled along the watercourse and at the watering places on Moqui land. These places taken by the Navajo are the very best on the reservation and control most of the water supply. The two tribes are bitter enemies, and there is constant friction, stealing of horses, destroying each other's crops, fighting and murder going on among them. When difficulty arises and the

159

superintendent tries to settle the matter, the Navajo says the superintendent is not their agent and refuses to be governed by his decisions" (U.S.
Department of the Interior 1899).

A few years later Thomas Donaldson, special agent for the 1890 census, similarly observed:

> From excursions I made into the desert and to the mesas, I fre-
> quently came across large herds of Navajo sheep and goats . . . far
> from their own reservation, monopolizing the feeding and watering
> places of the Moqui.
>
> These Navajos, with their herds roam up and down the cañons and
> over the plateaus to the Tusayan (Hopi) trading post [at Keams
> Canyon] . . . their hogans are found near all these points, which they
> unlawfully appropriate. They overrun the Moqui lands at will. . . . It
> will be seen that the Moqui has cause for complaint, and it is to be
> hoped that nothing will prevent the department from promptly ful-
> filling promises which have been made to these much deserving
> "people of the houses" (1893:60).

Emory Sekaquaptewa commented:

> The BIA at Keams Canyon was operating under the authority of the
> Navajo Agency, which was interested in promoting Navajo welfare,
> and everybody else was subordinate to the Navajo project. The super-
> intendent at Keams Canyon Agency was operating with great
> restraint as far as protecting Hopi rights against the Navajos. Even
> though there were lots of complaints by the Hopi of Navajos moving
> in, the superintendent at Keams Canyon was powerless to do any-
> thing. By that time, the BIA was beginning to interpret the language
> of the 1882 Executive Order as recognizing Navajo rights to dwell
> within that reservation, as well as the Hopi. The Navajo were not
> specifically named in the language. They were the "other Indians."
> But the "other Indians" later became the legal issue in the land case
> between the Hopi and the Navajo (Black 1984).

160   General Winfield Scott forcefully summed up the folly of the 1882
executive order: "It is quite apparent that in 1882 the authorities in
Washington either were densely ignorant of the situation in this country
at that time, or were utterly indifferent to it; and by laying out the
reservation with a desk ruler and an utter disregard of the welfare of

the Hopi, they laid the foundations for trouble and suffering which have developed a situation that calls for remedial action by the Indian Office" (in Crane 1925:298–99). Writing in 1950, ethnobotanist and student of Hopi culture Volney Jones agreed that the government's actions were ill-conceived and short-sighted: "The lack of realism in setting up the [Hopi] reservation became manifest in the difficulties of its later operation. Much of the area reserved for the Hopi was in 1882 already in the hands of the Navajo, where it has remained" (1950:22).

In the 1930s, when severe drought and overgrazing made much of the land unproductive, the commissioner of Indian affairs issued regulations affecting the carrying capacity and management of the Navajo range, rulings that were to have an adverse effect on the Hopis as well. In 1937, land management districts were established and the Hopis were restricted to one area—District 6—consisting of 631,194 acres, only one-fourth the original reservation (U.S. Bureau of Indian Affairs 1937). The Navajos were permitted to graze their livestock on most of the remaining land delineated in the 1882 executive order (see map of the partition of the Joint Use Area in illustration section). District 6 came to be identified by the BIA as the Hopi reservation and was considered sufficient for the Hopis' needs. Unofficially, the government adopted the position that the Navajos had coextensive, or equal, rights with the Hopis to the remaining 1882 area.

Dewey Healing told the following story:

Navajo would come over and try to take advantage of a water hole or spring . . . use it all up, so that the Hopis that were living there wouldn't get much water. The Navajo were stealing water and sheep. I had many of those experiences. . . . I catch two boys down here, a little way from that grove. They skinned a whole sheep and carried it on their backs. I caught up with them way north, about eighteen miles. They were still going when the sun was going down. I and another fellow tracked them, so we took those boys back to our sheep camp and we stayed overnight. Next day we brought them over to Keams Canyon. I guess they sent them up to school from there; that was the sentence (Black 1984).

Controversies over joint use of the land and its resources mounted, and the many efforts to resolve the problem by means of agreements, administrative actions, or legislation met with little success. The

Department of the Interior concluded that resolution could come only from court action.

In 1958 Congress passed legislation allowing the Hopi and Navajo tribal chairmen to bring suit against each other in federal court to settle the land dispute. After four years of testimony and hearings the lawsuit known as *Healing v. Jones* was conducted in the federal district court in Prescott, Arizona, on September 23, 1962, before a panel of three judges. Dewey Healing was chairman of the Hopi Tribe, and Paul Jones was chairman of the Navajo Tribe. The verdict of the special court disappointed both sides and left many issues unresolved. It decreed that the Hopis had exclusive rights and interests in all areas of that part of the executive order lying within Land Management District 6, as defined on April 24, 1943, including all surface and subsurface resources. The Hopi and Navajo tribes shared joint, undivided, and equal rights and interests in the remaining portion of the 1882 area. The Navajos contested the ruling and filed an appeal, but in 1963 the U.S. Supreme Court affirmed the decision and decreed that the tribes had equal joint use interests in the 1882 reservation. It became known as the Joint Use Area.

The Joint Use Area has been partitioned, giving each side "equal" areas for exclusive surface uses such as residential, farming, and grazing. But both tribes continue to have equal, undivided shares of subsurface interests in the whole of the Joint Use Area, a result of the 1962 ruling of the U.S. district court, which held that the Navajo tribe had an equal interest with the Hopi tribe to a portion of the Joint Use Area.

Pabanale talked about going to Prescott for the hearings:

The Navajo and the Hopi tribes were called to Prescott to testify about the land dispute in District 7. Some Hopis were there and they stayed a couple of days and the Navajos told their story one whole week. Afterwards, when they were through, the Hopis were asked to give their testimony of what they knew of this land, an 1882 problem with the executive order. I was called to Prescott to be a witness.

I went over there with my niece, Edna Sikwi. I also went with another man by the name of Preston Masa. We were the three that were called to Prescott to testify in the presence of three judges. We came there about four o'clock and there were other Hopis that were still there. They had already told their stories and they said to us that we'd tell ours the next day. They took us to the hotel and we stayed overnight and the next morning we went to court.

When we got to court there were a lot of people—white people,

Navajos, Hopis, and some others. And when we began, a young man by the name of Bennett Kootka [from Tewa Village] started to give his testimony. After he gave his testimony to the judges, my niece was asked to tell hers. She was telling her story because in 1916 her husband built a home in District 7. She told how the Navajos were treating them—how things were going at that time. Before she got through with her story, a Navajo lawyer said, "Is this all they are going to say against the Navajos?" That was the Navajo lawyer Lytell. Then one of the judges stood up and said, "It is their time to tell their story. The Navajos had their story told the whole week and now it is the Hopi turn and so she has a right to speak."

Right then the Navajo lawyer took up his briefcase and went out, saying that he wouldn't come back until Monday. My niece then finished her story. Then they asked me to tell mine. I went up to the stage and there was a Hopi man named Logan Koopi, who was interpreting. I said to the judges, of course, I can talk English but I can't say that I can talk perfect English, but we have an interpreter here. I want to ask that if I don't hear what the lawyer said to me, I want the interpreter to repeat it, so everything will be said and known that we are speaking of. This is what I said to the lawyers and judges.

Then I started to give my testimony. I told them that I tried my best to make my home away from the mesa in District 7, in 1914. I was working with Mr. Murphy from Washington when they were laying out the lines. I tried to build my home in District 7 but there was no backing for me so I didn't build there. Then I said, every time the white man comes from the office, from Washington, or from the land office, they always say it is our own fault that we are not living away from the mesa. But I told them that it is not so. We have tried to build our homes away from the mesa but there was never any backing for us and that is how come we didn't build there.

Dewey Healing also described the Prescott hearings:

I was the chairman [of the Hopi Tribe] when that happened. We had three judges there—one of them was [Judge] Welch. One of the others—he didn't act like a judge. He was always grinning or laughing. To me he didn't seem to know what he was doing.

We were kind of in a poverty stage—we made a trip in government trucks and we took our own tent and camping equipment—bedrolls, utensils. We couldn't afford to stay in any hotel. So we were just camping out in a forest just a little ways from there. And when we went to the meeting, the Navajos had all kinds of facilities, so that they could sleep in good places—they had money.

They had all kinds of evidence—and pictures that they took—old hogans, old springs at different places that they thought was theirs. There were a whole lot of papers and pictures that were taken from the airplane. The funny part of it is, lots of Navajos that we know around here, they refused to say that they knew us when they were cross-examined by the lawyers. Even though I know that person very well, they refused to say that they know us. I don't know why they do that.

Like one of the men over here, Kébingto. From childhood on he was raised here, working for old man Pavatea that used to have a store down below. And when he testifies he didn't know anybody out here, yet we know him from childhood on, and he settled a little ways from here. After he grew up he married and raised a lot of children, yet he can't know any Hopi.

And lots of our old people testified. And we took all kinds things we could get a hold of—which showed how far we claimed our land. We gathered herbs, different kind of medicine that we used, all the spruce trees that we used in our dances and all that stuff—everything.

They don't seem to be interested in those things. They just don't pay much attention to that. And about the old-time history that the old people told, how far our land was—all that stuff—but nothing doing, they're not interested. They even brought some kind of feather object that they used when they made peace with the Navajos, that they would never fight each other again—that was handed back and forth, but they don't want to recognize that. They think that we made it ourselves, but it was an old piece.

So all those things didn't work in a court; not much. Couldn't convince those judges.

It lasted a week. But in between we had to wait for some more things to dig up to show. But the final time when we go, that's when they gave us that little area, supposed to be District 6 grazing area (Black 1984).

Emory Sekaquaptewa commented on the Prescott hearings as well:

When the decision was announced, it was the greatest disappointment that befell the Hopi. In spite of this setback, the older Hopis with whom Emory [his father] spoke were very confident that they would get back all of their lands, because the Navajos would disappear—simply because that was his destiny. The Navajo as a Navajo would disappear. It goes back to the original times when the great deity, Masawu, laid out the different ways of life, after the Hopis emerged from the underworld. The people were asked to pick their different ways of life and before anyone could move to pick up their choice—corn—which symbolized a past way of life, someone [a Navajo] came running through the crowd, yelling, "Let me through." He pulled his way up to the front, and he went up and he picked the longest ear of corn. He held it up and announced to the throngs of people there, "Now you see me pick this long ear of corn; this is the way I'm going to live." And so he will continue to do this—he will take whatever it is, and his destiny is that that long ear of corn will not last very long, in comparison to the short one which the Hopis picked. Those who descended from those Navajos who survive in this world will be those who have become like the Hopi. We might accept them to live among us, but they will have to become like the Hopis.

We would press our grandfather, who lived in our house, for more particulars. "What do you mean, how can the Navajo become like the Hopis?" Then he described it like this: "When the Navajos come among us and we accept them to live here, that's the way they will cut their hair. That's the sign of the Hopi" (Black 1984).

The Results of the Indian Reorganization Act

THE HOPI TRIBAL COUNCIL

The landmark Indian Reorganization Act of 1934 made possible the establishment of limited Indian self-government through the adoption of tribal constitutions and elected tribal councils. Its implementation at Hopi was fraught with controversy and intervillage animosity.

When Irving Pabanale and the chiefs from the different villages met with Oliver La Farge at the Keams Canyon Day School in 1932 to consider the pending IRA legislation (the Wheeler-Howard Act), they helped set in motion a process that would forever change the relationship among the Hopi villages, as well as between the Hopis and the federal government. The Hopis were never a unified tribe. They existed as a series of independent, though related, theocratic villages. The IRA represented a historic departure from existing federal Indian policy, which was dominated by nineteenth-century assimilationist ideology and rooted in the Indian Allotment Act (1887), designed to rapidly reduce the remaining tribal landholdings.

Growing opposition to these policies developed during the 1920s with the appearance of such groups as the American Indian Defense Association, headed by John Collier, an Indian affairs crusader. In 1923 Collier helped defeat the onerous Bursum Bill, which was intended to defraud the New Mexico Pueblo Indians of their landholdings. In 1926 the prestigious Brookings Institution of Washington was asked to review federal policy and make recommendations for change. A team headed by Lewis Merriam undertook this study and in 1928 published its results, *The Problem of Indian Administration*, which became known as the Merriam Report. Highly critical of the government's failure to improve the conditions of Indian tribes, the report recommended the restriction of allotment policies, elimination of boarding schools, improvement of health care, decentralization of the BIA, institution of procedures to make better use of Indian resources, and adoption of a policy of "cultural pluralism."

Shortly after the release of the Merriam Report, the Senate Indian Affairs Committee, at Collier's urging, undertook a comprehensive investigation of conditions on the major reservations. The study, made between 1928 and 1933, added weight to the criticism of bureau policies, which resulted in the resignation of Commissioner Charles Burke in 1929 (Downs 1945:344). His successor, Charles Rhoads, former president of the Indian Rights Association, attempted to fulfill the recommendations of the Merriam Report but was unable to bring about the reforms he pledged to support. These goals included reform of the allotment system and encouragement of the establishment of tribal corporations to manage unallotted lands.

With the arrival of the Roosevelt administration in 1932, the stage was set for major changes in Indian policy. Harold L. Ickes was appointed secretary of the interior, and Collier was made commissioner of Indian affairs. Collier was not convinced that Indians were ready for self-government, but he must be credited with taking a number of bold steps to enable Indians to acquire some degree of autonomy in the conduct of tribal life and to institute measures of economic rehabilitation.

The IRA, as it finally emerged, constituted a major departure from existing federal policies. Though many innovative features of the bill were modified or deleted by Congress, the broad reforms intended by Collier were preserved. In order for the act to be implemented on any reservation, it had to be submitted to a referendum and approved by majority vote. The most significant part of the act was the prohibition of future allotments of Indian lands by the federal government. Tribes that voted to organize under the act would be able to negotiate with federal, state, and local governments; review all BIA budgetary matters relating to the tribe; establish tribal corporations; prevent further alienation of lands and tribal assets; and employ legal counsel. The act also established a revolving credit fund for economic enterprises and a fund for educational loans.

Following passage of the IRA by Congress in 1934, Collier was successful in persuading the Hopis to accept the new act, which they did in 1935 by a vote of 519 to 299. Collier then faced the most difficult task in enabling the Hopis to establish a tribal government: voting to adopt a constitution. Because of Hopi suspicion of the Bureau of Indian Affairs, Collier needed a nonbureau, nongovernment field worker— someone the Hopis would trust. He called on Oliver La Farge, president of the National Association on Indian Affairs, to help prepare a tribal constitution. La Farge was no stranger to the Southwest. In 1924 he

167

spent time on the Navajo reservation, where he became fluent in the language. He was something of a celebrity, having won the Pulitzer Prize in 1929 for his novel *Laughing Boy*. He had also visited the Hopis in 1924 and had been well received on First Mesa, where he became close friends with Irving Pabanale's brother Nelson Oyaping, then a member of the tribal police force. La Farge also met Pabanale that year and they too became friends. He visited villages on the other mesas but felt most at home at First Mesa, especially among the Tewas.

La Farge undertook the task of preparing a constitution, realizing that the great majority of the Hopis would reject a forced change. He wrote Collier in 1936: "I don't wish to assume the task of pushing the Hopis toward an organization which does not interest them. What I want to do is to make them come and get it" (Apr. 21, 1936, Private Papers of John Collier, Yale University, New Haven). This proved to be more difficult than he had anticipated. His sense of frustration would grow during the seemingly endless trips he made between villages. From June to September 1936 he kept a daily journal chronicling his activities and impressions (La Farge 1936).[1]

This unpublished document provides invaluable insights into the personalities La Farge encountered in the process of preparing the constitution. It also reveals his attitudes toward the Hopis; it is ironic that the man chosen to prepare their constitution was so biased against them. Although he admired the Hopis' intelligence and dedication to spiritual values, he was drawn to the group he termed progressives. These were people who "tend to absorb and master our material techniques and improvements, while retaining with full force their own aesthetic, religious, social and spiritual values" (La Farge 1937:9). He was contemptuous of another group, influential opportunists whom he called "smarties—self-styled progressives, sometimes Christians, sometimes not, who are social misfits and generally unstable and unreliable. Most of this group speak fluent English and know how to flatter the government officials. Unreasonable recognition of these individuals as leaders and spokesmen for their village has been a real factor in building distrust of the government and suspicion of any scheme of representation" (1937:10).

168   Though he clearly preferred dealing with the Arizona Tewas of First Mesa, La Farge had to face the enmity of the conservative Hopis, especially on Third Mesa. Collier's earlier association with the Christian interpreter Otto Lomávitu, leader of the progressives of Kiqötsmovi (New Orayvi), engendered deeply rooted mistrust of the government by

the traditional Hopis. By contrast, La Farge was drawn to qualities of the Tewas which most closely mirrored his own values. He admired their tenacity of conviction, their cleanliness, and their aggressiveness. He contrasted Hopi values of pacifism with the more forthright stance of the Tewas: "[The Hopis] abhor war and physical violence. Wherefore they quarrel constantly and the talking never ceases. In this respect, the Tewas, who will punch a man's head for him, are a great relief" (1936:3). "The Tewas believe in settling a row by giving the offender a poke in the jaw. They are not afraid of fighting. Although they possess the long Pueblo memory, they become impatient with too long dwelling in the past and take much more readily than do the Hopis to realistic action for settling present problems" (1937:4).

La Farge minced no words in enumerating his assessment of the many "unpleasant characteristics" of the Hopis, describing them as materialistic, self-seeking, smug, and quarrelsome (1937:14). He noted further: "These Indians are good business men, penny-squeezing, avaricious, fearful of the future, suspicious. Their good manners and friendly approach are from the lips out. They are intensely suspicious and great harbourers of the memory of wrongs received" (1936:3). La Farge found the Hopis of First Mesa commendable, in that they had adopted the more desirable values of the Tewas and Navajos: "Due to the influence of the Tewas, and considerable inter-mixture with the Navajos, this village [Walpi] shows the least of the unpleasant Hopi characteristics . . . it is the most accustomed to contact with the government, and in general the easiest to deal with" (1936:10).

La Farge embarked on his campaign to gain acceptance of the constitution, mindful of the difficulties he faced in overcoming the resistance of the Hopi religious leaders, whose power and authority reflected the theocratic nature of the villages. These village chiefs, or *kikmongwis*, could not become involved in secular affairs or quarrels. According to Hopi tradition, they had to be protected from all unpleasant contacts with the outside world. To be given any secular authority in village affairs would desecrate their religious status and authority. Entrusting authority to men of lesser religious rank, however, would result in their disavowal by the *kikmongwis*.

La Farge pursued the strategy of meeting with numerous leaders and village officials in an attempt to find some basis for consensus, a prospect that proved elusive as he faced the enmity of the traditional villages. Notwithstanding his frustrations with such villages as Orayvi and Hotvela, La Farge continued his efforts to prepare a draft constitution with the willing assistance of a joint committee of First Mesa villages (Tewa Village, Sitsomovi, Walpi, and Polacca).

The Tewas found this task to their liking. Over the years, they had formalized their role not only as protectors of the Hopis but as intermediaries and interpreters. They were recognized as conduits for new ideas that were introduced from the outside and slowly diffused to the other Hopi villages. Dozier notes that "Oliver La Farge was told at Songoopavi, at the time of the drafting of the Hopi Constitution, that the sequence of all new things was first the Hopi-Tewa, then First Mesa as a whole, then the body of the tribe" (1954:296 n. 28).

With the assistance of the progressives on First Mesa, the Tewas (including Pabanale) completed the draft, after which it was passed on to the other villages, where numerous meetings were held to debate the document. The sought-after consensus was unattainable. The conservative Hopis feared loss of autonomy and the intrusion of the BIA. They felt that the tribal council, mandated by the constitution, would infringe on village autonomy and the sacred traditions associated with the land.

The result was that the villages agreed to submit the acceptance of the constitution to a vote. If it was accepted, a tribal council would be established with clearly defined and limited powers. In the progressive Christian villages (Kiqötsmovi, Upper Munkapi, Paaqavi, and First Mesa villages) delegates would be elected by majority vote. In the conservative villages (Orayvi, Second Mesa villages, Hotvela, Lower Munkapi) the *kikmongwis* would appoint council members who would be responsible to them. Under the constitution the tribal council's authority was confined to the adjudication of intervillage disputes and relations with governmental agencies on the federal, state, and local level. The council would have no voice in village affairs; rather, each village would retain authority over domestic, religious, and internal matters; regulation of the inheritance of property; the assignment and use of land; and interpersonal and family relations.

Perhaps naively and optimistically, La Farge felt that "it is possible, with care, . . . to induce the Hopis to form a tribal organization which can speak for them, at least on matters which affect the whole tribe" (La Farge to Collier, Sept. 21, 1934, Collier Papers). He was later to express skepticism about the efficacy of the constitution. In 1950, in a postscript to his 1936 journal, he commented on the failure of his efforts: "The pattern of Tribal Council, decisive action, minority self-subordination, etc., simply did not suit them . . . no village . . . was prepared to surrender any part of its sovereignty, or to lay aside any of its quarrels with other villages." Collier was later to conclude that the constitution never worked because "it did not take into account . . . the conscious and unconscious motivations and accompanying resistances of the several quite diverse Hopi societies" (1963:218).

On October 26, 1936, the Hopis cast their votes. Of the estimated 2,800 eligible voters, only about one-quarter went to the polls. The vote was 650 in favor of adopting the constitution and 104 against. From its inception, the council established by the constitution met with marginal acceptance. The conservative villages of Orayvi, Hotvela, and lower Munkapi abstained from sending representatives. In 1937, the second year of the council's existence, a disputed ruling to adopt a law-and-order code written by the Department of the Interior resulted in the withdrawal of council representatives by the Second Mesa villages of Musangnuvi, Supawlavi, and Songoopavi.

A more serious crisis faced the tribal council shortly after its inauguration. In 1936, as Collier set about to implement further aspects of his "Indian New Deal," the council had to face the problem of reservation boundaries. At issue was the controversy over the 1882 executive order reservation established for the Hopis and, by implication, the Navajos. The rights of the Hopis to the 1882 area were not designated exclusive rights because Navajos were living there at the time. Since then, Navajos had infiltrated the reservation in ever increasing numbers (Collier to Supt. Ladd, Oct. 27, 1941, Collier Papers). The Hopis became more fearful of the continued encroachment of the Navajos as they sought new grazing areas for their stock. By 1935 the Navajos on the 1882 reservation numbered more than 45,000, and Hopi complaints to the bureau received little if any attention.

In 1937, as the BIA was proceeding with its regulation of livestock grazing and stock reduction on both Hopi and Navajo lands, District 6 was designated the sole and exclusive Hopi grazing area (U.S. Bureau of Indian Affairs 1937). This restricted area was established under the authority of the Navajo BIA Agency at Window Rock, which did not consult the Hopis in making the designation, an action that intensified Hopi grievances toward the Navajos and the U.S. government.

Collier visited Orayvi in July 1938 and met with council members to introduce Seth Wilson as the new superintendent of the Hopi Agency. He also attempted to allay Hopi fears about District 6 by answering questions concerning the district's boundary. Collier assured the Hopis that the new boundary would not represent a fixed and official boundary of the Hopi reservation. He told them "that [the grazing area] has nothing to do with the reservation boundary" (minutes of Collier's meeting with the Hopi Indians at Orayvi, July 14, 1938, Collier Papers).

Even Collier's supporters among the progressives found little satisfaction in his assurances. They had good cause to be apprehensive; by 1943 District 6 was turned over to the Hopi Agency, which began a stock reduction program exclusively for the district. The Navajo agencies were then responsible for implementing a similar program on the remainder of the reservation. District 6 became the de facto Hopi reservation, a far cry from what were vast Hopi lands (Clemmer 1978:533).

An interesting aside describes Collier's behavior during his visit to the Hopis. Dewey Healing was present at the time and made the following observations:

> I always am curious in how the white people act and how they could have respect for the people [Hopis]. So when Collier came here and met with the Hopis to make proposals—most of them were elderly— talking about reduction and reorganization and everything . . . you know what that crazy man did?
>
> If I was at that time, that kind of person [courageous], maybe I could tell him. But I felt I didn't have the right to say.
>
> There was a long table . . . from there to here. All those high-up men they sit at the table . . . most of them. Collier was right on this side with a few of his helpers. He lights his pipe, then he climbs up on that table and sits like that [cross-legged]! On the table!
>
> Looks around . . . grinning. See, nobody made anything of this kind of scene. I don't know why he did that; nobody told him to get off the table.
>
> They think that just because he had a high position he could do anything. But that's the craziest thing to do, even to us Indians. If somebody could have asked, "Why do you do that; is that something they told you to do from Washington?" Someone might make a remark of some kind. He was sitting there and talking and smoking his pipe.
>
> He talked about his program, then about the reorganization, what good it would do. Then, how we would respond to things, and so many other things that he brought out. But nobody could ask him any questions, even though he asked for them. They had fear! But that's the thing I just don't like. When he goes up on the table and sits up there like this [Dewey demonstrated: arms folded and legs crossed],

172

looking around, I don't know why that man would do that. I know Albert [Yava] was there, the superintendent; the clerks.

I asked Albert, "Why did Collier get up on that table?" He said, "I don't know. Oh, he's in a high position, maybe he could do anything. Maybe he got up there to see if we could say something." But nobody responded; nobody said anything. That showed Collier that we are afraid of him. We have a fear of him.

But if someone would have asked him, "What do you call this; is this the right thing to do?" Maybe that would have made him angry. But nobody said anything.

I don't know how I would have done it if it was now that this was done. I have a different attitude now—everything is different (Black 1984).

The Hopi Tribal Council did not fare well in the face of the crises. It managed a shaky existence until 1943, when the BIA superintendent ordered it disbanded because of a dispute on First Mesa concerning the enforcement of a stock-reduction ruling by the Department of the Interior. The council remained inactive until 1952 (Clemmer 1986:23). It was not until 1955 that the BIA was willing to reverse its previous ruling and resume official recognition of the council as the representative of the Hopi people. The BIA was persuaded by the increased influence of Christianity among the Hopis and the rising voices of younger, progressive Hopis who wanted more political influence in Hopi and broader Indian affairs. There was also clamor for increased economic development on the reservation and determination to weaken the powers of the dominating *kikmongwis* (Hopi Hearings 1955:288).

In retrospect, the sentiments of Oliver La Farge reveal a deeper understanding of the difficulty of his task. In 1936 he reflected on the IRA, the Hopi constitution, and its impact on the Hopis as another aspect of the "white man's burden":

I have thought of it ["the white man's burden"] often in the past fifteen years, in different ways. It is a snare and a delusion, it is also a reality and something not to be ducked. . . . The Hopis are going to organize, first, because John Collier and a number of other people decided to put through a new Indian law, the Reorganization Act. The Indians didn't think this up. We did. . . . We came among these people, they didn't ask us, and as a result, they are our wards. It's not any inherent lack of capacity, it's the cold fact of cultural adjustment. . . .

173

I said all the right things—"This is your decision, it is up to you"—but my manner was paternal and authoritarian. . . .We bring to these Indians a question which their experience cannot comprehend, a question which includes a world view and a grasp of that utterly alien, mind-wracking concept, Anglo-Saxon rule by majority vote, with everything that follows in the train of that (La Farge 1936:59).

Judge Pabanale and
the Tribal Court

Beginning in the 1880s, federal Indian policy sought to expand control over the reservations by adopting laws to control "Indian crime." In 1885 Congress passed the Major Crimes Act in response to a Supreme Court decision barring federal prosecution of offenses within Indian country involving only Indians (*ex parte* Crow Dog, 109 U.S. 556 [1883]); this law established uniform criteria for crimes and their punishment.[1] Federal courts were now empowered to try and punish Indians accused of these crimes, in keeping with the prevailing belief that tribal systems of justice failed to satisfy the goals of the civilizing process.

The BIA sought to further standardize the criminal justice system on Indian reservations by establishing the Courts of Indian Offenses in 1884. The conduct of judicial control over most of the reservations was exercised with authoritarian zeal by the Indian Service from 1887 to 1934. Intended to promote acculturation by discouraging practices felt to be detrimental to the process of assimilating the Indians, these courts sought to eliminate such "crimes" as plural marriages, native practice of medicine, destruction of property following the death of a tribal member, and certain dances and rituals (Hagan 1966; Kerr 1969). By 1900, Courts of Indian Offenses were established on two-thirds of the reservations. The BIA, through its regional superintendents, had absolute authority to appoint judges and to set forth a uniform code of offenses. From the more acculturated members of the Indian police forces, superintendents chose one to three judges for these courts.

Before the imposition of assimilationist policies, the responsibility for maintaining law and order among the Hopis was vested in the village chief, or *kikmongwi*, a man noted for his sagacity and charisma who served as an arbiter of disputes. Toward the end of the nineteenth century police agents of the court on the Hopi reservation began interfering in village disputes, imprisoning "troublemakers" and "hostiles" at Orayvi and Hotvela. These agents acted as both judges and law enforcers.

The Courts of Indian Offenses operated without clearly defined jurisdictional authority or procedures. Agency superintendents imposed their own rules for the operation of courts, judges, and police in their jurisdictions. Tribal judges received no systematic training in U.S. law, and proceedings often were conducted informally (American Indian Lawyer Training Program 1982:21).

The impetus to change the system did not begin until passage of the IRA, with its rejection of assimilationist policies and its provisions for strengthening tribal governments. It was the intent of the IRA to phase out the Courts of Indian Offenses and replace them with tribal courts, which would be more sensitive to the needs of Indian communities. Most tribal constitutions under the IRA provided for tribal courts to adopt a system of legal codes, generally patterned after the rules and regulations of the Department of the Interior, which continued to govern the Courts of Indian Offenses. Under the new law-and-order code adopted in 1941 the tribal court could begin to function as an arm of the Hopi tribal government. Judges could now be approved and dismissed by the tribal council, and the jurisdiction of the court extended over all Indians in the Hopi area, including Indians who were not Hopi. Even non-Indians working for the BIA were subject to the court's jurisdiction.

The replacement of the Courts of Indian Offenses with tribal courts was a slow and tenuous process. It was not until 1972 that the Hopis were able to abandon their Court of Indian Offenses and adopt a tribal court structure with its own criminal code.

Pabanale's tenure as judge, from 1940 to 1949, was not a placid one. Without legal training and experience in interpreting the complex federal code, he had to learn its application and limitations in the cases that came before the court. Perhaps his greatest difficulty was in learning to temper the strict enforcement of the laws, reducing the severity of the rules when warranted. Superintendent Seth Wilson made it clear to members of the tribal council that although the government recognized the leadership roles of the tribal chiefs and sought their support, the court and the police had written regulations that must be upheld, regardless of the opinions of the chiefs. Pabanale respected the authority of the government and the newly established status of the tribal court, and his strict interpretation of the rules and regulations of the court reflected his high regard for the white man's law.

Dissatisfaction with Pabanale's conduct of the court soon manifested itself. During his first year as chief judge (1941), a petition for his

176

resignation was circulated by members of the tribal council from First Mesa and was supported by the chiefs and ceremonial officials of First Mesa (Petition to the Hopi Indian Tribal Council for the Dismissal of the Judge, Feb. 26, 1941, Hopi Agency, Keams Canyon). Pabanale was accused of imposing overly severe punishment, showing favoritism in court, and ignoring the instructions of the chiefs of First Mesa in regard to issuing sentences in line with Hopi custom.

During that year there were further accusations of misconduct, followed by investigations by a committee of the tribal council, which failed to act on the petition for removal. Finally, examination of the court records by the chief special officer and the legal affairs officer of the Department of the Interior found no reason to remove Pabanale (Seth Wilson to the Commissioner of Indian Affairs, Apr. 11, 1941; Byron Adams to Burton A. Ladd, June 6, 1942, Hopi Agency, Keams Canyon).

Pabanale persevered in his role of chief judge and, despite the controversy, proceeded to build his reputation as a strict adherent of law and order. His term of office covered a period of pronounced change for the Hopis, beginning with the BIA's drastic restrictions on livestock grazing, implemented as part of an overall plan for livestock reduction and soil conservation. Most of Pabanale's cases dealt with enforcing these regulations.

Since before the turn of the century, government policy allowed the Navajos free access to pasturing and grazing lands adjacent to their original reservation. By 1940 the Navajos occupied nearly three-quarters of the original 1882 area, leaving the remainder as the unofficial Hopi reservation. The Indian Service did not foresee the detrimental effects of its encouragement of the expansion of the Indians' herds of sheep, goats, and cattle. Between 1933 and 1937, as drought, erosion, and overgrazing reached critical levels, the Collier administration instituted a far-reaching program of stock reduction, which was to have a devastating effect on both Hopis and Navajos. Under these restrictions the Hopi reservation was shrunk to a level far below that needed by the population to sustain itself.

By 1943 Hopi livestock herds were forcibly reduced by some 24 percent. The economic impact of the reduction was not distributed equally over the reservation. Hardest hit was Third Mesa, where sheep herds were cut back by 44 percent; First Mesa and Second Mesa herds were cut by 20 and 22 percent, respectively. The BIA justified the severe limitation on Third Mesa stock by claiming that its grazing areas were more

177

depleted than any others on the reservation (James 1974:206–7). It further required the superintendent to keep records of livestock ownership and tallies of livestock at all dipping vats. Each owner was to receive a grazing permit specifying the allowed number of livestock. All animals were to be branded, as specified by the superintendent, who was also instructed to keep a current register of all heads of families using the range and the number of each kind of stock owned by the family. In addition, he was to keep records of the carrying capacity of each part of the land management district and the periods during which grazing should be permitted in each part of the district (U.S. Bureau of Indian Affairs, Grazing Regulations for the Navajo and Hopi Reservations, June 2, 1937).

There was much bitterness over these rulings on the Hopi reservation, especially on Third Mesa. Many Hopis refused to obtain the temporary stock-reduction permits issued by the agency at Keams Canyon. The enforcement of the grazing permit rules was left up to the tribal court, and there was resentment toward Pabanale as he proceeded to enforce these rules. Hopi stockmen on First Mesa and Second Mesa cooperated for the most part and were commended by Collier for "recognizing the gravity of the situation" and agreeing to reduce their livestock holdings. Collier warned the Third Mesa stockmen that unless they complied with the reduction by obtaining the required permits, they would be liable for prosecution in the federal courts (John Collier, Memorandum of Dec. 23, 1943, Hopi Agency File, Forestry and Grazing, Keams Canyon). Those Hopis who refused to accept the permits and the reduction of their herds would be subject to arrest and the confiscation of their stock.

Pabanale's court dealt with a number of cases involving the grazing of livestock without permits in the 1940s. Some of the Hopi stock owners involved in the arrests later gave testimony at the Hopi Hearings held by the BIA at Hotvela, July 15–18, 1955. Four Hotvela men refused to accept the temporary permits in 1945. They were arrested and sentenced to ninety days in jail, and all their sheep and horses were confiscated. In his testimony at the hearings one Hopi told of being arrested for refusing to accept the permit. Judge Pabanale said to him, "Well, you are going to have to be put in jail then because Washington officials have given me authority to do this, and I want you to know that I am a white man and I have to do this to you" (Hopi Hearings 1955:14–15). In addition to the jail sentence, the defendant's 185 head of sheep and five horses were taken from him, most of them butchered before they were sold.

178

Dewey Healing commented on the stock reduction:

That Paul Jones [chairman of the Navajo Tribe] up there, when the reduction time comes, he worked it out among his Navajos to give each child one sheep. That way they didn't have to reduce them.

It's because of the ruling, when you have a big bunch of sheep, there's a scale that you go by. If you go beyond your limit, you have to come down with your sheep [reduce them]. So that's the way Paul Jones figured it out. So he told them Navajos to give all their sheep away. So that's why they couldn't very well reduce them. Every child has a sheep.

Everybody—Tewas too—were hard hit by the sheep reduction. It happened that I was put on a committee where the recommendations were our job, but I think we did pretty good. Only a few [men] had more head of sheep. They're the ones that were reduced. Like my father—he had a herd of close to 500; he was cut in half.

Nobody went over a thousand head when the reduction came. They had between 600 to 800. When the reduction came, they cut them in half and left them about 400 head.

The bad part was this: they put the price on those sheep too cheap. If they had men who could think of how much time it took for those people to raise those sheep, they could have raised the price on them, but a dollar a head is what the old government gave. That's why it's wrong; the government pay them a dollar a head, whatever they were going to kill off. Then all they do is let the people kill them off for themselves. They don't get nothing from it. But the government is not paying too much for them; a dollar a head. That's why the people don't like it. If they were given what the sheep were worth, then it would have been easier . . . maybe ten dollars a head, at the most (Black 1984).

Pabanale had a distinguished record of public service that lasted almost a half-century. From his early days as a policeman to his culminating years on the bench, he strove to serve the tribe as well as the government. He accepted the responsibility of leadership for both the Arizona Tewas and the Hopis and was instrumental in furthering greater contact with the Euro-Americans; he welcomed the challenges presented by contact with the outside world. He served best as an intermediary between the world of the Hopis and the Tewas and that of the Euro-Americans. Especially in his role as judge, he strove for greater Hopi

179

acceptance of American culture while maintaining his loyalty to the customs of his people.

Pabanale was accepted by most of the Hopis, though he had to contend with the resentment of the more conservative members of the tribe. His representation of authority was viewed with suspicion and disapproval, especially in his enforcement of the livestock reduction program. Despite the antagonisms, he pioneered the establishment of a fledgling court system that was to become a respected and integral part of Hopi government.

Pabanale's peers generally commented favorably on his work. Dewey Healing noted:

I think he did the best way he did. He would ask a defendant, "How many times did you do that?" "My first time." "All right, don't do that again. Next time you're going to get the penalty." He would make it easy for the person. Irving tried to make it easy for offenders because the court allowed for him to decide whichever way he should go. Yes, he was a fair judge. He used that probation deal a lot of times.

I remember a funny thing happened one time. They took an old man from First Mesa into court. He was an old-timer; he didn't know nothing. They took him to court for having a black ram in his bunch. The tribe didn't allow any colored sheep in the herd, so they charged him with that.

Irving was judge and Albert [Yava] was interpreting. Irving asked, "How is it that you have that black sheep in your herd?" "It's because of your dad," he said [referring to Albert's father]. "Your dad is always after me for the black wool, that's why I keep that black sheep. He's been after me for that black wool and I have it so I put that one in my herd." Irving grinned, then he said, "I want to know, did you raise that black sheep yourself?" "Are you crazy? How could I raise that sheep? I'm no sheep and I have no tits to nurse that black ram." You can't blame that old-timer. You're not supposed to laugh in a court, but everybody did. Then Irving asked him, "Why don't you put him in the corral over here?" "How can I do that? Don't you understand the condition I'm in? I'm crippled; I can't drive him all the way from Second Mesa." It was the correct answer. Then Irving told him to get some help to bring the sheep in here.

A lot of funny things happened long ago. But nobody ever complained about the way the judge goes. He tried to go along the old-fashioned way that a man [who] is judging you is supposed to go in olden times. So he just got in that line. He never stick to what the regulations say. He just do halfway what the regulations say, and make it easy on people (Black 1984).

Emory Sekaquaptewa commented:

Pabanale was appointed, not elected. The superintendent's practice was to let the people think that they made a choice.

Before the 1940s, there were Hopi policemen in each village. They acted as referees in disputes; there was no great need for a court at that time.

When the Court of Indian Offenses was being formed, the superintendent had absolute authority to pick who was going to be the judge. He could just go to one village and say, "I'm looking at these two men, now what do you think?"

It made sense to pick a judge from First Mesa because he would be close to the office of the superintendent. Perhaps the superintendent felt that he could work more effectively with the Tewa than with the Hopi.

The judge must enforce the rulings of the criminal code of the United States, as required by the BIA through its agent, the superintendent.

At the same time, he is trying to balance the decisions he makes with Hopi customary law. When people object, it is not because they are concerned with his being progressive. They object on the basis of factionalism. Under Pabanale, it was the Court of Indian Offenses that had jurisdiction over any violations of grazing regulations. There were many Hopis who resisted the regulations, particularly at Hotvela. Many of them refused to get grazing permits to continue their livestock operations. It was a standoff between them and the BIA. They were forcibly reduced but the livestock owners would not follow up with permits (Black 1984).

Abbott Sekaquaptewa, former chairman of the Hopi tribe, said:

Under the circumstances, I think he did a pretty good job, if you take into consideration his lack of formal education. I think he probably was more responsive to BIA regulations and policies than he was to what the man in the village street felt. But as far as I know, there were no excesses as far as his holding down his judgeship.

181

Some people disliked him because he had the misfortune of having been on the bench when the livestock reduction program was being implemented. He looked at it as being a law, and "a law is a law." I think that when he met up with people who knew as much about the law and the regulations, he was not able to handle that real well, without the presence of the BIA to lend technical support. He needed that to handle the more difficult cases. I know this because during that period of time, my father was charged with a breach of the regulations—the reduction program. He, along with some of the other officers, members of the Hopi Stockmen's Union, as they called it—it was a cattle association—were charged before the court, Pabanale's court. They argued the case themselves and they were able to make a good enough argument against the superintendent and the range riders. I don't know what happened. They either abandoned Judge Pabanale, or the court couldn't make the case stick. And so they left my dad and the other defendants in the courtroom and didn't come back. So my dad and the other members of the stock association just sat there looking at each other and said, "What do we do next?"

I think ultimately they assessed them fines. But the point is, that unless he had that strong support of the BIA in a technical sense, it was difficult for him.

There were others who disliked him, but it was not on very good grounds. He probably got tough with the liquor violators at times. Maybe he did not work with them very closely in a counseling mode. But if you look at the total picture nationwide in Indian country, he probably was a pretty good judge. I can't say he was, 'cause I don't know. Knowing what I do, subsequent to his tenure of office, when I became tribal chairman, in 1961 and traveled over a good deal of Indian country seeing the judges, etc., for his time, he was probably a good judge . . . as long as things didn't get too technical.

The couple of times I talked with Judge Pabanale, he told me about what the old people said and kind of encouraged me because I was with the council at that time. He gave me a few words of encouragement—not the kind that I got from other people—but, nonetheless, he gave me encouragement (Black 1984).

In response to a question about the treatment of traditional people, Abbott noted:

What I think happened was that everybody resisted [the livestock reduction program], particularly here, at Third Mesa. So they were charged before the court. But what happened was that when the decisions finally came down, like the stock association here, they finally complied with it because it was the system—it was the law. So they complied with it and reduced their livestock, but they fought it as long as they could. When it came down to the final decision, they complied.

The others [Third Mesa traditionalists] just plain refused to comply. They even refused to appear in court. So the BIA went out and reduced the livestock for them. They just took numbers of them and drove them away. They offered compensation for the livestock but the Hopis refused to take the compensation (Black 1984).

Abbott elaborated on the problem of livestock reduction:

It doesn't compute well with a lot of things in Hopi life, you know, because, see, this is not the first time that the Hopis ever encountered droughts and overgrazing. It happened in Spanish times. They've always said that we shouldn't allow too many livestock to graze because it will destroy the raiment of mother earth, as it happened after Spanish times when they just got too many livestock going, and the drought occurred. So we are taught not to overstock, to maintain control over the numbers of livestock. And when there's too many, you've got to do away with them. Yet, because they become too dependent on livestock in many ways, when a drought occurred and when overgrazing occurred, they fought it. Nobody's talked about that. That's part of it. The big cloud over this whole thing was it didn't have to happen to us, because we had sufficient land to have used, to meet all our needs without livestock reduction. But what happened was that when the Navajo Agency passed a resolution authorizing the livestock reduction program, they also set up the land management districting system and then they squeezed us into District 6 and took the rest of the land for their people. And if we had been able to use our land, we wouldn't have had to reduce livestock.

I think probably that during Pabanale's time, the judicial system began to take on a little more formal organization, where before his time, there were practically no procedures.

But I think, generally, Hopi people would react the same way to any judge if he's willing to take strong action. He'll have support, but

183

he will always have resistance and suspicion, because in the Hopi traditional system of government, where the leader is [more of] a spiritual father than a ruler, that's very strong. Absolute rule, or rule by a
code of laws, especially those governing criminal conduct, does not go
well with Hopi people. One of the principles of Hopi leadership and
what they really are taught (and clan leaders are always knocking that
into my head), "It is said that we are not in our positions of leadership to be rulers over our children, but to be fathers to them." That's
why a priesthood leader is called a father—a father of his people. And
traditionally he cannot push anybody away; he cannot cast anybody
aside. He has to embrace them all to himself. That's why their rule did
not include handling disputes, either families or individuals, because
if he had to handle a dispute between individuals or families, he
would have to make a decision in favor of one against the other, and
when he does that he has cast the other person away. That's a no-no
for the priesthood leaders. They cannot do that. That's why they were
insulated from the secular life of the people.

For that reason, anybody in any responsible position would run
into that problem, even though he's a judge, you see. But the business
of judging is what is not part of the Hopi system of leadership. And
in the traditional society, even the people who had the responsibility
for making decisions frequently, they didn't try to judge the offenders.
They found ways of identifying the wrongdoers or the culprits, and
public criticism or ostracism was their punishment. Then also, there's
the fear of being held responsible for something. Anybody who would
belong to a priesthood society, or would come from a clan, the
wrongdoing would result in some bad things, and they would be held
responsible for them. Fear of that is what held them together—kept
them in line (Black 1984).

Becoming a Mormon

The Hopis called them *moomonam,* Mormons, as distinguished from *pahaanam,* other white people. The Mormons were probably the most successful and best liked of all missionary groups among the Hopis. Their first mission was established at Munkapi by Jacob Hamblin in 1862, and they have since spread throughout the villages.

In 1952, after becoming blind, Pabanale sought solace in Mormon teachings, believing that the *Book of Mormon* paralleled the life of the Tewas and supported his belief in a living God. In his earlier years Pabanale was an active participant in the ceremonial life of First Mesa. He was one of the few Tewas who was initiated into the important Wuwtsim Society at Walpi and was also a member of the Central Plaza Kiva in Tewa Village.

Many of the Hopis who converted to Mormonism retained their affiliation with Hopi religion, feeling that the Mormons were tolerant of Hopi beliefs and ceremonies and that there was no conflict in maintaining both belief systems. Dewey Healing held a similar opinion: "When the Mormons came in, a lot of them [Hopis] fell for them, because they can't try to tell these people to stay away from Hopi doings or whatever is going on. They just let them attend it, so that they can take part. So that's what interested them, I guess. There's a lot of them that joined the Mormon Church" (Black 1984).

Pabanale was not the first in his family to become a Mormon. His daughter Edith and her husband, Sylvan, had been baptized by the church some years earlier. Sylvan's opinions about being a Mormon reflect this feeling of acceptance:

Irving had the support of his family when he became a Mormon. They all were Mormons. They liked the Mormons because they helped the Hopis. Being a Mormon doesn't make you less Hopi.

It's the faith that goes—whatever you believe in. We have our traditions here. We want to go to church.

We sing and say prayers, maybe for everyone. The prayer comes from the book. We want to go straight, follow the book. It's up to an individual how you feel. We got no hard feelings against nobody. As long as they want to put their stuff out for someone to learn, try to do something that's good.

Try to keep people in peace; try to keep them happy. All that goes under God. Nobody sees any god, but we still believe in something to protect us, to guide us, keeping us going. But it's up to an individual. If you want to do this, go!

If you want to work, keep yourself alive, don't beg off.

I think all these books of Christian life is the same book all the way.

We know our traditional ways, but we still want to learn someone else's life.

Baptists used to come up here [Sitsomovi]. They had a portable organ in a suitcase. They'd come up in a car. They pull the legs out and open the top. They used to sing right in the plaza, there in Sitsomovi. A lot of men and ladies sit around and talk and sing—tease. A lot of these old people they used to sing with them. They had songs in Hopi, too.

Mormons used to come and go from house to house. We're always glad to see somebody—strangers or something—they want to help. We're right there. In return they try teaching us this little English. I want to turn right back and try to help them out. They brought food (Black 1984).

The Mormons may well have been tolerant of Hopi religious beliefs and practices, but their prescriptions for converting the Indians entailed a persistent and doctrinaire program for assimilation. David Flake, in his study of Mormon missions among the Hopis, Navajos, and Zunis, wrote: "The Mormon religion was rigidly based upon European culture and would not yield to lowering itself until a common ground with the Indians was reached. . . . The Church was quite willing to wait for as many generations as necessary for the Indians to learn modern civilization . . . then the Mormons hoped to step in and find the Indians more able to live and accept their religion" (1965:85–86). Guidelines for the program of rapid assimilation included "making friends, getting into the homes as soon as possible, with pictures of Indian people . . . they like pictures" (Buchanan 1960:5, 12).

Nonetheless, the Hopis found the Mormons to be helpful. Bourke (1884:330) noted that "Mormons have greater influence over the Oraybe Moquis who decline to have any relations whatsoever with other Caucasians." The Mormons' willingness to offer assistance, especially in time of great need, was noted by Albert Yava. In the wake of severe food shortages following the devastating smallpox epidemic of 1898, Albert's mother and stepfather went down to the Mormon settlement at present-day Joseph City, where they were allowed to gather the unharvested remains of wheat and trade clothing for food (Yava 1978:13).

Yava also had some critical observations about Hopi and Tewa responses to missionaries: "One thing is clear. The Hopis and Tewas who convert from our traditional religion have taken themselves out of our traditional ways. The missionaries have had a great deal to do with the destruction of Hopi-Tewa religion. In a way, they are competing with each other to see who can do the most destruction. I guess you can't blame the missionaries too much. They are doing what they believe they are supposed to do. If our traditional religion is passing away, you have to blame the Hopis and Tewas themselves" (1978:136).

Alcohol on the
Reservation

Pabanale voiced concern about the impact of alcohol on the future of the Hopis. He saw the problem primarily as a matter of stopping the illegal supply of whiskey from sources in the border areas. He was frustrated with the unwillingness of the tribal council to recognize the problem and take appropriate action to deal with it.

At the Hopi Hearings in 1955, David Mononge, an influential Hopi traditionalist from Hotvela, said that unless something was done to stop the drinking, "not much good will be had from these new ideas of [providing] more schools and better education." He, too, felt that it was the responsibility of the white man to "close down this liquor. . . . They must not allow this to come to our Hopi land" (Hopi Hearings 1955:27).

Alcohol has made its way to the Indian country for the past three hundred years. Alcohol was available from numerous trading centers, especially Taos, Jemez, and Zuni, as well as from Mexican villages where Navajos and Pueblo Indians frequently traded. The Zuni Pueblo was also a supplier to the Western Apaches, Navajos, and Hopis (Bailey 1964; McNitt 1962).

When the railroad reached Flagstaff after 1870, border towns such as Holbrook, Winslow, and Flagstaff became new sources of alcohol for the nearby reservations. In the 1880s Indians under the influence were visible in all these growing urban centers (McNitt 1962:530). By the turn of the century a well-established bootleg industry was flourishing along the southern fringes of Navajo and Hopi country. People on white ranches participated in this illicit trade, which operated north of Lees Ferry on the Colorado River (Levy and Kunitz 1974:65–66).

Neither the Indian agencies nor their police were effective in curtailing the flow of alcohol among the tribes. When Pabanale was a policeman, in 1915, he observed Navajos freely selling bootleg whiskey to Hopis near Keams Canyon. Agent Leo Crane also reported the increased use of liquor among the Navajos (Crane 1915). In the ensuing years public drunkenness became the major cause of arrest on the reservation.

Indian drinking soon became a major area of study for social scientists and specialists from a wide range of disciplines. These early investigations were generally too broad, poorly constructed, or based on illogical and ethnocentric premises. Thus, many of the stereotypes of Indian drinking, developed by non-Indians, remained unchallenged until recent years.

By contrast, early alcohol researchers Jerrold Levy and Stephen Kunitz were credible and responsible: Levy trained as an anthropologist, and Kunitz had both a medical degree (specializing in epidemiology) and a Ph.D. in sociology. Focusing on southwestern tribes, particularly the Hopis and Navajos, they looked at whether drinking patterns were culturally regulated or stemmed from social and personal disintegration within tribal communities. They found that drinking behavior was highly patterned and socially regulated by traditional culture and that this pattern was stable over time (Levy and Kunitz 1974). For example, Hopi drinking tended to be covert, steady, excessive, and prevalent in all communities (Levy and Kunitz 1974:104–5). In the progressive villages the police handled problems of deviancy, whereas in the traditional villages alcoholics were isolated and later forced to leave (Levy and Kunitz 1971).

Although Levy and Kunitz found no correlation between drinking and acculturation, they concluded that changes in certain basic regularities in a culture, such as child-rearing practices and family organization, could affect patterns of social deviance. Other possible contributors included social frustration and cultural conflict with white society, producing symptoms of anomie.

More current research on alcohol use includes Beauvais 1993, Duran 1990, Leland 1976, and May 1992.

The Smoki Dancers of
Prescott, Arizona

In 1923 a group of businessmen in the former territorial capital of Prescott organized a new tourist attraction, an entertainment pageant in which non-Indians performed Indian dances. It was conceived as an attraction to help the financially troubled Frontier Association continue with its failing rodeo.

This group of white men adopted the name Smoki People (pronounced "smoke-eye") for its attraction. The name was taken from the reviled derogatory term *Mooki*, which whites applied to the Hopis in earlier years. The word is similar to a Hopi word meaning "to die."

The Smoki Snake Dance was a source of considerable irritation to the Hopis for many years. Their efforts to persuade the Smokis to end the sacrilegious mimicking of the sacred ritual were to no avail. The dance became a successful commercial venture, and its organizers strongly resisted the wishes of the Hopi tribe.

Held each year in August, close to the date of the real Hopi Snake Dance, the Smoki pageant was dedicated to the recreation of "authentic" Indian ceremonial dances, particularly those of the southwestern Indians, and featured the Smokis' version of the Hopi Snake Dance. Some three thousand paying tourists attended this annual event. The Smokis wore costumes closely modeled after those of the Hopi snake dancers. They painted their bodies brown, wore long wigs, and clutched live bull snakes in their teeth. As recently as 1990, the chief of the white dance group, Iron Eagle, said, "We are an educational organization which represents the preservation of an ancient culture. We educate ourselves about the dances and we educate the public when they come to our shows. What we do is very serious" (*Arizona Daily Sun*, Aug. 12, 1990).

The Hopis saw these events differently. Hopi snake priests who observed the dance said it was an abomination and a blatant mockery of one of their oldest sacred rites. Said one priest: "We work at it spiritually with serious meditation because that is our belief. The Smokis work at it with billboards. It is a business attraction for a big dollar" (*Arizona Daily Sun*, Aug. 10, 1990). In 1980 tribal chairman Abbott Sekaquaptewa said performances such as the Snake Dance by persons not possessing the necessary priesthood authority can be nothing but a corruption and desecration of the sacred nature of Hopi religion (*Qua Toqti*, Sept. 11, 1980).

In 1990 tribal chairman Vernon Masayesva brought a group of Hopi religious leaders and councilmen to Prescott to demonstrate against the dance. He noted that though it is unusual for Hopis to protest anything publicly, years of useless diplomacy led his people to come to Prescott to voice their indignation. Continuation of the Smoki dance, against the wishes of the Indians, will give Prescott a "negative image as a very redneck, insensitive town," he said (*High Country News*, Oct. 8, 1990).

Reluctant to abandon such a lucrative enterprise, the Smokis indignantly maintained the justness of their efforts by affirming their love of Indian culture. One woman at the 1990 pageant blamed the Hopis for not understanding what the Smokis were trying to accomplish: "It's just a lack of communication. That's the whole thing of it. . . . It's like when you have a TV program about the Bible, about Jesus. It's like a pageant" (*High Country News*, Oct. 8, 1990).

The governor of Bacavi, who attended the protest, noted: "I see a bunch of white people acting like fools there. I probably would have shown disrespect [if I] walked off, but that is one thing they have to learn, respect" (*Arizona Daily Sun*, Aug. 10, 1990). The head councilman of the Zuni tribe added his voice to those of the Hopi protesters. He came to Prescott to see the Smokis' presentation of his tribe's Kianakwe dance. Both angry and amused, he observed: "It's just totally out of contact with the real world. They say they want to preserve the Indian ways, but I'm sure that they can have better luck trying to preserve refried beans in a Mason jar" (*High Country News*, Oct. 8, 1990). The 1990 demonstrations by the Hopis played an important role in bringing to an end the Smoki Snake Dance, which was last performed in 1991.

Migration Accounts

Fourteen variants of the Tewa migration account were examined for purposes of comparison. In addition to the one related by Pabanale as part of his story, a narrative was collected from Dewey Healing; the remaining twelve variants appear in the published literature.[1] Although varying in length, narrative content, and emphasis, the fourteen stories have similar components: the Tewas came to the Hopis in response to a plea for assistance; after defeating the Utes, the Tewas suffered from the Hopis' ingratitude and unfair treatment. Ultimately, the Tewas' honor was upheld through the imposition of a "curse" on the Hopis. These variants can be compared in terms of eight motifs structuring the story:

    I. Prologue
    II. Invitation by the Hopis and the Tewas' responses
    III. Migration to First Mesa and reception there
    IV. Mistreatment by the Hopis
    V. Battle with the Utes or other enemies
    VI. Aftermath
    VII. Confrontation over land
    VIII. Tewa curse on the Hopis

In the comparisons of the various elements of the texts, the names of the narrators are given in parentheses. Where such names are unavailable, the author's name and date of publication are noted. Table A.1 is provided as a reference guide.

I. Prologue

Two introductory themes set the stage for the story. First, the origin of the Tewas is specified. The Tewas came from C`e'wadeh/Tsaewari on the Rio Grande (Pabanale, Naranjo); they came from Paharito (Youvella); the Tewas were not Tanos (Yava). Second, the condition of the Hopis at First Mesa (Walpi) is described. The Hopis were being raided by Utes, Apaches, Navajos, Paiutes, and Comanches—"enemies" (Pabanale, Yava, Kwalákwai, Naranjo); the Hopis were "few," down to only seven families (Pabanale, Yava, Kwalákwai).

II. The Invitation

All accounts agree that two to four emissaries, representing the Hopi Snake and Bear clans, were sent as delegates to the Tewa villages at Tsewageh/C`e'wadeh on the Rio Grande.[2] In one story a Hopi Coyote clan chief accompanied the delegation (Parsons 1925:175). In another version (Youvella) the delegation was

TABLE A.I. Migration Accounts.

NARRATOR	PUEBLO	CLAN	SOURCE
Irving Pabanale	Tewa Village	Stick-Spruce	Field collection, 1968
Dewey Healing	Tewa Village	Corn	Field collection, 1982
Albert Yava	Tewa Village	Bear-Spruce	Yava 1978
Kwalákwai	Walpi	Rain-Cloud	Mindeleff 1891 Fewkes 1899
Unknown			Parsons 1925
Hatco		Bear	Fewkes 1900
Wéhé		Katsina	Stephen 1936
Naranjo	Santa Clara		Harrington 1916
Tayhün			Stephen 1936
Bert Youvella		Snake-Sand	Hopi Hearings 1955
Polakka			Nelson 1937
Unknown			Courlander 1971
Unknown	Tewa Village		Dozier 1954

sent to a Tano village to ask for assistance, and the Tano chief (Mustard clan) readily agreed. The eagerness of the Tanos worried the Hopis, who were afraid the Tanos might turn against them in the future, making war on the Hopis instead of on their enemies.

Each delegation made four visits to the Tewas requesting their help to fight the Utes. The first three requests were rejected: the Tewas wanted time to reflect on the matter, did not want their people to get killed, or did not want to leave their home at C`e'wadeh. On the fourth visit the Hopis brought offerings of *pahos* (prayer sticks) for the Tewa chief. The number varied between three and eight, representing a pledge or "sacred promise" made to the Tewas in return for their assistance. The predominant grouping of three *pahos* of different lengths, painted blue and yellow and tied with feathers, represented land, women, fertility, water, a place to build a village, and rain.

In one variant the Hopis made a sand painting of large stalks of corn that were grown on lands promised to the Tewas. Extending both arms to indicate the size of the ears of corn that grew on this land, the Hopis promised that "all this will be yours if you will come and live among us as our protectors. In our land you will have plenty to eat and your storehouses will be full" (Dozier 1954:353). The pledge was usually made in the first person, emphasizing its significance (Yava, Pabanale, Youvella, Dozier).

In Pabanale's account the Hopi chief instructed the delegation to take along the woven cape (*atö'ö*) worn by the female Katsinas. It was embroidered in red, blue, and white and represented fertility.

In Youvella's story the Hopi delegation mistakenly visited a Tano village, where it was received enthusiastically, the Tanos agreeing to what was asked of them. The Hopis returned home and later made a second visit to "that country," losing their way at night and entering a Tewa village. There they offered tobacco as a greeting, smoked with the Tewa chief, and made a similar request for assistance, as in the other tales. On the third visit, after the offering of *pahos* and the pledge, the Hopis were questioned concerning their treatment of people: "Do you have the habit of taking food away from people after it is placed before them? When they reach out, maybe you have a habit of taking it away from them?" The Tewa chief also asked whether there was any pestilence or disease, indicating that he did not want his children to go hungry or be sick. The Hopis answered that their children usually had a gum disease, a slight fever, and a rash. The Tewa replied that there were too many illnesses and that they were not present at Tewa. Having made the point of the Tewas' greater cleanliness, the chief agreed to allow some of his people to go to Hopi.

In all variants the Tewas accepted the Hopi invitation, but only on the fourth visit and only after receiving offerings and pledges of land and living space.

III. The Migration

Subthemes include the preparations for departure, the clans involved, and the itinerary and length of the journey. Preparations for departure were made in eight days and included the making of weapons, clothing, and the like. The Tewa chief selected participants from "half the houses in a certain row" (Pabanale) or decided that "only those on a certain side of the village would be allowed to go" (Youvella). All the Tewas wanted to go, but the chief said that "only half the village would go," led by a man named Agaiotsay (Yava); the Tewa chief called out, "'Who wants to go to Kosoówinge (Walpi) can go in four days, but not all.' All wanted to go, so they started" (Parsons 1925:176).

The departure from the Rio Grande involved two hundred men, women, and children (Yava); two to three bands, the first consisting of 146 women (Kwalákwai); "everyone left Tsaewari" (Naranjo).

Three variants list the Tewa clans that are believed to have participated in the migration. Pabanale cites eight clans that went to First Mesa: Stick, Sun, Cloud, Cottonwood, Tobacco, Katsina, Sand, and Butterfly. Youvella notes that the Bear clan took the lead, followed by the Tobacco, Sun, and Corn clans. Dozier observes that the narrative mentions only the Bear clan, which left ahead of the

195

others: "When our clan arrived at Hopi, they secured a village site and farm lands, and then sent for the other clans" (1954:338).

According to Youvella, the Tewas had to send for a Corn clan person to lead them, as they did not have cornmeal to bless the path they were to take. A Corn clan woman came and sprinkled cornmeal on the pathway and they all followed. Pabanale says a Stick clan man sprinkled cornmeal on the ground, putting a feather down on it.

Four accounts specify the itinerary. According to two variants collected by Fewkes (from Kwalákwai and Hatco), the Tewas made the following stops along their journey: Jemez, Duck Water (Pawikpa), Bear Spring (Kepo, or present-day Fort Wingate), Fort Defiance, Pueblo Ganado (Wukópakabi), and Keams Canyon (Puñci). At East Mesa they built a pueblo near Isba, or Coyote Spring (near the present trail to the mesa), traces of which can be found at Yellow Rock Mound (Sikya'owatsmo), a ridge of land above the spring.

Yava's itinerary includes four stops: Cañoncito, a little north of Laguna Pueblo; Duck Spring (Awpimpaw), near Grants, New Mexico; Reed Spring (Bopaw), near Ganado, where they "planted some sacred things" and rested; and the Place of Bubbling Water in Keams Canyon (Kwalálata, or Pawsaiyeh in Tewa). Here more "sacred things" were planted and temporary houses built. From there they came to Walpi.

Pabanale makes scant reference to the route taken by the migrants. They stopped at Santa Clara, then came to some pueblos, and finally to Ganado, where they buried some *pahos*. This was done as a protective measure; should they be mistreated by the Hopis, they would settle here instead of going back to C`e'wadeh. On their arrival at Keams Canyon, they came to Kwalálata (Place of Bubbling Water), where they saw the water standing a foot high above the ground. They moved on from there to First Mesa, where they were instructed by the Hopis to build homes "on a high rock" (Yellow Rock Mound).

In Youvella's narrative the Tewas also reached First Mesa after making four stops along the way—Ganado, Steamboat Canyon, Peach Springs, and Keams Canyon—staying a while at the last two places. When they reached Steamboat Canyon, some old men decided to settle there, offering as their reason, "Should we stay here and become something different, we will help you in your struggle." Unable to proceed because the distance was too far for them, the old people were left there and the remaining Tewas continued westward.

According to Youvella, the Tewas employed an element of magical assistance in their trek across the desert: "We were equipped with an object that when placed in the soil, would produce a spring of flowing water whereby on our way we would quench our thirst" (1955:354). At First Mesa they were told to settle on the ridge south of Coyote Spring, where they stayed "quite a while."

All accounts agree that the Tewas settled in an area removed from the mesa—Yellow Stone Hills, on the east side below the Gap. Kwalákwai refers to this settlement as Kohti, where the ground plan reveals much debris from long occupation (Fewkes 1899:257).

IV. Mistreatment by the Hopis

All variants strongly condemn the Hopis for their mistreatment of the Tewas on their arrival. The Tewas were received rudely, Ute raids had ceased, and the Walpis reneged on their promise to provide land and water (Kwalákwai). The Tewa were refused access to the mesa and were forced to stay below (Parsons 1925:176; Dozier 1954:339, 1966:17; Pabanale; Youvella 1955:354; Polakka).

The Hopis are scorned for their callous treatment of the Tewas when they came up to Walpi requesting food. As the Tewas had no vessels to receive the food, the Walpi women told them to cup their hands and poured boiling hot cornmeal gruel on them, or they had to lick cornmeal off the stirring sticks (Dozier, Kwalákwai, Youvella, Pabanale, Healing). The Tewas burned themselves and let the food slip through their hands to the ground. The Hopi women observed, "You're probably not hungry." They then laughed at them and berated them for being weak and soft. The Tewas got angry and said, "We shouldn't have come" (Healing).

V. The Battle with the Utes

The specific details of the battle differ, but ultimately the Utes were defeated and returned to their home country after promising never to attack the mesa again.

The account by Dozier treats the battle summarily: the enemy was defeated, and life was made safe for the Hopis. All the other narratives provide varying degrees of detail with some unusual variations. In Yava's account "the Walpis did a strange thing; they contacted the Utes and challenged them to attack Walpi. They said, 'We have some real fighters here now. Why don't you come and try to drive them off?'" Yava speculates that the Hopis had a change of heart and wanted to get the Tewas out before they had a chance to settle, or perhaps "they just wanted to test them." Healing, too, introduces the element of testing: "To see if the Tewa lived up to their reputation as warriors, the Hopi brought the Utes from the north to fight them. Just to test these people out, they hired some warriors from somewhere—the Utes" (Healing).

Yava is skeptical about the appearance of the Utes. Four days after the Hopis challenged the Utes, a messenger from Walpi came down to the Tewa camp and said that the Utes were coming. Yava speculates: "Now, how in the world did the Walpi people know that the Utes were coming? It's something our people often thought about" (1978:29). The Tewas refused to engage the enemy immediately, as recounted by Pabanale and Youvella. In both instances the Tewas said they were hungry. They finally agreed to do battle after four requests were made. Youvella reports a seemingly angry interchange between the Hopis and the Tewas in the course of these requests. In addition to stating hunger as their reason for not engaging the Utes, the Tewas said "that they were afraid and did not have the courage to go out and meet the enemy." At the fourth request the Hopis

197

told them, "You came here to fight for us and that is the purpose of coming out here" (1955:355).

Preparations for the battle included the fixing of bows and arrows, spears, shields, and war clubs (Yava, Pabanale, Wéhé); painting the body with red paint and donning eagle war bonnets (Pabanale); tying buckskins around the loins, applying white clay to the legs, and staining the body and arms with red ocher (Kwalákwai).

The Tewas moved to the top of the Gap to engage the Utes when several Hopis appeared, ready to take part in the fight. The Tewas said, "You can stay at home; we will go out and meet the enemy and suffer the consequences" (Youvella 1955:355).

The Tewas sent scouts out on three successive nights and reported the Utes traveling at night on horseback. The following day they recognized these horsemen as Utes because they were wearing mirrors that reflected the light (Yava); from the top of the Gap the Tewas saw the Utes, some of whom were on horseback, a mile and a half away (Pabanale). The Tewas ran down the other side of the Gap (to the east) to meet the enemy, perched on a high ridge (Youvella, Wéhé).

Detailed descriptions of the battle are given by Pabanale, Yava, and Youvella. Yava singularly identifies the Tewa leader as Agaiotsay, a village chief, spokesman, and war chief. He divided his forces in two, to hit the Utes in the front and in the rear.

The Tewas drove the Utes up toward Wepo (three miles north of Tewa Village), where they had built their defenses on a ridge by piling up sacks of pounded meat made from the carcasses of sheep run off from the Hopis (Healing, Yava, Youvella, Parsons, Kwalákwai, Wéhé, Hatco). The battlefield became known as Meat Point, Meat Pinnacle, or Flesh Gap (Sikwítukwi in Hopi, Touchyoowidi in Tewa).

The Utes were defeated through various flanking maneuvers and frontal assaults (Youvella, Wéhé, Yava). The number of survivors is given variously. No Utes survived (Kwalákwai in Mindeleff 1891); one boy survived (Parsons 1925:176); all but two were killed (Kwalákwai in Fewkes 1899; Healing); all but one were killed (Wéhé); all but four were killed (Tayhün); all but two or four were killed (Hatco); all but three were killed (Yava). No indication of the number of Utes who survived is given by Pabanale or Youvella. In the fragment from Naranjo the enemy is identified as the Navajo and all but one were killed (Harrington 1916:257).

Before the survivors left to return home to report their defeat at the hands of the "Tewa Bears" or the "Warrior Tewas," there is a dramatic exchange between the surviving Ute (usually a chief) and the Tewa chief. It is one of the pinnacles of the tale, for it enhances the status of the Tewas as exceptional and respected warriors. The Utes learned that their victors were not Hopis but Tewas. They called the Tewas their brothers or cousins (Youvella, Yava, Pabanale) and expressed regret that they had fought them; they vowed never to fight them again, as the Tewas were the best fighters to have defeated the Utes. In Youvella's more expansive account the Ute chief praised the Tewas: "I am a great fighter, but I have never encountered anyone who has beat me in battle . . . it is no wonder that you fought like you did." In the same account there is a final expression of remorse by the Ute chief: "I have never met an enemy like I did today. I am just like a wasp; whenever I am molested, I follow the person who has molested me and I don't let go of him. You have done me misery, my brother."

A final symbolic ceremony of farewell occurred between the former antagonists when the Ute chief exchanged his bow, made of elk horn, for the Tewa bow, saying, "Take my bow as a token. It is not made of wood but elk horn; it will never rot. Only when this bow rots will we ever meet you again in battle. So you see, we will have peace forever" (Yava, Pabanale, Youvella).

VI. The Aftermath

On their way back to their camp the Tewas took some scalps and removed the hearts from four of the bravest fallen Ute warriors (Yava); according to Pabanale, only the heart of the first Ute killed was removed; or the Tewa took the hearts of the fallen enemy, their scalps, and also some of the hands and the flesh inside the palms (Youvella). These trophies were buried in a pit on a sandhill one mile from the Gap (Pabanale), or they were buried where the Tewas first met the Utes (Yava). The Tewa chief marked the place with a ring of stone, saying, "Let us see what will grow out of their grave. Whatever it is, we'll protect it and keep it growing" (Yava). "If anything grows above this, do not chop it down, let it stand" (Youvella). In Pabanale's text the chief said, "The ones who will be living here will know what will grow on this hill—maybe a tree of some kind. That place is called 'Place of the Hearts'" (Píngto'i in Tewa, 'iwáktana in Hopi). "A juniper tree is growing there inside that ring of stones" (Yava).[3]

The Tewa victory over the Utes is memorialized by carvings of Ute shields in the sandstone cliffs on the road up to First Mesa. This event is noted only in Pabanale's tale: "They went to the foot of the mesa and they drew a round shield, a Ute shield, on that rock. They carved lines near that shield for each one [Ute] that was killed. That is our record; that is proof of what the Tewa had done when they got here."

VII. The Confrontation over Land

On their return to the mesa the Tewas engaged in a confrontation with the Hopis over the distribution of land and the location of a village site for themselves. Four of the narratives present this confrontation in the form of three offers of land and settlement which were rejected by the Tewas. A fourth offer was made, and it was accepted. The thrust of this exchange is the loyalty of the Tewas to their agreement to help fight the enemy and the reluctance of the Hopis, who are portrayed as fearful of Tewa encroachment and intransigent in fulfilling their pledge.

Land offered the Tewas below the mesa was refused because it was too vulnerable (Pabanale); similarly, a village site north of the Gap was rejected because the Tewas would be unable to protect the Hopis on the mesa (Yava, Healing, Youvella). The second offer of a village site on the south side of the Gap was also refused (Pabanale, Yava, Healing, Youvella). A third offer of land which was somewhat larger was again refused because of lack of room for expansion (Pabanale, Youvella); an offer to settle the Tewas in the middle of the mesa was turned down for similar reasons. In Yava's account the Tewa chief, Agaiotsay, accepted the third offer of land for settlement, which was marked by a shrine of petrified wood. In the remaining accounts the fourth offer was accepted (Pabanale, Youvella, Healing).

Farming land was also given the Tewas north and west of the mesa. The shorter narratives merely note that farmland and a place on top of the mesa were offered (Parsons 1925; Kwalákwai in Fewkes 1899). An interesting reference to an earlier occupation of Hano (Tewa Village) by the Asa clan is found in Kwalákwai's account (Mindeleff 1891), in which the Hopis gave the Tewas old houses built by the Asa in Hano.

The offer of women, promised by the Hopis, was rejected by Agaiotsay, who admonished, "Wait, let us not go too fast. First we have to see how well our villages live together" (Yava).

VIII. *The Tewa Curse*

The final motif of the Tewa migration account concerns the curse placed on the Hopis by the Tewas as revenge for their mistreatment. In five of the tales the Tewas exacted retribution from the Hopis by promising that they "will never learn the Tewa language, but the Tewa will learn to speak Hopi."

The ritual by which the curse was effected involved an exchange of corn, representing the Tewa and Hopi languages. The Hopi chief was the first to chew the piece of corn and handed it to the Tewa chief, who swallowed it, thereby acquiring the Hopi language. When the Hopi asked the Tewa to do the same—to chew a piece of corn and hand it to the Hopi so that he might learn the Tewa tongue— the Tewa refused, saying, "I won't be able to; I had a hard time swallowing yours, I almost vomited. You look handsome and good. I am afraid you will vomit if you take what I place in your mouth" (Youvella, Healing, Pabanale, Yava).

In Yava's version the Tewa chief took the initiative in the exchange by giving the Hopi the corn, telling him to chew it. When the Tewa had ingested the corn, the Hopi asked, "What is the meaning of this?" The Tewa replied, "It means that we will take from your mouth the language you speak. We will speak Hopi." According to Healing, the Hopi spit the corn into the Tewa's mouth, then asked the Tewa to do the same. The Tewa chief, having refused to give the Hopi his chewed corn, dug a deep hole in the ground and he and all the Tewas spit the corn into the hole, filling it with earth and rocks (Yava, Healing,

Pabanale, Dozier); or the Tewa chief gathered his people on top of the mesa and had each one dig a hole. He spit into his and bade the rest do the same (Youvella).

In what may be a Hopi version of the tale, or a mix-up in its telling, Kwalákwai's rendition of the events is reversed, with the Hopi refusing to accept the Tewa's chewed corn. The reason given is similar to the other tales: "It would make us vomit." The final affront to the Hopis is found in the remarks of the Tewa chief on sealing the pit(s), rendered in several of the accounts. "You will never have our language in your mouth. We will speak Hopi and Tewa but you will never speak Tewa. If you were to speak our Tewa, you would be able to infiltrate our rituals and ceremonies and you would interfere with our way of doing things" (Yava). "If the Hopi learn our language they might mistreat us and lose respect for us. So our secrets are going to be hidden away and they won't be able to learn them" (Pabanale). "I did this because if the Hopi wanted to learn our language they will just mock us because of our language. You, my children, are quick tempered and I know you will be angry and probably fight back because they would be mocking you. We don't want to have any trouble. I think we will be able to learn their language" (Youvella). "Because you have behaved in a manner unbecoming to human beings, we have sealed knowledge of our language and our way of life from you. You and your descendants will never learn our language and our ceremonies, but we will learn yours. We will ridicule you in both your language and our own" (Dozier).

The shorter, fragmentary accounts of Kwalákwai (Fewkes), Naranjo (Harrington), Tayhün, Wéhé, and Parsons do not contain the elements of the corn exchange and the curse.

The migration account and the effective stigma of the curse have perpetuated the saga of Hopi ingratitude, functioning as a mechanism of revenge on the Hopis. To this day the Hopis do not speak Tewa; those who are married to Tewas understand it but are ridiculed if they attempt to speak it.

Drilling for Oil on the Reservation

Emory Sekaquaptewa commented:

The geodetic surveys were the first kinds of surveys that came into the reserve after the IRA. As a result, these surveys, which put iron pipes into the ground, raised a lot of suspicion about those survey markers. This included the possibility that the white man has come in now and had located some rich minerals and they marked places that they were going to take away from the Hopi people, and give it to the Navajos.

We were warned by our parents not to disturb these markers. I knew where they were in our area—marked 1936. Section markers. Steel posts with government warnings on them. Probably the first official survey done on the Hopi land itself—1936.

The superintendent of the time had to have some explanations for them, in order to allay any fears and suspicions of the Hopi people.

About 1955–56 they began to approach the Hopi concerning the possible development of coal mining by Peabody. The first ten thousand dollars that the Hopi ever earned was the money offered by Peabody, for exploration for coal.

Peabody wanted to put a hold on any prospecting—to be done at a later time. The money was "good faith" payment for future lease. This was on Black Mesa. Thereafter, that materialized into a full-fledged lease. By 1958 the lease was a fact, when the Hopi entered into a lawsuit with the Navajo tribe.

Somewhere between 1958 and 1962 the Hopi Tribe signed a full-fledged coal mining lease with Peabody. One of the reasons was the Navajos had already entered into a lease agreement with Peabody, and there was a possibility that the feds would give their approval to this lease agreement—a legal requirement. Even with only the Navajo signature, if the Hopis wanted to preserve their right in the coal, they were forced to enter into this leasehold for half of the interest. They wanted to be sure to do that while the suit was pending, to protect their interest in it.

This was another area where the BIA was very lax. To my knowledge, that was the first official lease that paid Hopis money for valuable minerals. I also believe that it was also at the same time that various major oil companies got interested in the area for exploration. The tribe followed the rule of asking the BIA to announce bids for exploration leases. Five or six companies made offers for exploration leases, for oil, which covered only District 6, at that time. They did not want to bring the Navajo in or give them any opportunity to be a party to any lease agreement for exploration.

After 1962 the Navajo acquired an interest in [the] 1882 [area] outside of District 6, by the decision of the federal tribunal established to hear a quiet title suit to the 1882 reservation.

Out of these exploration leases the tribe raised $3.4 million. That is what got the tribal government on its feet and it really became significant. The council was paying its way; people began to look at the council for employment opportunities. It also stimulated the resistance movement by the so-called traditionalists.

Toward the end of the oil exploration leases, one company—not a successful bidder—somehow was able to discover that the Baptist church on the north side of Musangnuvi held a leasehold on its land site, which was accomplished before the tribal council was formed. It did not require tribal council approval to legitimize the leasehold. It was strictly between the Baptist church and the BIA, who was interested in bringing mission churches in there because they were given some responsibility for Indian education.

Apparently, this was quite an open-ended lease, so this oil company assumed that the lease was private and they needed only an agreement with the church, to come in with their equipment. At this point, mid-1960s, Abbott [Sekaquaptewa] was chairman—the term of the office was still one year.

Abbott was still working as a court clerk and also at the same time he was chairman of the tribal council. Somehow he discovered that the oil company was moving in their rigs. He then went on the highway and challenged this great big caravan of rigs, between Musangnuvi and Polacca. He argued with them that they may have a lease right to explore at that place, but they have to go through the Hopi country, for which they have no authority or permission. The court ruled in his favor.

There were several places within this area that were drilled during the exploration period. Now all those leases have run out. It's not certain whether they ever found any oil (Black 1984).

Pabanale noted:

When I was first a delegate [to the tribal council], that had been brought up and we agreed, the council agreed to have them drill when Mr. Ladd was our superintendent. But on account of all this talk that the Navajo made against the Hopi, it hasn't yet been drilled. However, they found the oil all right. They drilled an oil well at Second Mesa. I don't know what company came out and did that, but because they didn't report that to the agency before drilling, that is why they were stopped. It is right there by the mission church, right there is where they drilled. I don't know what company. But as they didn't ask first, that's why they stopped it. They got the oil all right but

203

without Second Mesa knowing that they were drilling that well. The only thing that Second Mesa people agreed on is just the church but not drilling. Just to have the church, they agreed to that, but it was just a little way from the church where they drilled for oil. They found it, see, and so that proves that we have oil, but I don't think I will see it myself. I don't think I will have time to have any money from the oil, as I am old now. I don't know when they will drill that. That time, as I have said before, when I was a councilman, we agreed to it, but on account of one man, that hasn't been done, on account of a man named Maho, Hopi Fire clan. He's also a subchief and he's the one that said that until we get the land that will be exclusively Hopi, there will be no drilling. And so it was not drilled, see. But they did find the oil all right and they know that oil because they came and went around the reservation looking for oil and they found it. As I said, it was on account of these Navajos that they haven't drilled it yet.

NOTES

Introduction

1. In earlier times when food was scarce the Paiutes would sell their children to other tribes, knowing that they would be taken care of. Talasayo was a Paiute who grew up among the Arizona Tewas. It is likely that he kept Pabanale from returning to school because he was needed to herd sheep and assist in other ways.

2. Wuwtsim, in November, is the time for celebrating the renewal of life and the rebirth of all living things. The Wuwtsim ceremony, which marks the symbolic emergence of the Hopis from the underworld, begins with the preparation of new fires in all the houses. Wuwtsim is also the occasion for inducting young men into full adult status. After their initiation they are eligible to join the religious societies.

3. The newly created northern Tewa town of San Cristobal was also known as C'e'wadeh (Dozier 1954:237) or C'ewareh (Fewkes 1899:258). In the San Juan dialect of the Tewa language it means "broad white line," referring to a conspicuous belt of soft white rock. Both the Arizona Tewas and the Rio Grande Tewas recognize the ruined remains as the place from which the Arizona Tewas migrated to First Mesa. The ruin is also known as Yam P'ham-ba, the village the Tanos constructed in the vicinity of Santa Cruz after the 1680 uprising, when they forsook the Galisteo region and moved north to be closer to their Tewa relatives (Harrington 1916:254).

The Coming of the Tewas

1. *Paho*s are prayer sticks or prayer feathers, ritual offerings used to communicate with the supernaturals. Prayer sticks usually consist of a pair of painted sticks to which are attached feathers, a corn husk, or parts of plants. They are tied together with native-grown cotton and placed at wells, shrines, and fields. Prayer feathers consist of eagle-down feathers on a cotton string which are similarly tied to special offerings and places. There are many varieties of *pahos* made for different ceremonial occasions.

2. Rooftop announcements were made in all the Hopi villages to announce upcoming events, ceremonies, and village activities. They were usually done at dusk or just before dawn when atmospheric conditions were ideal for carrying the human voice to all parts of the village.

3. Before all sacred events, as a blessing, Pueblo priests spread a path of corn-

meal on which the participants must walk. Sometimes eagle-down prayer feathers, signifying the breath of life, are laid down along the cornmeal path.

4. The Gap is a visible cleft or separation in First Mesa.

5. Wepo is the site of a prehistoric wash that made possible extensive flood farming around A.D. 1000. It is located twelve to fifteen miles north of the Hopi villages of First Mesa.

6. The Cottonwood clan (*t'eh*) at Tewa Village is the equivalent of the Katsina clan. Both Cottonwood and Katsina clans are known as Okuwa, or Cloud clans. Okuwa is the Rio Grande Tewa term for Katsina. In Hopi tradition the Katsina clans came from the east and included Crow and Cottonwood (Fewkes 1900:584).

7. Albert Yava's account of the migration also makes reference to the taking of Ute scalps by the Tewas (1978:31). Harold Courlander notes the occurrence of scalping among the Hopis. In one of the oral narratives of the Warrior Twin Gods, Pokianghoya, the younger of the two brothers, took an Apache scalp (1971:74).

8. See Appendix 1 for different versions of the clans that traveled to the Hopis.

The Early Years

1. Talasayo was a Paiute Indian adopted by Tewa Village in the late nineteenth century. His Paiute name was Yane', and he was Pabanale's adopted uncle. Fewkes (1900:621–22) notes that a Yane' belonging to the Cloud clan lived in Tewa Village.

2. This is the household to which Pabanale refers:

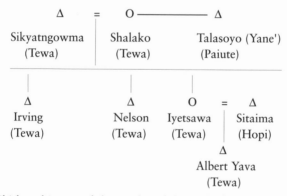

3. Piki bread is one of the staples of the Hopi diet. It is a wafer-thin bread made of a mixture of blue cornmeal, ash, and water and is spread thinly by hand on a hot stone. As it bakes, it is folded like a long napkin.

4. During the smallpox epidemic of 1898 the disease spread from the New Mexico Pueblos to the Hopi villages. Pueblos could not be quarantined because the traditionalists insisted on participating in communal dances or visiting other

Pueblos to watch the dances (U.S. Department of the Interior 1899:249). Not all Hopis were susceptible to smallpox. They had suffered repeated epidemic attacks, including a particularly serious one in 1853. Consequently, all or nearly all the adults in the population over forty-five years of age had acquired some immunity (Dobyns 1984:13–14).

5. Fred Harvey was an enterprising businessman who saw the need for providing quality dining facilities along the route of the Santa Fe railroad, beginning in 1876. His Harvey Houses soon became common along the route, providing fresh food prepared by well-groomed chefs and served in a hospitable environment with Irish linen tablecloths, fine china, and a cadre of trained and attractive attendants known as the Harvey Girls.

6. The Indian Allotment Act of 1887 mandated the breakup of reservation lands into individual plots to be distributed to adult males and used for farming and grazing. The goal of this policy was to instill in the Indians the value of private ownership and individualism and to abolish what whites saw as the insidious practice of communal ownership. After the land was allotted, extensive "surplus" lands could be sold to white settlers. Beginning in 1891, several attempts were made to allot Hopi lands. More than one hundred thousand acres were surveyed and allotted, and stakes were driven into the ground to mark the plots. The Hopis vigorously opposed allotment, and they pulled up and destroyed the survey stakes. Communal land tenure was tightly interwoven in the fabric of traditional clan structures and religious beliefs, and therefore allotment was doomed before it began. Further attempts at allotment were abandoned in 1911. Matthew Murphy was a special allotment agent for the Hopis from 1908 to 1911.

A Trip to Zuni

1. The Arizona Tewas have been participants in Hopi religious life for more than a century. Their young people become initiated into both Hopi and Arizona Tewa religious societies. Among the Hopis the Powamu Society is responsible for initiating boys and girls between the ages of eight and ten into the Katsina religion. After their initiation the boys take an active part in Katsina ceremonies. At about the age of fourteen an Arizona Tewa boy prepares for the full status of manhood by being initiated into the Winter Solstice Society, a ceremony usually held every four years in November. The newly acquired status of manhood enables him to participate fully in religious affairs.

2. During the public portion of the final night of the nine-day curing ceremony known as the Nightway, masked impersonators of the supernaturals appear as dancers in a public exhibition known as the Yebechai Dance. The Nightway is performed to cure a variety of head ailments, including eye and ear diseases, as well as mental illness.

3. San Juan Paiutes were in the area of Tuba City as early as 1776, as reported by Escalante (Bolton 1949:23–31). In 1823 Vizcarra encountered them

on White Mesa. The Paiutes claim to have been the first occupants of the Tuba City area, and a group of them has been living around Moenave, west of Tuba City, for many years. Paiutes, as well as Navajos and Hopis, used the Tuba City area as far as the Little Colorado River for farming and grazing, especially during the summer months. Paiutes at Willow Springs were stealing cattle from settlers and selling them in the Flagstaff area as early as 1890. A brief note in the Tuba City letterbooks for October 27, 1914, indicates that "Utes are included with the Paiutes as one of the two marauding groups" (Tuba City Letterbooks, I.1 and I.2, Misc. Coll., Museum of Northern Arizona Library). Third Mesa Hopis agreed that the Paiutes and Utes were traditional predators on the Hopis, especially during trading days (Black 1984).

4. The Hopis and Navajos have clans with similar names, and people of the two tribes who share a clan believe themselves to be clan relatives. Pabanale's Bear clan is grouped with the Stick and Fir clan. It is also possible that the woman was a Hopi, taken as a captive by the Navajo. A third possibility was given by Dewey Healing: "Navajos have clan—Bear clan—but if you have something good on you, they always ask first what clan you are. Then if you tell them what clan you are, then without hesitation they'll tell you, I'm your clan, too."

5. This was preparation for the Tewa Winter Solstice Ceremony (Tahntahy), which corresponds to the Hopi Soyal Ceremony. It is a time for initiation into manhood and is also a ceremony of rebirth. Prayer feathers are made by each family for placement at plaza shrines in the village.

Becoming a Policeman

1. Nelson Oyaping, Irving Pabanale's older brother, was an aggressive, restless person who looked to herding rather than farming to make a living. He was not afraid to tackle anything and was appointed a policeman by Tom Polacca. He also was active in the government agency's attempt to modernize the Hopis and introduce Euro-American technology and ideology to the reservation. In addition, he strongly supported establishing a school at Keams Canyon.

2. Tsaihaskai is a Navajo settlement located north along the Polacca Valley at the third artesian well, where Pabanale was building a house.

3. In attempting to curb the traffic in liquor on the Navajo reservation, the undermanned agency police force faced an impossible task. Indian agents dutifully reported the incidence of liquor among the Navajos, as Leo Crane did in his superintendent's report for 1915:

> The Agency court record for the year 1915 shows a number of cases of minor importance and one of the introduction of liquor by an Indian. With respect to liquor it must be reported that while the Hopi continues a sober tribe, absolutely opposed to the use of intoxicants, the Navajos of the reservation have been procuring more and more liquor. The whiskey is brought in by visiting Indians traveling over unfrequented

208

trails, from the direction of Gallup, New Mexico, the only "wet" [area] within reasonable distance of the jurisdiction. These Indian whiskey peddlers have to cross the Fort Defiance Navajo Reservation, and whereas it is understood considerable effort has been made to apprehend them, it is undoubtedly true that at practically every Navajo dance whiskey has been reported. The Moqui Superintendent has on many occasions given as his judgment and opinion that for the restriction of the liquor trade, gambling, and general loose living, the only officers at hand (full-blood Indian police) are well nigh worthless. It has been found impossible on the Moqui Indian Reservation to procure the services of efficient Navajo police. The Hopi police are well enough in their way with their own people, but are useless in the control of areas where the Navajos reside. The Navajo policeman will report concerning gambling and liquor using many days after the occurrence and he will have vague evidence with which to support his charges. He will never report against his friends or members of his clan, and seldom it is that he will arrest any Indian except for personal reasons. Then, too, the Navajos do not present practical possibilities of strict supervision in any respect, for the reason that they are nomads, here today, and 40 miles away tomorrow, and such a condition in an area of reservation larger than many eastern states presents problems that it is likely no Government official could control satisfactorily without the assistance of intelligent and energetic peace officers. (Crane 1915)

"Blossom Bride"

1. Anita Baldwin was a wealthy woman related to the Baldwin estate in California. She came to the reservation to determine what was needed by the Hopis and eventually collected wagons, harnesses, shovels, and other farming implements. Much of it was sent to Tom Polacca, who distributed it to the people. *Blossom Bride* was a dramatization of a traditional Hopi wedding; Pabanale acted the part of a brother of the bride. The play showed how the young unmarried girls wore their hair in the traditional side whorls, representing the squash blossom (*naasomi*), the emblem of fertility. After marriage the hair is worn long and uncurled (*poli'ini*).

2. The Arizona Tewas traditionally used eagle-feather headdresses (*cheeteh*) in social dances, a form of dress probably borrowed from the Southern Plains tribes. Some extended to the knees, and others were shorter. The Hopis never used them.

3. The store was located in Pabanale's old house, which he had built some years earlier. It was first used by his sister, and he then added to it and lived in it himself. In more recent years his daughter Edith and her husband lived there with some of their children.

209

Becoming a Medicine Man

1. In December the Soyal ceremony begins the new year. At this time the earth is frozen and danger lurks in the villages because witches are active. It is the occasion to welcome the return of the sun and, with its warmth, the rebirth of all living things. The first Katsinas of the new season also arrive at this time.

2. The deity Sootukwnangwu helped create the earth. He also appears as a Katsina during the Powamu, or Bean Dance procession, on Third Mesa. He has a white conical cap and a short cape. He follows the procession very quietly after a wide gap, then stops and makes a circle around the top of the kiva. He stops at the far end of the ladder leading into the kiva and strikes his lightning, which is a frame that is made to stretch out. He does this four times, then swings his bull roarer. This act is symbolic of the earth's fertility.

The Indian Reorganization Act

1. The buttes and cliffs where eagle nests are located designate the extent of Hopi land. They are the property of different clans and are related to the former migrations of the clans. Members of one clan do not trespass on buttes that are the property of another clan (Beaglehole 1936:18; Fewkes 1900:690–707; Voth 1912). "Eagles build permanent nests in those buttes and cliffs, which they come back to each year. That's how the Hopi know just where to go to get them. Clan groups each have certain places which are marked out. Eagles mark out clan lands" (Black 1984).

2. Comment by Emory Sekaquaptewa:

> After the emergence, these people who were to become Hopi set out to find their promised land. There was disagreement among them as to which way was the "right" way. They didn't know that this was part of the plan set out for them by the god Masawu, who set out the Hopi Way of Life, symbolized by that short ear of corn. In the course of their separate migrations, the Hopis relied on the corn to find suitable planting areas to survive. Eventually, the people who went into separate directions were to come back to where the Hopis are today. It was their destiny to come back together, but they would come back with more knowledge about the world. So they were bringing all this knowledge gained from their migrations and when they settled together they would have made "footprints" along the migration route, as the Hopis would call it. These footprints consisted of ruins as well as *kwaatipkya* [eagle-shrine nests]. When they arrived here, each of those clans, becoming part of the whole, retained certain separate rights as clans. So thereafter, they would continue to revisit their footsteps in order to capture the eagles, the feathers of which they used in order to commemorate their history in prayers, rituals, and ceremonies.
>
> Wherever people left those eagle nests, they were marks of the

boundaries of their traditional domain. This happened a long time ago. According to prophecy, the Hopis would be settled here when the *pahana* [white man] arrives. When the *pahana* asks the chief how far his territory lies, he would climb to the tower of his house to point to places around (as far as the eye can see) and say, "This is my country." The white man would have to accept this that this is Hopi country. Other tribes would also recognize this. (Black 1984)

3. Five Houses is a landmark across the wash from Polacca. Dewey Healing noted: "You take the road from Walpi, go across the Polacca bridge going to Keams Canyon. One mile or so after you cross the bridge, you take the turnoff from the Keams Canyon road to Badger Butte Crest. The old Winslow road went around Polacca Butte and on down into Cedar Springs, to Winslow. Right about where the road to Badger Butte turns were five houses. The old Walpi term for them was *tavuptsomo* [quilting hall]. It was possibly established by missionaries for holding quilting sessions. Early converts to Christianity gathered around there. The five houses established the boundaries for the jurisdiction of Hopi farm lands near Polacca" (Black 1984).

4. A comment by Emory Sekaquaptewa:

The account given by Pabanale regarding the woman and her instructions was a local version. That may have happened at Walpi, perhaps to reinforce the concept of matrilineality. The woman is not as profaned as the men; therefore she could take certain kinds of actions without being endangered. A man is profaned and he would be doing it to his own peril if he tried to take the initiative.

Clan lands were established as a result of different migrations. The first ones to reach Third Mesa [the Bear clan] were the ones who set up conditions for admitting all others that were to come. As each clan came to Third Mesa, they had to demonstrate to those already there that they were legitimately Hopi and carried certain knowledge about Hopi teachings. They had to demonstrate this knowledge and power by contributing a ritual or a particular kind of technology . . . growing certain crops, etc., to the satisfaction of the Bear clan, then they were admitted.

They had to agree to share their knowledge and ritual so that it would be beneficial for all who were there. In return, the Hopi chiefs gave the new clan particular plots of land. It was done in a spiritual way so that others who would come along and violate another clan's land would be in spiritual danger and would suffer the consequences of being a violator. (Black 1984)

Becoming a Judge

1. Pabanale was formally appointed by Superintendent Seth Wilson on February 3, 1940, to serve as chief judge for four years.

2. Soyokos are known as ogre Katsinas; their primary purpose is to discipline

young children who have misbehaved. Parents arrange for these Katsinas to confront naughty children with their misbehavior and threaten to carry them away or cook and eat them. As prearranged, the parents come to the child's defense, promising that the child will behave himself in the future. The parents then ransom the child by giving the Katsina a large quantity of food.

3. Pabanale saw the court as a "parent," a stern disciplinarian who had to teach the children—the Hopis—how to behave under the new system. He had great reverence for the power of the court, with its rules, procedures, and protocol, and felt it was his duty to carry out the laws as prescribed. In sentencing a defendant for refusing to accept a stock permit, he reportedly said, "You are going to have to be put in jail . . . because Washington officials have given me authority to do this, and I want you to know that I am a white man and I have to do this to you" (Hopi Hearings 1955:14–15).

4. District 7 is one of the land management units established within the boundaries of the Navajo reservation. It lies adjacent to District 6, which is the Hopi reservation (see map of the Hopi villages and Rio Grande Pueblos in the illustration section). These districts were intended to maintain a balance between the number of livestock and the carrying capacity of the range.

5. Gene Lowry was a government stockman under Burton Ladd, who was made superintendent by John Collier to replace Seth Wilson. According to Simon Scott, a Hotvela Hopi, Wilson was a man of much sympathy with the Hopis, but he was not able to fulfill the things the Collier administration wanted him to do, so he left. "Then they made Ladd superintendent, who was a stockman and a man who is willing to do any kind of work for Collier, and being a cowboy, he is willing to act any authority he had with the help of Gene Lowry who was a stockman under Ladd" (Hopi Hearings 1955:39). As part of his testimony at the Hopi hearings in 1955, Scott related the following incident involving Lowry and the branding of a mule:

> Then he started with branding the Hopi stock, and one evening I was returning from my corral below Oraibi I came to a place just below Oraibi Village where these men have rounded up many Hopi horses to brand. When I arrived at that branding spot, I saw many Hopi people gathered there, and it seems they are up against something, so when I came closer they are arguing with these stockmen, and David Monongye came to me and said it is a bad situation here because look at the mule over there. It is about ready to die, and this man is doing everything to force a brand on them. And I looked to the chute where this white mule was laying and struggling, and it makes me very angry because I have been raised with the stock and know how to treat them. But this white man has been doing this kind of work on these animals, and I said in the white man's language because it makes me so mad. The mule was struggling in the chute and being forced so much that his rectum was out, yet he was still kicking him all over in trying to do what he wants to this mule. Gene Lowry is still kicking this mule while I was standing there so

I said to Gene Lowry, "What the hell is going on here?" I said to him that animals have feelings just like humans, but the only trouble is they can't speak and tell you they are hurt. Animals have feelings just like anybody else. They must be raised. They are tame animals, and you are a stockman, supposed to know better than that.

Then he turned around and said, "I don't give a damn what you say, I am going to finish the job." This is what happened, and it makes me so sick of seeing these things being done in this manner by the stockman and we were told by the white man that we shouldn't speak these words in this language, but I had to use it because I cannot stand the sight. And when the mule got up he walked away very weak and wobbling, but the owner tried everything to save the animal, but later it died. (Hopi Hearings 1955:39)

6. Lee Zee is located on the top of Jeddito Mesa, east of Keams Canyon.

7. Records from Superintendent Ladd's office indicate that in 1944 Pabanale was reappointed chief judge of the Hopi court, to serve until 1947 (Ladd to Pabanale, Feb. 1, 1944, Hopi Agency, Keams Canyon).

The Early Years

1. Many organizations in the 1880s, purporting to have the Indians' best interests in mind, set forth recommendations that reflected the anti-Indianism of the time. For example, J. B. Harrison, a member of the Indian Rights Association, wrote in 1887: "Education for Indians should consist of instruction and training adapted to prepare them for the life of laborers. A few Indians will rightly be teachers and preachers, but the mass of them nearly the whole number indeed must work with their hands, as farmers and mechanics, and their wives. Most Indians who try to live by their wits are likely to be worthless idlers. The competition of white men will be too intense for many Indians to succeed in the learned professions. They are, as a race, distinctly inferior to white men in intellectual vitality and capability, and their wisest friends will advise them to look forward to the life of toilers, and to make their persistent appeal to the conscience of the nation for opportunity to make their own living by their own industry" (*The Critic* [New York], Dec. 24, 1887).

2. Tom Polacca was an uncle of Albert Yava, Irving Pabanale's nephew, and a member of the Tobacco clan. He was a pivotal agent for accelerating change on the reservation around 1900 and gave his full support to the implementation of government policies and practices. He was a prosperous cattle owner and trader, the first reservation policeman, and (because of his fluency in English) an interpreter for all the Hopi villages. He was the first Tewa to build a house below First Mesa, in 1900, around which the town of Polacca later grew up as a secular, nonaffiliated village. Over the objections of the Hopi chiefs, he helped establish the first day school in Polacca in 1894 by providing the building. He was resented by the conservative Hopis, who called him a progressive and

resisted his efforts to implement "white" education. Despite this controversy, which split Tewa Village in the mid-1880s, Polacca was convinced that some of the white man's ways had to be learned if the new generation was to survive (Yava 1978:10–11). Until he was forced by conservative Hopis to move his residence some miles from First Mesa, he was respected for his participation in Hopi and Tewa life.

Tribute to Polacca was paid by E. S. Clark, a special enumerator for the U.S. Census, in 1893: "It would be an injustice to a good and worthy man should I fail to make favorable mention of the Indian of Tewa who devoted his time so generously in the height of the harvest season to our interests, who has forsaken the home of his fathers and many of their ways by moving his home down from the mesa and breaking away from many of the customs and superstitions of his tribe, thereby invoking the anathemas of his people; a man whose highest ambition is to learn and adopt the ways of the white man in all things (except possibly the vices). It is with profound respect and admiration of a good, true, and brave man that I commend to the fostering care and generous treatment of those who have charge of the nation's wards the big, kindhearted Tom Polacca" (in Donaldson 1893:50).

3. Hopi reminiscences of the early years at Keams Canyon School can be found in Sekaquaptewa 1969:91–108, 121–31; and Simmons 1942:89–133.

4. The Navajo Agency was established at Fort Defiance, Arizona, in 1852. It had charge of the Navajos who lived in the northwestern part of New Mexico and adjoining areas of Arizona, Utah, and Colorado. From 1876 to 1877 the Navajo agent handled the business of the Moqui [Hopi] Pueblo Agency.

5. The 1905 "List of Moqui Boys" for the Phoenix Indian School shows that Pabanale arrived May 1, 1901, at the age of eleven.

6. Students at the Phoenix Indian School were encouraged to sign the following pledge: "God being my helper, I promise to abstain from the use of intoxicating liquors as a beverage, and to do all that I can to encourage others to do likewise" (Native American 2, Mar. 2, 1901).

7. The superintendent of the Hopi Agency adopted the policy that Indians who had received educational advantages must marry under state license. This rule did not necessarily prohibit the tribal form of marriage (Annual Report, Superintendent, Moqui Indian Reservation, for 1914 and 1916).

Trading

1. O'Kane provides an interesting account of his experiences in the company of a Hopi trader in his book *Sun in the Sky* (1950:150–61).

Rabbit Hunting

1. Dozier notes that in Tewa Village the war chief announced secular activities and took charge of tribal hunts (1954:346).

Notes

2. In the old style of hunting on foot the men would divide into two long lines surrounding a wide area of the range, "then walk towards the center of the circle beating the bushes and killing the rabbits with throwing sticks as they are flushed" (Beaglehole 1936:12).

The Indian Police

1. See Crane 1925:122–80 for further exploits of Nelson Oyaping.

Medicine Men

1. In 1966 the Shumakolil Society was headed by the only remaining Cloud clan member (Dozier 1966:78).

2. Pabanale was an initiated member of the Wuwtsim Society on First Mesa.

The Results of the Indian Reorganization Act

1. La Farge also wrote on important historical developments during his time on the reservation, in an unpublished report called "Notes for Hopi Administrators" (February 1937). A copy is on file at the Museum of Northern Arizona Library in Flagstaff.

Judge Pabanale and the Tribal Court

1. The crimes included manslaughter, rape, assault with intent to kill, arson, burglary, and larceny. In 1932 the law was amended to include incest, robbery, and assault with a dangerous weapon.

Appendix 1: Migration Accounts

1. Courlander 1971; Dozier 1954; Fewkes 1899, 1900; Harrington 1916; Youvella 1955; Mindeleff 1891; Nelson 1937; Parsons 1925; Stephen 1936; Yava 1978.

2. There is a Hopi corroboration that the delegation to the Tewa was made up of men of the Snake and Sand clan. Duke Pahona, of the Sand-Snake clan and crier chief at First Mesa, noted, "According to our clanship tradition, it was we [Snake-Sand clan] who wanted to go get the Tewa people" (Pahona 1977).

3. In Parsons (1925:7) Crow Wing refers to an old cedar tree beneath which the heart of a Navajo chief is buried, considered a protection for First Mesa.

REFERENCES

Adams, David W.
1979   Schooling the Hopi: Federal Indian Policy Writ Small, 1887–1917. *Pacific Historic Review* 48:335–56.

Adams, E. Charles
1978   *Synthesis of Hopi Prehistory and History: Final Report for the National Park Service, Southwest Region, Indian Cultural Resources Assistance Program.* Flagstaff: Museum of Northern Arizona, Department of Anthropology.

American Indian Lawyer Training Program, Inc.
1982   *Indian Self-Determination and the Role of Tribal Courts.* Oakland, Calif.

Bailey, Jessie B.
1940   *Diego de Vargas and the Reconquest of New Mexico.* Albuquerque: University of New Mexico Press.

Bailey, L. R.
1964   *The Long Walk: A History of the Navajo Wars, 1846–68.* Los Angeles: Westernlore Press.

Bandelier, Adolf
1890–92 *Final Report of Investigations Among the Indians of the Southwestern United States, Carried on Mainly in the Years from 1880 to 1885.* 2 vols. Papers of the Archaeological Institute of America, American Series, vols. 3 and 4. Cambridge, Mass.

Bartlett, Katherine
1934   Spanish Contacts with the Hopi, 1540–1823. *Museum Notes* 6:1–12. Museum of Northern Arizona, Flagstaff.

Beaglehole, Ernest
1936   *Hopi Hunting and Hunting Ritual.* Yale University Publications in Anthropology 7. New Haven.

Beauvais, Fred
1993   Trends in Indian Adolescent Drug and Alcohol Use. *American Indian and Alaskan Native Mental Health Research* 5:1–12.

Black, Robert A.

1967   Hopi Grievance Chants: A Mechanism of Social Control. In *Studies in Southwestern Ethnolinguistics,* edited by Dell H. Hymes with William E. Bittle. The Hague: Mouton.

1965   *A Content Analysis of Eighty-One Hopi Indian Chants.* Unpublished Ph.D. dissertation, Department of Anthropology, Indiana University.

1984   Field Notes. In possession of author.

Bloom, Lansing B.

1931   A Campaign Against the Moqui Pueblo under Governor Phelix Martinez, 1716. *New Mexico Historical Review* 6(2):158–371.

Bolton, Herbert E.

1949   *Coronado, Knight of Pueblos and Plains.* Albuquerque: University of New Mexico Press.

Bourke, John Gregory

1884   *The Snake Dance of the Moquis of Arizona.* New York: Charles Scribner's Sons.

Brew, J. O.

1949   *The History of Awatovi.* Papers of the Peabody Museum of American Archaeology and Ethnology Vol. 36, No. 3. Cambridge: Harvard University.

Brumble, H. David

1988   *American Indian Autobiography.* Berkeley: University of California Press.

1981   *An Annotated Bibliography of American Indian and Eskimo Autobiographies.* Lincoln: University of Nebraska Press.

Buchanan, Golden R.

1960   *Teaching Aids for Lamanite Missionaries.* Salt Lake City: Church of Jesus Christ of Latter-day Saints, Indian Relations Committee.

Clemmer, Richard

1995   *Roads in the Sky: The Hopi Indians in a Century of Change.* Boulder: Westview Press.

1986   Hopis, Western Shoshones, and Southern Utes: Three Different Responses to the Indian Reorganization Act of 1934. *American Indian Culture and Research Journal* 10(2):15–40.

1978   *Continuities of Hopi Culture Change.* Ramona, Calif.: Acoma Books.

Collier, John

1963   *From Every Zenith: A Memoir.* Denver: Sage Books.

Cordell, Linda S.

1984   *Prehistory of the Southwest.* Orlando: Academic Press.

218

Cordell, Linda S., and George J. Gumerman
1989   *Dynamics of Southwest Prehistory.* Washington, D.C.: Smithsonian Institution Press.

Courlander, Harold
1971   *The Fourth World of the Hopis: The Epic Story of the Hopi Indians as Preserved in Their Legends and Traditions.* New York: Crown. Reprint. Albuquerque: University of New Mexico Press, 1987.

Crane, Leo
1925   *Indians of the Enchanted Desert.* Boston: Little, Brown.
1918   Annual Report of the Superintendent of the Moqui Indian Reservation. Mimeograph. Manuscript Collection (135-3-4B). Museum of Northern Arizona, Flagstaff.
1916   Annual Report of the Superintendent of the Moqui Indian Reservation. Mimeograph. Manuscript Collection. Museum of Northern Arizona, Flagstaff.
1915   Annual Report of the Superintendent of the Moqui Indian Reservation, Narrative Section. Mimeograph. Manuscript Collection (135-2-3). Museum of Northern Arizona, Flagstaff.

Daniel, Robert E. L.
1921   Annual Report of the Superintendent of the Moqui Indian Reservation, Narrative Section. Manuscript Collection (135-4-2). Museum of Northern Arizona, Flagstaff.

Davis, Irvine
1959   Linguistic Clues to Rio Grande Prehistory. *El Palacio* 66(3):73–84.

Dobyns, Henry F.
1984   Native American Collapse and Recovery. In *Scholars and the Indian Experience,* edited by W. R. Swagerty. Bloomington: Indiana University Press.

Dockstader, Frederick J.
1985   *The Kachina and The White Man: The Influence of White Culture on the Hopi Kachina Culture.* Rev. ed. Albuquerque: University of New Mexico Press.

Donaldson, Thomas
1893   *Moqui Indians of Arizona and Pueblo Indians of New Mexico: Extra Census Bulletin.* Washington, D.C.: U.S. Census Office.

Downs, Randolph D.
1945   A Crusade for Indian Reform, 1922–1934. *Mississippi Valley Historical Review* 32:331–54.

Dozier, Edward P.

1966　　*Hano: A Tewa Indian Community in Arizona.* New York: Holt, Rinehart and Winston.

1956　　The Role of the Hopi-Tewa Migration Legend in Reinforcing Cultural Patterns and Prescribing Social Behavior. *Journal of American Folklore* 62:176–80.

1954　　*The Hopi-Tewa of Arizona.* University of California Publications in American Archaeology and Ethnology 44, No. 3. Berkeley.

1951　　Resistance to Acculturation and Assimilation in an Indian Pueblo. *American Anthropologist* 53:56–66.

Duran, Eduardo

1990　　*Transforming the Soul Wound.* Berkeley: Folklore Institute.

Eggan, Fred

1966　　*The American Indian: Perspectives for the Study of Social Change.* Chicago: Aldine.

1950　　*Social Organization of the Western Pueblos.* Chicago: University of Chicago Press.

n.d.　　Panel on Land Problems in the Pueblo Southwest: 5. Modern Hopi Land Problems. Duplicated. Museum of Northern Arizona Library, Flagstaff.

Ellis, Florence Hawley

1974　　*The Hopi: Their History and Use of Land.* New York: Garland.

1967　　Where Did the Pueblo People Come From? *El Palacio* 74(3):35–43.

1966　　Pueblo Boundaries and Their Markers. *Plateau* 38(4):97–106.

1961　　The Hopi: Their History and Use of Land. Defendant's Exhibit No. E-500, Docket No. 229. Duplicated. Indian Claims Commission, Washington, D.C.

1951　　Pueblo Social Organization and Southwestern Archaeology. *American Antiquity* 17(2):148–51.

Espinosa, José Manuel

1940　　*The First Expedition of Vargas into New Mexico, 1692.* Albuquerque: University of New Mexico Press.

Ferguson, William M.

1996　　*The Anasazi of Mesa Verde and the Four Corners.* Niwot: University Press of Colorado.

Fewkes, Jesse Walter

1923　　*The Use of Idols in Hopi Worship.* Annual Report of the Smithsonian Institution for 1922. Washington, D.C.

1900　　Tusayan Migration Traditions. In *Nineteenth Annual Report of the Bureau of American Ethnology, for the Years 1897–1898.* 2 vols. Washington, D.C.

1899   Winter Solstice Altars at Hano Pueblo. *American Anthropologist*
            (n.s.) 1(2):251–76.

Fewkes, Jesse Walter, and A. M. Stephen
1892   The Mam-zrau-ti: A Tusayan Ceremony. *American Anthropologist*
            (o.s.) 5(3):217–45.

Flake, David K.
1965   *A History of Mormon Missionary Work with the Hopi, Navajo, and
            Zuni*. Unpublished Master's thesis, Brigham Young University, Provo,
            Utah.

Forbes, Jack D.
1960   *Apache, Navaho, and Spaniard*. Norman: University of Oklahoma
            Press.

Ford, Richard I., Albert H. Schroeder, and Stewart L. Peckham
1972   Three Perspectives on Puebloan Prehistory. In *New Perspectives on
            the Pueblos*, edited by Alfonso Ortiz. Albuquerque: University of
            New Mexico Press.

Hack, John T.
1942   *The Changing Physical Environment of the Hopi Indians of Arizona*.
            Papers of the Peabody Museum of American Archaeology and Eth-
            nology Vol. 35, No. 1. Cambridge: Harvard University.

Hackett, Charles Wilson
1937   *Historical Documents Relating to New Mexico, Nueva Vizcaya, and
            Approaches Thereto, to 1773, Vol. 3*. Carnegie Institution Publica-
            tion No. 330. Washington, D.C.: Carnegie Institution.

Hackett, C. W., and C. C. Shelby
1942   *Revolt of the Pueblo Indians of New Mexico and Otermin's
            Attempted Reconquest, 1680–82*. Albuquerque: University of New
            Mexico Press.

Hagan, William T.
1966   *Indian Police and Judges: Experiments in Acculturation and Control*.
            New Haven: Yale University Press.

Hale, Kenneth, and David Harris
1979   Historical Linguistics and Archaeology. In *Handbook of North
            American Indians, Vol. 9: The Southwest*, edited by Alfonso Ortiz.
            Washington, D.C.: Smithsonian Institution Press.

Hammond, George, and Agapito Rey, editors
1953   *Don Juan de Oñate, Colonizer of New Mexico, 1598–1628. Parts I
            and II*. Albuquerque: University of New Mexico Press.

Hargrave, Lyndon L.
1931   First Mesa. *Museum Notes* 3(8):1–6. Museum of Northern Arizona, Flagstaff.

Harrington, John P.
1916   The Ethnogeography of the Tewa Indians. In *Twenty-Ninth Annual Report of Bureau of American Ethnology, for the Years 1907–1908.* Washington, D.C.: Smithsonian Institution.

Hill, W. W.
1982   *An Ethnography of Santa Clara Pueblo.* Edited by Charles H. Lange. Albuquerque: University of New Mexico Press.

Hodge, Frederick W., editor
1907   *Handbook of American Indians North of Mexico.* 2 vols. Bureau of American Ethnology Bulletin 30. Washington, D.C.

Hodge, Frederick Webb, George P. Hammond, and Agapito Rey, editors and translators
1945   *Fray Alonso de Benavides' Revised Memorial of 1634.* Albuquerque: University of New Mexico Press.

Hopi Hearings
1955   Mimeograph. 2 vols. Hopi Indian Agency, Bureau of Indian Affairs, Keams Canyon, Ariz.

Hough, Walter
1915   *The Hopi Indians.* Cedar Rapids, Iowa: Torch Press.

James, Harry C.
1974   *Pages from Hopi History.* Tucson: University of Arizona Press.

Jones, Volney H.
1950   The Establishment of the Hopi Reservation and Some Later Developments Concerning Hopi Lands. *Plateau* 23(2):17–25.

Kerr, James R.
1969   Constitutional Rights, Tribal Justice, and the American Indian. *Journal of Public Law* 18:311–38.

Kroskrity, Paul V.
1993   *Language, History, and Identity: Ethnolinguistic Studies of the Arizona Tewa.* Tucson: University of Arizona Press.

Krupat, Arnold
1994   *Native American Autobiography: An Anthology.* Madison: University of Wisconsin Press.
1985   *For Those Who Come After: A Study of Native American Autobiography.* Berkeley: University of California Press.

La Farge, Oliver

1950   Postscript to Running Narrative of the Organization of the Hopi Tribe of Indians. Memorandum. Museum of Northern Arizona Library, Flagstaff.

1937   Notes for Hopi Administrators. Manuscript. Museum of Northern Arizona Library, Flagstaff.

1936   Running Narrative of the Organization of the Hopi Tribe of Indians. Journal. La Farge Collection, Humanities Research Center, University of Texas, Austin.

Leland, Joy

1976   *Firewater Myths: North American Indian Drinking and Alcohol Addiction.* New Brunswick: Publications Division, Rutgers Center of Alcohol Studies.

Leonard, Irving Albert

1932   *The Mercurio Volante of Don Carlos de Siguenza y Gongora: An Account of the First Expedition of Don Diego de Vargas into New Mexico in 1692.* Vol. 3. Los Angeles: Quivira Society.

Levy, Jerrold E.

1992   *Orayvi Revisited: Social Stratification in an "Egalitarian" Society.* Santa Fe: School of American Research Press.

Levy, Jerrold E., and Stephen J. Kunitz

1974   *Indian Drinking: Navajo Practices and Anglo-American Theories.* New York: John Wiley.

1971   Indian Reservations, Anomie, and Social Pathologies. *Southwest Journal of Anthropology* 27(2):97–128.

May, Philip A.

1992   Alcohol Policy Considerations for Indian Reservations and Border-town Communities. *American Indian and Alaska Native Mental Health Research* 4(3):5–59.

McNitt, Frank

1962   *The Indian Trader.* Norman: University of Oklahoma Press.

Mindeleff, Victor

1891   A Study of Pueblo Architecture in Tusayan and Cibola. In *Eighth Annual Report of the Bureau of American Ethnology, for the Years 1886–1887. Part 2.* Washington, D.C.: Smithsonian Institution.

Montgomery, Ross G., Watson Smith, and John O. Brew

1949   *Franciscan Awatovi: The Excavation and Conjectural Reconstruction of a Seventeenth-Century Spanish Mission Established at a Hopi Indian Town in Northeastern Arizona.* Papers of the Peabody

Museum of American Archaeology and Ethnology Vol. 36. Cambridge: Harvard University.

Narvaez, Valverde, Fray José
1937   Notes upon Moqui and Other Recent Ones upon New Mexico. In *Historical Documents Relating to New Mexico, Nueva Vizcaya, and Approaches Thereto, to 1773, Vol. 3*, edited by W. C. Hackett. Washington, D.C.: Carnegie Institution.

Nelson, John Louw
1937   *Rhythm for Rain*. Boston: Houghton Mifflin.

O'Kane, Walter Collins
1953   *The Hopis: Portrait of a Desert People*. Norman: University of Oklahoma Press.
1950   *Sun in the Sky: The Hopi Indians of the Arizona Mesa Lands*. Norman: University of Oklahoma Press.

Ortiz, Alfonso, editor
1979   *Handbook of the North American Indians, Vol. 9: The Southwest*. Washington, D.C.: Smithsonian Institution Press.
1972   *New Perspectives on the Pueblos*. Albuquerque: University of New Mexico Press.

Pahona, Duke
1977   Clansman Speaks His Mind. *Qua Toqti*, July 14, pp. 5–6. Oraibi, Ariz.

Parsons, Elsie Clews
1939   *Pueblo Indian Religion*. 2 vols. Chicago: University of Chicago Press.
1936a Early Relations Between Hopi and Keres. *American Anthropologist* 38:554–60.
1936b The House-Clan Complex of the Pueblos. In *Essays in Honor of A. L. Kroeber*. Berkeley: University of California Press.
1933   *Hopi and Zuni Ceremonialism*. Memoirs of the American Anthropological Association No. 39. Menasha, Wis.
1926   The Ceremonial Calendar of the Tewa in Arizona. *American Anthropologist* 28:209–29.
1925   *A Pueblo Indian Journal*. Memoirs of the American Anthropological Association No. 32. Menasha, Wis.

Powell, John Wesley
1891   Indian Linguistic Families of America North of Mexico. In *Seventh Annual Report of the Bureau of American Ethnology, for the Years 1885–1886*. Washington, D.C.: Smithsonian Institution.

Reed, Eric K.
1952   The Tewa Indians of the Hopi Country. *Plateau* 25(1):11–18.

1944   The Abandonment of the San Juan Region. *El Palacio* 51(4):61–74.

1943a   The Origin of Hano Pueblo. *El Palacio* 50(4):73–76.

1943b   The Southern Tewa Pueblos in the Historic Period. *El Palacio* 50(11):254–64, (12):276–88.

Robinson, Robert

1988   *Black Mesa–Kayenta Mine: Socio-Economic Analysis and Final Technical Report.* Denver: U.S. Office of Surface Mining Reclamation and Enforcement, Western Field Operations.

Scholes, F. V.

1942   *Troublous Times in New Mexico, 1659–1670.* Publications in History, Vol. 11. Albuquerque: Historical Society of New Mexico.

1936   Church and State in New Mexico. *New Mexico Historical Review* 11(1):9–76, 12(1):78–106.

Schroeder, Albert H.

1972   Rio Grande Ethnohistory. In *New Perspectives on the Pueblos,* edited by Alfonso Ortiz. Albuquerque: University of New Mexico Press.

1968   Shifting for Survival in the Spanish Southwest. *New Mexico Historical Review* 43(4):291–310.

Sekaquaptewa, Emory

1972   Preserving the Good Things of Hopi Life. In *Plural Society in the Southwest,* edited by Edward H. Spicer and Raymond H. Thompson. New York: Arkville Press.

Sekaquaptewa, Helen

1969   *Me and Mine: The Life Story of Helen Sekaquaptewa as Told to Louise Udall.* Tucson: University of Arizona Press.

Simmons, Leo

1942   *Sun Chief: The Autobiography of a Hopi Indian.* New Haven: Yale University Press.

Simmons, Marc

1979   History of Pueblo-Spanish Relations to 1821. In *Handbook of North American Indians, Vol. 9: The Southwest,* edited by Alfonso Ortiz. Washington, D.C.: Smithsonian Institution Press.

Spicer, Edward H.

1962   *Cycles of Conquest: The Impact of Spain, Mexico, and the United States on the Indians of the Southwest.* Tucson: University of Arizona Press.

Spindler, George, editor

1963   *Education and Culture.* New York: Holt, Rinehart and Winston.

Stephen, Alexander MacGregor
1936   *Hopi Journal.* 2 vols. Edited by Elsie Clews Parsons. New York: Columbia University Press.

Swadesh, Morris
1967   Linguistic Classification in the Southwest. In *Studies in Southwestern Ethnolinguistics,* edited by Dell H. Hymes. The Hague: Mouton.

Swagerty, W. R., editor
1984   *Scholars and the Indian Experience.* Bloomington: Indiana University Press.

Thomas, Alfred B., editor and translator
1932   *Forgotten Frontiers: A Study of the Spanish Indian Policy of Don Juan Bautista de Anza, Governor of New Mexico, 1777–1787.* Norman: University of Oklahoma Press.

Thompson, Laura, and Alice Joseph
1944   *The Hopi Way.* Chicago: University of Chicago Press.

Titiev, Misha
1944   *Old Oraibi: A Study of the Hopi Indians of Third Mesa.* Papers of the Peabody Museum of Archaeology and Ethnology Vol. 22, No. 1. Cambridge: Harvard University.

Trennert, Robert A.
1988   *The Phoenix Indian School: Forced Assimilation in Arizona, 1891–1935.* Norman: University of Oklahoma Press.
1979   Peaceably if They Will, Forcibly if They Must: The Phoenix Indian School, 1890–1901. *Journal of Arizona History* 20(3):297–322.

Twitchell, Ralph E., compiler
1914   *The Spanish Archives of New Mexico.* 2 vols. Cedar Rapids, Iowa: Torch Press.

U.S. Bureau of Indian Affairs
1940   *Code of Federal Regulations, Title 25—Indians, Chapter 1.* Washington, D.C.
1937   *Grazing Regulations for the Navajo and Hopi Reservations.* Washington, D.C.

U.S. Department of the Interior
1904   *Annual Report of the Commissioner of Indian Affairs.* Washington, D.C.
1899   *Annual Report of the Commissioner of Indian Affairs.* Washington, D.C.
1894   *Census Office: Special Report on Indians Taxed and Not Taxed in the U.S. 11th Census, 1890, vol. 10.* Washington, D.C.

1890   *Annual Report of the Commissioner of Indian Affairs.* Washington, D.C.

1889   *Annual Report of the Commissioner of Indian Affairs.* Washington, D.C.

1884   *Report of the Commissioner of Indian Affairs to the Secretary of the Interior.* Washington, D.C.

1878   *Annual Report of the Commissioner of Indian Affairs.* Washington, D.C.

Voegelin, C. F., and Robert C. Euler

1957   Introduction to Hopi Chants. *Journal of American Folklore* 70:115–36.

Voth, H. R.

1912   Notes on the Eagle Cult of the Hopi. In H. R. Voth, *Brief Miscellaneous Hopi Papers.* Field Museum of Natural History, Publication 157, Anthropology Series 11(2):1–149. Chicago.

Waddell, Jack O.

1980   Similarities and Variations in Alcohol Use in Four Native American Societies. In *Drinking Behavior Among Southwestern Indians: An Anthropological Perspective,* edited by Jack O. Waddell and Michael W. Everett. Tucson: University of Arizona Press.

Whiteley, Peter M.

1993   The End of Anthropology (at Hopi)? *Journal of the Southwest* 35(2):125–57.

1988   *Deliberate Acts: Changing Hopi Culture Through the Oraibi Split.* Tucson: University of Arizona Press.

Yava, Albert

1978   *Big Falling Snow: A Tewa-Hopi Indian's Life and Times and the History and Traditions of His People.* Edited by Harold Courlander. New York: Crown.

Youvella, Bert

1955   Account of Tewa Migration to Hopi. In Hopi Hearings, vol. 2. Mimeograph. Hopi Indian Agency, Keams Canyon, Ariz.

INDEX

Adams, Bob & Hale, 56
agriculture: and Pabanale as farmer, 41; traditional Hopi methods of, xx. *See also* cattle; sheep
Albuquerque Indian School, 71
alcohol and alcoholism: and Pabanale as judge, 52; and Pabanale as policeman, 35–36; Pabanale on problem of on reservation, xvii, 78–82, 188–89; and police, 80, 210–11n3
alienation, and boarding schools, 133
American Indian Defense Association, 166
Apaches, xxiii
Arizona Tewa language, xx–xxi, 13, 121, 200–201
Arthur, Chester, 159
assimilation: and boarding schools, 127; and land allotments, 134; and Mormons, 186
Avayung, Charlie, 147
Awatovi (Hopi town), xxiv

Baldwin, Anita, 40, 211n1
Baptist Church, 79
Big Falling Snow (Yava 1978), xiv, xvi
Book of Mormon, 73, 74, 185
Bourke, John Gregory, 187
Bowman, John H., 129
"Boy Who Became a Girl, The" (Hopi folktale), 89–94
Brookings Institution, 166
Brumble, H. David, xiii
Bureau of Indian Affairs (BIA), 72, 132, 157–65, 171–73, 175

Burke, Charles, 167
Burton, Charles E., 159–60

California: and dramatization of traditional Hopi wedding in Los Angeles, 40–42; and Pabanale's travels as young man, 26
Carson, Kit, 157
cattle: and improvement of Hopi livestock, 68–69; and trading, 27–28, 29–30
ceremonial practices: and migration of Tewa to First Mesa, 122; rabbit hunting and Hopi, 140. *See also* Katsina ceremonies; medicine men
Christianity. *See* Baptist Church; missionary groups; Mormons; Spanish
clan system: of Hopis and Tewas, xxi, 123–24, 210n4, 212–13n1–2; of Navajo, 210n4. *See also* kinship system
Clark, E. S., 216n2
climate: drought and livestock on Hopi reservation, 68–69; of Hopi mesas, xx
Collier, John, xv, 166, 167, 171–72, 214n5
constitution, Hopi tribal: and La Farge, 168, 169–71; and Pabanale, xiv–xv, 49–50; and water supply for livestock, 69
councilman, Pabanale as, 68
Courlander, Harold, 208n7
Court, Hopi Tribal. *See* judge
Courts of Indian Offenses, 175–76
courtship, and rabbit hunts, 143–44. *See also* marriage

229

public service, Pabanale's record of, 179–84. *See also* councilman; culture broker; judge; police

Pueblo: and Spanish colonial period, xxii–xxiv; and prehistoric sites in Four Corners area, xviii; and special status of Tewa, xx–xxi. *See also* Hopis

Pueblo Revolt (1680), xxiii, xxiv

rabbit chant, 141, *142–43*

rabbits. *See* hunting

religion, Hopi: and Mormonism, 185, 186, 187; and Pabanale as medicine man, 43, 45; Pabanale on traditions of, 23, 73, 77; and Snake Dance, 83–84, 191; and Tewas, 209n1. *See also* ceremonial practices; *pahos*

repetition, and traditional style of Native American storytelling, xiii

Rhoads, Charles, 167

Rio Grande Tewa language, xx, xxi

Santa Clara Pueblo, 155

schools. *See* education; Keams Canyon Boarding School; Phoenix Indian School

Scott, Simon, 214–15n5

Scott, Winfield, 160–61

Second Mesa: and Hopi villages, xix; and reduction of sheep herds, 67

Seeni, Herbert, 47

Sekaquaptewa, Abbott, xxv, 181–84, 191

Sekaquaptewa, Emory, xxv, 139, 158, 160, 164–65, 181, 203–204, 212–13n2, 213n4

Sekaquaptewa, Helen, 130, 131

Senate Indian Affairs Committee, 167

Sergeant, Elizabeth Shepley, 125

Shalako (mother of Pabanale), 14

Shalako Dance, 23, 24, 25

sheep: and Pabanale on improvement

of herds on Hopi reservation, 59–60, 68–69; permits and Hopi Tribal Court, 58–59; and reduction of Hopi herds, 66–67, 171–73, 177–79, 183–84; theft of and Pabanale as policeman, 36–37

Shumakolil Society, 155, 217n1

Sichoma, Andrew, 51

Sikyatngowma (father of Pabanale), 14

smallpox, xxiii, 15–16, 208–9n4

Smoki Dancers (Prescott, Arizona), 190–91

Snake Dance, 83–85, 190–91

Snake Society, 156

Sootukwnangwu (deity), 212n2

Soyal ceremony, 212n1

Spanish, and history of Arizona Tewas, xxii–xxiii

Stephen, Alexander MacGregor, 142–43

store, operation of by Pabanale, 41–42, 211n3. *See also* trading

storytelling, patterns of repetition in traditional style of Native American, xiii. *See also* narrative

"Sunflower Girl" (Hopi folktale), 101–108

Supreme Court, and Hopi-Navajo land dispute, 162

Talasayo (uncle of Pabanale), xiv, 14, 19, 207n1, 208n1

Tano Revolt (1696), xxiii

Tanos (Southern Tewas), xxii, xxiii–xxiv, 207n3

Tengyo'tse, Effie (niece of Pabanale), 124

Tewas: brief history of Arizona Tewas, xxi–xxiv; and culture brokers, xiii–xiv; culture differences between Hopi and, xvi, xvii; and folktales, 95–100, 109–17; and Hopi traditional religion, 209n1; and La Farge, 168–69; language of,

xx, 13, 121, 200–201; and medicine men, 155; and migration to
Hopi lands, xxi–xxiv, 3–13,
121–25, 193–201, 208n7; and
Mormons, 187; and Pabanale's role
as cultural innovator, xviii; and
police on Hopi reservation,
145–54; and repetition in traditional narrative style, xiii; special
status of among Pueblo peoples,
xx–xxi; and structure of formal
discourse, xvi; and trading, 138–39
theft: and Pabanale as policeman,
36–37; at Pabanale's store, 41–42
Third Mesa: and Hopi villages, xix;
and reduction of sheep herds, 67;
and resistance to land allotments,
134
Thompson, Laura, 134
Titiev, Misha, 140
trading, and life story of Pabanale,
27–28, 29–30, 70, 71, 138–39. *See
also* store
Tuno'a (Hopi chief), 46, 47, 48
Tuwapongtumasi (Mother of All
Animals), 140
typhus fever. *See* disease

Utes, 10–11, 197–99, 210n3

Vandever, C. E., 128
Vargas, Diego de, xxii, xxiii

Walpi Snake Dance, 83–85
Ward, John, 157
warfare, and Tewa culture, 124–25
Warrior Twin Gods, 208n7
water, and livestock on Hopi reservation, 68–69
Wilson, Seth, 51–52, 176, 213n1,
214n5
Winter Solstice Ceremony, 122,
209n1, 210n4
witches and witchcraft, 155, 156
Wuwutsim Society, xv, 140, 156, 185,
207n2, 217n2

Yava, Albert, xiii–xiv, xvi, xvii, 14,
46, 47, 51, 55, 56, 59, 125, 149,
187, 196, 197, 198, 200, 208n7
Youvella, Bert, 196, 197–98, 199

Zuni, 23–25, 191

Robert Black retired in 1995 from the University of California at Berkeley, where he was on the faculty of the Native American Studies Program. He received a doctorate in anthropology from Indiana University and taught at Western Michigan University, the University of Wisconsin at Milwaukee, and California State University at Hayward. While at Berkeley he was editor of the *American Indian Quarterly*.